How to
Be Your Own
Management Consultant

KENNETH J. ALBERT

How to
Be Your Own
Management
Consultant

McGRAW-HILL BOOK COMPANY

New York St. Louis San Francisco Auckland Bogotá
Düsseldorf Johannesburg London Madrid
Mexico Montreal New Delhi Panama
Paris São Paulo Singapore
Sydney Tokyo Toronto

Library of Congress Cataloging in Publication Data

Albert, Kenneth J., date.
  How to be your own management consultant.

  Includes index.
  1. Business consultants. I. Title.
HD69.C6A44   658.4′6   78-2722
ISBN 0-07-000751-9

1234567890 DODO 7654321098

*The editors for this book were Robert A. Rosenbaum and Joan Zseleczky,
the designer was Naomi Auerbach, and the production supervisor
was Teresa F. Leaden. It was set in Elegante
by KBC/Rocappi.*

Printed and bound by R. R. Donnelley & Sons Company.

To Carol—my wife, and my best friend

Contents

Preface   ix

INTRODUCTION: Why This Book?   1

part *1*   The Management Consulting Approach
            to Business Problem Solving

1. About the Management Consulting Business   11
2. Defining the Problem   22
3. Gathering the Necessary Information   38
4. Analysis and Conclusions   49
5. Recommendations and Implementation   62

part *2*   Putting the Management Consulting
            Approach to Work

6. Planning for Future Success   69
   (Corporate Growth Planning)
7. Avoiding Bad Apples   80
   (Acquisition Screening and Analysis)
8. Predicting the Success of Newness   90
   (New Product and New Venture Analysis)
9. Achieving Marketing Success   101
   (Marketing Strategy)
10. Using the Crystal Ball   111
    (Sales Forecasting)
11. Drawing Lines and Boxes   120
    (Organizational Planning)
12. Finding Good People   136
    (Executive Search)
13. Keeping Good People   153
    (Executive Compensation)

14. Bricks and Mortar   161
(Facilities Planning)

part 3 Solving Your Business Problems

15. Establishing Your Own Problem-solving System   175
16. When to Seek Outside Help   189
17. How to Buy Management Consulting Services, When Necessary   196

Index   205

Preface

This book is not intended as an attack on management consultants or their work. They serve a real and necessary purpose in many situations. Rather, its purpose is to explain the approach that management consultants have used so successfully for years to solve unstructured business problems. Small companies who can't afford consultants, large companies who limit their use of management consultants because of budget constraints or policy, and companies who use unnecessary or excessive consulting services should understand and be able to implement, when appropriate, the pragmatic and extremely effective problem-solving methods employed by management consultants. The potential benefits of more skillful problem solving by businesses and institutions and the resulting improvements in products and services that can be offered to consumers are substantial.

I would like to thank the management consulting firms I have been associated with for the last decade. It has been enjoyable and stimulating work. And, more significantly, the experience I gained while working on dozens of clients' problems made it possible for me to write this book.

Thanks, also, to all the clients whose problems I've used as examples. I think these real-life situations helped bring to life a potentially dull subject. By the way, I've changed all the client names and some of the background in each illustration, both to protect the innocent and, perhaps more important, to disguise the not-so-innocent!

Finally, a fond "thank you" to two special people—Jim Petal, and my wife's mother, Ethel Vavruska. Jim gave me some sound advice when I was starting my writing career and helped me again by providing invaluable material for one of the chapters in this book. And my wife's mother, whom my kids affectionately call Granko, typed most of the manuscript.

Elmhurst, Illinois   *Ken Albert*

How to
Be Your Own
Management Consultant

Introduction

Why This Book?

Have you ever gotten a dinner invitation that you didn't understand? My
wife and I received just such an invitation recently. It was from a casual
acquaintance I hadn't seen or talked to in well over two years. His name
was even crossed off my business Christmas card list. And I couldn't remember his wife's name for the life of me. Why was he inviting us to
dinner? I wondered what he was up to. After some discussion we decided to
accept the invitation, more out of curiosity than in anticipation of an enjoyable evening. . . .

As I swallowed my last bite of dessert, Frank (my long-lost friend) suggested that he and I take our coffee into the den, and the reason for the
dinner invitation soon became clear.

Frank, who was now the vice president of marketing for a division of a
major manufacturing company, had a problem. A business problem.
"Ken," he said, "our sales have turned sluggish for some mysterious reason. And worse yet, I don't know what to do about it. I guess I should
probably be hiring a management consultant to help me out, but we just
can't afford it now. I know what you guys cost!"

After filling me in on some of the symptoms of the problem (he just
happened to have all his sales records in his briefcase), Frank said, "Can
you give me some direction on what I can do to go about solving the
problem myself?"

My feelings were mixed. I felt as though I were being used, and yet I was
flattered. At this moment, a dyed-in-the-wool career consultant would have
gone into his "buy now—pay later" routine. (It goes something like this:
"Maybe we can work out a monthly payment plan, or even defer the payments a bit to get you into next year's budget.") But I'm not a dyed-in-the-
wool career consultant. In fact, I'm neither dyed-in-the-wool nor career, as
I'll explain later, so I decided to try my best to help Frank out.

Two hours later, I had given Frank the basis of solving a marketing-
related problem. More important, I had convinced him that there wasn't

1

anything that I could do to solve the problem that he couldn't do just as well. In fact, I said, "Frank, there are some things, like implementing the solution, that you may be able to do much better than any consultant."

Frank telephoned me several times in the next two months to tell me how he was doing and to seek further guidance. I helped him all I could. Then, three months later, he bought me lunch to thank me for all I had done for him. He had defined and solved his problem (a poor incentive compensation system for sales personnel), and sales volume was showing signs of moving up again.

This brings us to the answer for the question "Why this book?" It is to explain and to show you how to apply, when appropriate, the management consulting approach to unstructured business problem solving.

A BOOK FOR ALL
BUSINESS MANAGERS

My original concept was to write this book for companies that can't afford professional management consulting services because of small size or budget limitations. But my publisher suggested that a self-help management consulting book would be helpful to almost all business managers, regardless of their company's size. This feeling was borne out by my experience with Frank. His profit-centered division honestly didn't think they could afford outside consulting help, even though they were part of a large company. Incidentally, this is often the case with ailing companies. Even though they always have room in the budget for lawyers and accountants, the management consultant is considered a discretionary, nonessential expense. Thus a small or nonexistent professional service budget is not the only motive for seeking a self-help approach to consulting. You may be working for a company that has a policy which limits your use of consultants. If so, this book is a natural for you, too.

Further, even if you're associated with a company that *does* use consultants on a regular basis, you should find this book of interest. You will learn how to use consultants more effectively, how to get the most out of your consulting dollar, and in what circumstances you can eliminate the use of consultants altogether.

In summary, this book is intended for all business managers who are interested in improving their business problem-solving skills.

PURPOSES

This brings us to the four purposes of this book:

1. To give you an understanding of the management consultant's approach to problem solving. Obviously, this is a necessary first step to apply-

ing the approach to your own problems. Notice that I refer to the "management consultant's approach" as a singular topic. That's because there is only one basic problem-solving approach. It is used almost universally to solve all types of business problems.

This universal approach makes it possible for you to solve most problems in any area of business management. You don't have to be a compensation specialist to solve compensation problems, or an industrial engineer to solve inventory control problems. In fact, one of my first consulting problems involved the location of a fast-food chain store. I knew nothing about this area, but I solved the problem by applying the universal management consulting approach.

2. To show you how to apply the approach to many types of common problems. This will be done primarily by illustrating business problem solving with actual (and I think very interesting) management consulting case histories. You'll see how the basic approach works in many different situations, and learn how to make modifications to fit a particular circumstance.

3. To show you how to set up an internal problem-solving system in your organization. Several alternatives are suggested for organizations of different sizes and types.

4. To make you an informed buyer for when it becomes necessary for you to purchase outside consulting services. This is important because it isn't always wise to avoid management consultants. They can bring some very desirable attributes to specific situations and in some circumstances their services are indispensable. More on this subject later.

THE MANAGEMENT CONSULTING APPROACH TO BUSINESS PROBLEM SOLVING

Many management consultants would say that it is impossible to explain how they solve business problems because each problem is unique and, therefore, requires a unique solution. I say nonsense! The key to solving any business problem is to use a logical, straightforward approach. Some consultants try to disguise and mystify their work, as if their results were somehow obtained by magic. But, in fact, no magic exists. Consultants solve business problems with a simple, pragmatic approach, and they successfully use the same approach for almost all problems, regardless of the problem's nature or type.

This universal approach seems so simple to me now that it would appear to require no explanation. But as I think back on my first exposure to what management consultants did, before I became one, I remember being impressed by their very presence. Early in my business career, I was a junior marketing manager for a division of Allis–Chalmers. Booz, Allen and Hamilton were hired at the corporate level to do a strategic planning study for our division. I was mesmerized by the confident, almost cocky, well-dressed young consultants who scurried down the hallways and rummaged through reports and files. Little did I know that they were just involved in step 2 of the universal approach to business problem solving.

I'm getting a little ahead of myself. But before I go on to introduce each step in the approach, I want to emphasize the importance of understanding that the approach, although "universal," is customized to fit *individual* problems. Application is really the key to using it effectively, and later on, a great deal of material is presented to illustrate proper application. I say this now so you won't be deceived by the apparent simplicity of the approach.

1. Defining the Problem   This sounds like an almost trivial first step, but in practice, it is not trivial at all. This observation is borne out by the fact that in many cases consultants begin client engagements without the vaguest idea of what the problem is, not because the consultants are inept (although surely some are), but because the problem is buried under a heap of symptoms, memos, records, opinions, and egos. Finding the problem, and getting everyone involved to recognize it, often requires cutting decisively through this heap.

2. Gathering Information   Clear definition of the problem leads directly to a specific indication of the factual material that must be gathered to solve it. Information gathering is the most mechanical step of the universal approach, and it quite often requires expenditure of a great deal of physical energy. Frequently, it involves running all over the country to meet with and to interview the right people.

In many situations, consultants have a tendency to overdo this phase. Some people would suggest it's because the consulting firm knows "the meter is running," and in some instances this is probably true. But more often it's caused by a preoccupation with thoroughness on the part of the consulting team and its managing principal. Junior consultants live in fear of having the principal find out that some source of information (no matter how obscure) was not investigated thoroughly, and the managing principal lives in dread of his client's top executives finding out the same thing.

Nothing is worse than the silence that hangs in the air at a final client presentation when the president of a client company says, "That doesn't sound right. Did you check that with Jim, our planning guy?" Answers like "No, but we did check with . . ." or "Well, not exactly. . . ." will not do. The only acceptable answer is "Yes, and Jim said. . . ." So consultants have a preoccupation with thoroughness or they're not consultants for very long.

3. Analysis and Conclusions   This is probably the most nebulous part of the problem-solving system and the phase where consultants like to emphasize their extensive experience and specialized staff qualifications. In some circumstances extensive, specialized analytical ability is important, but frequently, judgment and common sense carry the day. This is a critical point because it means that you don't have to be an expert; anyone with judgment and common sense can use the universal approach to solve most business problems.

It's my finding, based on exposure to hundreds of business problems, that the old 80:20 rule applies here. Eighty percent of business problems can be solved effectively without specialized analysis tools or expertise. The expertise and specialized skills that are so highly touted by consulting firms are only applicable to 20 percent of their assignments. The application of common sense and good judgment to a thorough collection of facts will solve most business problems. (There is some need to learn how to weigh the facts and judge their relative importance, and this is illustrated in Chapters 4 to 14.)

A good example of the commonsense approach is a study I once did for a modestly sized family-owned business that had a very enviable problem. They were making too much money and paying too much in taxes. The company was being operated in a trust and there were divergent family interests. I'm not a tax expert, but it became apparent rather early that all that was required was a comparative analysis of the available tax and income options. After pumping a tax lawyer for several days and developing a pro forma five-year income statement, all that was left to do was to crank through the resulting taxes for each ownership and salary option. After the cranking was completed, the most attractive alternative was obvious. I did nothing in this study that an employee of the client couldn't do. The analysis was tedious but very straightforward.

4. Recommendations and Implementation Implementation is the step in the business problem-solving approach where the manager who has used the self-help approach to problem solving may be able to do a better job than a hired consultant. Implementation is probably the most important step in the process, but it's the step where many outside consultants do the poorest job. Even consultants admit their shortcomings in the area of implementation. In a recent magazine article, the president of a well-known consulting firm wrote, "Too many of us are content to advise, recommend and write elaborate manuals. . . . As many consultants learn to their dismay when they return to industry in a line-operating capacity, it is one thing to make recommendations and quite another to put those recommendations into effect." [1]

This "failure to implement" is one of the reasons for the growing trend in some larger companies to using internal management consultants. Internal consultants can't close up their briefcases and move on. They have to

[1] J. A. Patton, "Consultants at the Crossroads," *Duns Review*, September 1974, p. 123.

live with their recommendations and the success or failure of the implementation process. The use of one or more internal management consultants is one of several effective ways to institute a self-help consulting approach (see Chapter 15).

CONSULTING A CONSULTING FIRM

Another approach to instituting an internal business problem-solving system without the use of outside management consultants involves the use of special assignments. I raise this topic early in the book only to illustrate another option that managers have available to them to practically implement a self-help problem-solving strategy.

I know that the special assignment approach works because I was personally involved in such a process. On several occasions I served as a consultant to a consulting firm while I was a member of the firm. This is akin to serving as the doctor to all the other doctors in a doctor's office. People second-guessed my every move; every statement, conclusion, and recommendation I made was challenged.

Nevertheless, it worked out very satisfactorily. How do I know? I got repeat business, which is the way all consultants measure the success of previous engagements. The president of our firm came to me three or four times asking me to conduct studies. I did an incentive compensation study for the firm (which is discussed in Chapter 13), among others. I turned down a request to do a long-range planning study for the firm, and on one occasion, recommended they use a specialized outside consultant to solve a staff motivation problem. (I felt an outsider's expertise was essential.)

The fact that a special assignment problem-solving system works in a consulting firm says to me that it will work in almost any business organization. Details on this and other ways of integrating the philosophy of this book into your organization are covered in Chapter 15.

MY BACKGROUND AND EXPERIENCE

I want to briefly touch on my personal background and experience to put the perspective I bring to this book into clear focus. I am an engineer and M.B.A., and spent six years in engineering and sales before entering the general and marketing consulting business.

My hope was that the consulting profession would bring me the personal satisfaction and freedom that seemed to be lacking in industry. But as I got older and got to know myself better, I realized that I could only be happy as my own boss and doing something I truly enjoyed. So after almost a decade in the consulting business, I struck off to sink or swim as an independent consultant and writer. My first success came in the form of a book that explains how to use management consulting techniques to achieve success in a small business (*How to Pick the Right Small Business Opportunity*, McGraw-Hill, 1977).

A FORMER INSIDER'S VIEW

Being an independent management consultant and a writer creates a special situation for me. I'm in the unique position of knowing enough about the management consulting business to explain how to solve problems without using consultants, and I also have the need to write about it to earn a living. Early in this chapter I said I was not a dyed-in-the-wool career consultant. Now you understand what I was referring to. A consultant in a large firm, an insider, would never write this book.

Now don't get me wrong. I'm not knocking the management consulting business, and this book is not intended to be a vendetta. Most management consultants do a good job, and consultants are essential in many situations. All I'm saying is that frequently, probably most of the time, you can do just as good a job solving problems yourself, at a substantial savings and with good implementation of the solution.

BOOK ORGANIZATION AND STYLE

This book is organized into three parts. The purpose of Part 1 is to explain in some detail the management consultant's approach to business problem solving. A single complex business problem, from its first symptoms to its solution, is used to illustrate the key points.

In Part 2, a series of common business problem areas are presented. You'll see how you can apply the basic management consulting approach to business problems in such diverse areas as strategic planning, acquisition selection, executive compensation, and facilities planning. (These topics may not all be of equal interest to you, so feel free to skim the material as you wish.)

Part 3 is devoted to showing you how to set up an internal system to solve your business problems. Variations are discussed which are applicable to large businesses, small businesses, and just about everything in-between. Also in this section are guidelines that point out when it is best to seek outside management consulting help and how to most effectively buy consulting services.

A word about writing style. I'm going to try to make this book fun to read as well as informative; I don't like reading stodgy business books any more than you do. So my style will be informal (unlike most consulting reports). This way it will definitely be more fun to write, and, I hope, more enjoyable to read.

part 1

The Management Consulting Approach to Business Problem Solving

1

About the Management Consulting Business

> There are one-story intellects, two-story intellects, and
> three-story intellects with skylights. All fact collectors,
> who have no aim beyond their facts, are one-story
> men. Two-story men compare, reason, generalize,
> using the labors of fact collectors as well as their own.
> Three-story men idealize, imagine, predict; their best
> illumination comes from above, through the skylight.
> — OLIVER WENDELL HOLMES

Before getting into the specifics of the management consulting approach to business problem solving, I think it might be a good idea to explain some of the basic characteristics of the management consulting business. Despite the title of the book, as I've said before and probably will say again, every manager should probably use management consultants in certain circumstances. In order to use them effectively, you should have some "insider" perspective of their business. Also, it's true that who consultants are relates directly to how they solve problems. Since the primary purpose of this book is to illustrate how to solve the types of problems that management consultants deal with, without the use of expensive consultants, I think a brief overview of the management consulting business is appropriate.

BACKGROUND

What we now refer to as the management consulting business was started by Edwin Booz in 1914. During the first twenty years his firm expanded slowly, reaching a modest two dozen members by the early 1930s. During this period many of the historic names of the consulting business were associated with the Booz organization. George Fry joined the firm in 1924. James Allen followed in 1929. In 1934 Richard Paget and Mark Cresap came aboard, followed by Carl Hamilton the next year.

Ed Booz founded what eventually became known as Booz, Allen and Hamilton in Chicago, where its headquarters remained until 1975. In 1926 in Chicago, another famous firm in the consulting business was born—James O. McKinsey and Company. Four years later, A. T. Kearney (also to become the founder of a landmark consulting firm) joined McKinsey in the firm that is now McKinsey and Company.

World War II and the economic growth that followed helped the expansion of the management consulting business. Today it is estimated that there are in excess of 3000 firms, with more than 50,000 consultants. Consulting revenues are estimated by some to be approximately $2 billion a year.

Some consulting firms are now very large businesses. Booz, Allen and Hamilton's revenue is approaching $100 million. Other modern giants include A. T. Kearney, Arthur D. Little, and McKinsey. But for every giant there are hundreds of one-person firms. Last year I submitted a proposal to a new client who had also solicited six other proposals. I had never even heard of five of the other firms. This is not typical, but it illustrates an important point. Entry into the consulting business is ridiculously easy. All you need is a telephone, a company name, some stationery, and a place to sit. That's not to say that most small firms are not competent. It just says that you should be careful when dealing with small, lesser-known firms.

Another major distinction other than the size of the firm now exists in the consulting business. There are generalist firms and specialist firms. And to confuse matters, some generalist firms are relatively large and some one-person firms consider themselves capable of solving almost any problem (which makes them generalists). A generalist firm is departmentalized into groups like operations research, marketing, personnel, and executive search, while a specialist firm may concentrate solely on executive search.

It used to be that back in the fifties and sixties membership in ACME (Association of Consulting Management Engineers) separated the "class" firms from everybody else. But this is no longer true. Some very good younger firms have shunned ACME membership because of its pompous and often unrealistic regulations (for example, advertising and aggressive sales activity are forbidden). Recently, McKinsey and Company and Booz, Allen and Hamilton dropped out of ACME, further tarnishing ACME's image. Organizations in competition with ACME have also sprung up. There's a whole laundry list, including The Society of Professional Management Consultants, The Association of Management Consultants, and The Institute of Management Consultants. The list goes on and on. What all this tells us is that membership in a consulting association is probably as meaningful as membership in an employee credit union. There's just no way you can judge a consultant by his or her membership cards.

WHO ARE THE CONSULTANTS?

There are three basic types of consultants. The first and probably most numerous group are the full-time members of established consulting firms. The second type of consultant is the moonlighting professor (they also have their own organization, by the way). And finally, there is the executive who is between jobs or indefinitely unemployed. In this section I will concentrate my remarks on the first group—the full-time employees of established consulting firms.

In almost all established consulting firms there are three functional levels. The reason it isn't always obvious to people in industry that these three distinct levels exist is that there are just about as many titles for these three levels as there are consulting firms. To confuse matters even more, firms seem to change titles periodically. My second job in the consulting business was with a major firm in Chicago. I was hired at the lowest of the three levels, which this firm called senior associate (an impressive title for a junior consultant, don't you think?). Two years later I was promoted to the middle level and given the title program manager. But soon afterwards one of those periodic title changes came along. The program manager title was changed to associate. So after a little more than two years with the firm I had gone from senior associate to program manager to associate. My title was less impressive after two years of hard work and a promotion than it was when I started. Try to explain that to clients, friends, and especially to your spouse.

The three functional levels have distinct responsibilities. The lowest-level employees (whatever they happen to be called) are the doers. They gather the information, make the analysis, write the reports, and do the less critical portions of the client presentation. After two to five years of experience, the acceptable junior men are promoted to the middle level (which may be called associate, principal associate, or managing associate, to name a few). Middle-level responsibilities include program management, proposal writing, and limited sales responsibility. Middle-level consultants usually also share some project work with the doers. I call the highest, or third, level in the consulting organization the sellers. Their primary responsibility is getting business and running the firm. Of course, sellers (often called vice presidents or partners) have ultimate project responsibility. But their true involvement in project work is minimal. They attend client meetings, review drafts of final reports, and buy lunches. They do get more involved in a project if something goes wrong. When a seller has a long meeting with a project team in his office, you know something's wrong with one of the seller's reports! Sellers have a sixth sense about problems in client reports, which they usually verbalize with the phrase, "This doesn't sound right." They're usually, but not always, accurate in their judgment—not because of their vast experience or expertise, but because of plain common sense. They exercise their common sense before the final client meeting, because they know the client also possesses the same common sense.

The qualifications of the lowest-level consultants, the doers who are responsible for the bulk of client project work, are woefully lacking. Some consulting firms hire M.B.A.'s right out of college (I was told of one firm that hired an M.B.A. so green he didn't even know how to get to the airport in Chicago—and he *lived* in Chicago!). Most consulting firms hire M.B.A.'s with three to five years of industrial experience. But even with five years of experience and an M.B.A., most new doers are not capable of handling an unstructured business problem, and the sellers are too busy selling to get involved in business problem solving. So it's the middle-level person who really does the problem solving in most firms.

CLIENT ASSIGNMENTS AND CLIENTS

There are as many different types of client assignments as there are problems in a client organization. Consultants operate in all functional areas of business and in all phases of the product life-cycle. They'll solve anything from people problems to a plant location problem. Specialized consulting services are available for specialized clients like retailers, banks, and hospitals. Over the years, just like any other astute business people, consultants have catered to whatever business problem areas would bring them the most work.

The size of client assignments also varies. Sellers at times will sell one day of their time to a client for $500 to $1000 plus out-of-pocket expenses. But this practice is rare and is not considered desirable, because the sellers feel that their effort is better spent in selling major assignments than in billing a client for one day at a time. Extremely large studies (those costing more than $100,000) are unusual, but they do occur. Government agencies are more likely than private industry to purchase these large programs. The typical consulting assignment is probably in the $15,000 to $75,000 professional effort range. Out-of-pocket expenses, which are also billed to the client, are in addition to professional fees.

Although the variety of client assignments is seemingly endless, a small group of consulting specialties probably accounts for half to two-thirds of all consulting revenue. In this small group I would include six specialties: (1) strategic and long-range planning, (2) market research and related marketing studies, (3) computer systems, (4) executive search, (5) industrial engineering and operations research, and (6) organization planning. I know of one general consulting firm which has over 90 percent of its business concentrated in these six areas.

Consulting firms generally do the vast majority of their business with large clients. Most industrial clients have sales in excess of $100 million, and Fortune 500 companies are an important client group to all the larger general consulting firms. That's not to say that consulting firms don't serve small companies. All consulting firms could probably rattle off a list of small clients they have worked for. But small clients (companies of less than $50 million) rarely make up a significant share of a consulting firm's annual revenue. This is true for several reasons: (1) Consulting studies for small firms inherently have small budgets because of the limited resources of the client. (2) Small clients generate less repeat business for consulting firms since problems don't seem to arise very frequently. (3) Because of reasons (1) and (2), consultants don't usually pursue small clients aggressively.

The limited resources of the small company and the lack of interest in them on the part of most consultants means that most small entrepreneurs do not have the benefit of professional problem-solving services.

In addition to the industrial sector, many of the large consulting firms and some of the small specialized firms cater to two other client groups. One of these important groups are government agencies at the federal, state, and local levels. The U.S. Postal Service has spent millions over the years on consulting services. (As a consumer, I sometimes wonder if it has done any good—but who knows, without consultants' magic, first class postage might now be 25 cents.) The other important nonindustrial client group are institutions. Institutions include hospitals, colleges, libraries, and museums. Some of the larger general firms generate more than half of their total revenue from institutional clients.

Many people have the impression, and this impression is no doubt encouraged by the consulting firms themselves, that the "client" in a client company is the president or the chairman of the board. Consultants would probably like this to be true, but it is not. In fact, frequently top-level management in large companies doesn't even know that a consulting firm has been hired to perform a specific task. If the top executive is aware of and interested in the study, he or she may at best sit through a brief summary presentation of the findings and conclusions. Most management consulting does not involve shirt-sleeve sessions with the president of a powerful conglomerate. The "client" in the client organization could be anybody from the market research manager to the vice president of corporate planning.

THE ECONOMICS OF CONSULTING

The consulting business is obviously a service business, and is extremely labor intensive. Profit margins are set (as you'll see later in this section) so that profits are very good when the staff is busy. But management consulting is a cyclical business. Consulting activity is good while the economy is good. When the economy turns down and clients' profitability begins to suffer, the consulting business begins to suffer too. There's an old fallacy that in a soft economy companies spend tons of money on cost reduction consulting services. This is not true. On the contrary, companies cut budgets for outside consulting services when things begin to tighten up. The image of management consultants being doctors for sick companies is not accurate. The vast majority of consulting firms' clients are healthy organizations.

When the economy begins to weaken, the first thing that happens in a consulting firm is shrinkage, or total disappearance, of the backlog of assignments. When the economy worsens further, it becomes impossible to find work for the entire professional staff (which cuts severely into profits because the payroll still comes around every month). When the economy gets very bad, some consulting firms have no choice but to let some of their professional staff go. I was in a consulting firm in 1970 when this happened. Before I was asked to leave, I relocated with a more recession-proof firm. When I resigned, one officer was naive enough to ask me to reconsider, even though we all knew that things were going to get a lot worse before they got better.

Consulting firms generally try to avoid discussing staff billing rates with clients (and a surprising number of clients don't ask). Billing rates are not a popular topic for discussion because they sound so unreasonably high. The doer (or consultant) billing rate in an established firm is about $300 to $400 per day. Middle-level consultants (or project managers) bill in the $400 to $500 per day range. Sellers' billing rates are from $500 to a phenomenal $700 to $800 per day. Sellers bill very few days to a typical project, mainly because they're so busy selling more projects, but also because each day billed at $700 chews up too much of the budget. A typical program budget (for a $27,000 study) might allocate four days for the seller, fifteen days for the manager, and fifty days for the doers. In passing, I'd like to note that of the sellers' four project days, three are probably consumed in meetings (kickoff, interim, and final) with the client and one is allocated for reviewing the interim and final reports. Because of the sales and promotional responsibility of sellers, they usually end up billing less than half of their time during the year to client projects.

There's a "one-third/one-third/one-third" rule of thumb in the consulting business. It states that one-third of a staff member's billing rate (say one-third of $330, or $110) goes for salary. (This means an annual salary of about $25,000.) Another third of the billing rate goes to the firm's overhead (office space, secretarial services, training, insurance, etc.), and the final third goes to the sellers in the form of salary and the firm's bottom-line profit. This is why, as I noted earlier, when the staff is fully billable, consulting can be very lucrative to the sellers in the firm. This is also why sellers don't want to sell themselves to clients one day at a time. Rather, they prefer to multiply their efforts by selling large blocks of the staff's time, and potentially collecting one-third of every day's billing by the staff.

POTENTIAL SAVINGS
OF AN IN-HOUSE CONSULTING
APPROACH

If your company now purchases outside management consulting services, the savings by transferring that work to insiders can be significant. Companies that have instituted internal management consulting groups figure they can do an assignment for 35 to 50 percent less than outsiders can. This magnitude of savings is an accumulation of a number of smaller incremental savings.

First, internal groups don't have to make a bottom-line profit. A typical profit in a well-run consulting firm is about 15 percent pretax. So there's a 15 percent savings to start with.

Next, there's a savings associated with start-up costs and "learning the company." Outside consultants put time in their quotation for day-long orientation and kickoff meetings (which are often attended by the full study team). I attended a meeting like this that lasted three working days. Three representatives of my firm were present, and the cost to the client of the orientation session, including travel expenses, was about $6000. Professional time alone cost the client $1400 per day. Also, consulting firms tend to put contingencies into their quotation for unpredictable learning time. I would guess that eliminating the start-up and learning-the-company efforts by using an internal consultant or a special projects approach could amount to a saving of 10 to 20 percent.

Other savings are also possible. If managed properly, an internal consulting effort can save the portion of an outside consultant's billing rate that is needed to cover the firm's contingency expenses. Internal consultants also have no marketing expense. Consulting firms spend 5 to 20 percent of revenue on selling efforts. A final saving is possible in out-of-pocket expenses. If your company in Denver has an inventory-control problem and you hire a consulting firm in Chicago, you'll pay for five to ten round-trip air fares (maybe first class) from Chicago. You'll also pay for fifteen to thirty days of travel expenses (car, motel, meals) for the doers when they are working on your problem in Denver. This expense can add up fast. Out-of-pocket expenses can amount to an additional 40 to 50 percent on top of professional fees. If you assigned your inventory control problem to a company employee who lives in Denver, you could save almost all the out-of-pocket expenses.

All things considered, I think it's *conservative* to estimate that the internal approach to consulting saves 35 to 50 percent of the cost of an outside firm.

MANAGEMENT CONSULTING SHORTCOMINGS

In the last section, one of the major shortcomings of using management consultants probably became obvious: Management consultants are just plain expensive! Before I get into some of the other shortcomings, I want to emphasize that this section is not intended to put down consultants, but to give you, as someone who may be buying consulting services, an idea of some things to keep in mind. This section will probably come across sounding very one-sided, because none of the inherent management consulting strengths are included. I've decided it's more in keeping with the flow of the book to hold them for Chapter 16.

It has been my observation over the years that management consulting firms have a continuing problem with maintaining consistent high quality in their work. No matter how large or small the firm, every consulting organization seems to put out its share of botched studies. One firm I'm familiar with does about fifteen to twenty projects a month, and invariably one or two of these will be lemons. The one factor that probably contributes most to this is the constant movement of people into, within, and out of consulting organizations. Some new consultants are good and stay on for an indefinite period, while others are dreadful and are asked to leave (but they do their share of damage while they're there). Doers move up to become managers, and managers sometimes shortchange project work so they can do enough selling to merit promotion to the seller level. There doesn't seem to be enough stability in any consulting organization to guarantee consistent quality.

Another situation that contributes to inconsistent quality is the lack of involvement of sellers in most project work. After all, the sellers are the most experienced consultants, yet they contribute little or nothing to the problem-solving process. The lack of problem-solving experience at the doer level compounds the problem associated with the sellers' lack of involvement. Usually 50 to 75 percent of a typical project's budget is consumed by a consultant with less than three years of consulting experience, and little or no relevant industrial experience. The lack of involvement by the most experienced and the predictable mistakes by the inexperienced can combine to create terrible results.

I suggested earlier that management consulting firms are sometimes poor at implementing their recommendations. This is another major shortcoming of management consulting. More often than not the project budget is gone at presentation time. So if there was any time put in the program for implementation, it's usually gone (or insufficient) when implementation time rolls around. So what do many consulting firms do? They close out the report with a next-step section that suggests subtly that more work is needed. Or, if it's felt that this next-step strategy will be unacceptable to the client, the firm may resign itself to absorbing the added cost of implementation. Unforeseen difficulties always seem to crop up during the implementation process, and there's definitely no contingency in the implementation budget for such difficulties. Implementation is difficult under any circumstances, but it's almost impossible when done as part of a project overrun. Another reason for poor implementation is a feeling on the part of many clients to the effect that "there's no need to pay consultants to implement, we can implement just as well, so let's not have them quote on that phase of the program." I feel that management consultants generally underestimate how much effort is involved in doing a good job of implementation.

Another shortcoming of some management consulting firms, typical of smaller firms and one-person operations, is a misguided attempt to try to be all things to all clients. This type of consultant has a tendency to tackle any kind of problem and also tends to be overoptimistic about the value of the result that will be delivered. The operating philosophy of such consultants seems to be, "I'll sell the job now, and figure out how to do it later." Fortunately, know-it-all consultants are in a small minority.

TRENDS IN THE MANAGEMENT
CONSULTING BUSINESS

A group of business school students recently did a study of the management consulting business. They concluded that management consulting is becoming a mature business and that the days of rapid growth and steady expansion are over. No longer can consulting firms expect to grow 15 to 20 percent a year. Rather, they have to learn to live with 10 to 15 percent annual growth, or less. Several factors account for the maturing of the management consulting business. First, the country and its economy are no longer growing the way they used to. Secondly, the management consulting market is becoming saturated. There are no longer truly new clients. Everybody who is ever going to use consultants probably already has. Firms just trade them back and forth. Finally, clients are getting more sophisticated. They no longer rely on consulting firms for the more routine tasks. Instead, they're beginning to call in consultants only when they're really needed.

Not only is the market for consulting services growing at a more modest rate, but to make matters worse for consultants, they're now facing more competition than ever before. Almost all major accounting firms now operate large management services divisions. Worse yet, companies that might once have been clients are now doing much of their consulting work on an in-house basis. Some are even selling their management consulting services to other companies!

Slower market expansion and increased competition have cut deeply into many management consulting firms' growth and profitability. In an attempt to regain lost ground, most consulting firms are involved in diversification programs. Firms that once dealt exclusively with industrial clients are now emphasizing government and institutional prospects. Domestic consultants are expanding into world markets. Overseas revenue now accounts for a third to a half or more of all professional billing in some larger firms.

One Chicago-based consulting firm that specializes in marketing has expanded very successfully into foreign operations. Five or six years ago, their foreign business was minimal. But now they have offices or affiliates in Europe, the Middle East, Japan, Australia, and South America. Interestingly enough, even though foreign business now accounts for a third of their total revenue, this incremental business has not been enough to recapture the rapid growth attained in the booming 1960s.

If you're being "visited" more frequently now by consultants than you were in the past, there's a reason for this also. In the old boom days, it was possible to be very passive and still succeed in the marketplace. Consultants joined clubs, gave speeches, and wrote magazine articles, and then sat back waiting for the phone to ring. Aggressive selling was not only considered unnecessary, it was labeled unethical. However, "ethics" yielded to pragmatism when sales began to soften. Sure the club memberships, speeches, and articles are still around, but so is the unsolicited proposal and the "cold call." For those who haven't been exposed to the cold call, it starts when you answer your phone and a consultant on the other end of the line says, "Hi! My name is Bob Smith and I'm with XYZ Consultants. I'm going to be in Pittsburgh to see a client tomorrow morning. I wonder if it would be convenient for me to stop in in the afternoon to just get acquainted and tell you a little bit about our firm?" Consulting firms are knocking on doors and following up leads more than they've ever done before.

Consultants are also trying to attack the credibility gap that they sense has developed between potential clients and themselves. This is probably one of the motives behind all the professional management consulting organizations that have been popping up recently. There is even talk among consultants about the desirability of setting up some form of licensing system. Consultants (myself included) have always liked to put themselves in the same class as C.P.A.'s and lawyers. There seems to be some feeling among consultants that licensing would help validate this comparison.

In Chapter 2, we begin a detailed examination of a typical consulting engagement from its inception to its conclusion. My plan is to use this study to illustrate, in detail, how management consultants go about solving problems.

2
Defining the Problem

My clearest recollection of a long-ago interview with Thomas A. Edison is a single sentence that was painted or hung on the wall of his room. In effect, the sentence was: "It is remarkable to what lengths people will go to avoid thought." That is tragically true. Some of us think, more of us think we think, and most of us don't even think of thinking.
— POLLACK

In the Introduction, I discussed the universal approach to business problem solving. This is the system used by almost all management consultants to solve the great majority of business problems. You may recall that there are basically four steps:
1. Defining the problem
2. Gathering necessary information
3. Analyzing and drawing conclusions
4. Making recommendations and effecting implementation
"In essence, management consulting involves *defining* and analyzing a management problem, and providing a timely, practical and acceptable solution." This statement is taken from a staff recruiting brochure of one of the leading management consulting firms. It emphasizes beautifully the topic at hand—defining the problem.

In this chapter, I'm going to concentrate on the methods used by management consultants to concisely define clients' problems. In the latter part of the chapter, the consulting assignment I'm currently involved in will be introduced to point out how complex and time consuming problem definition can be.

PRELIMINARY DISCUSSIONS

Typically, discussion concerning a client's problem will be initiated by a telephone call from the potential client. The client will ask the consultant if he or she does work in such and such a problem area, and if he or she is interested in getting involved in a specific assignment in the near future. If the answers to these questions are "yes" (and they usually are), most consultants will suggest a personal meeting to discuss the situation. The consultant's main purpose during the meeting will be to gain enough understanding of the problem to write a winning proposal.

Preliminary discussion meetings are generally held at the client's offices. The meeting may last from an hour to an entire day, depending on the situation.

During the intitial phase of the meeting, the consultant will do a lot of listening and note taking. Sometimes the consultant will ask open-ended questions like, "How did that come about?" or "Why do you think that decision was made?" As the session progresses, consultants frequently begin to get more inquisitive: "Do you have any data on that?" "Can I have a copy?" They will gather up all available reports, memos, sales records, or other documents.

However, in all the questioning that a consultant does, he or she tries to avoid the often fatal mistake of asking dumb questions. A dumb question is defined as any question that gives away a consultant's lack of knowledge or understanding of the client's business. It's sometimes hard for a consultant to recognize a dumb question even after asking it. But potential clients always recognize them instantly.

Although consultants at this stage of a client engagement are doing their best to define the client's problem, they don't ever let this be known to the client. Rather, they exude an air of understanding and confidence. There's one other thing consultants do not do at this point—they will not correct a client who mistakes one problem for another. The client may think, for example, that a declining profitability is caused by competitive price pressure. The consultant may have another opinion, but will usually keep quiet about it. "Why rock the boat?" the consultant thinks. "After I get the assignment, I'll gradually bring this person around to my way of thinking."

LIMITING THE SCOPE

Consultants have a sincere interest in keeping a consulting assignment within manageable bounds. If a problem's scope is not controlled, the consultant has little chance of satisfying the client at the end of the program. It's a lot more practical to limit the scope of a problem in the early stages than to disappoint the client with a seemingly incomplete job at the end of a study.

Limiting the scope of a problem is done in many ways. The primary aim, in most cases, is to exclude secondary facets of an issue. If a product audit is being discussed, a consultant may suggest limiting the study to the six products that account for 70 percent of the company's sales volume. The three dozen or so products that make up the other 30 percent are excluded from the study. In this way, the consultant will not dilute his or her efforts on less important products and the client will only expect recommendations about the six major products.

Another example of scope limiting that comes to mind was on an acquisition study I did. The client had an option to buy a manufacturer of home entertainment products. These products were manufactured in the Far East and sold in the United States, Canada, and Europe. Because of time pressures it was mutually decided to limit the scope of the acquisition analysis to the United States market. If the results of that effort were inconclusive, further markets would be included later.

I want to emphasize that limiting the scope of a problem is not a management consultant's ploy, but rather an essential part of effective business problem solving. It's always important to focus effort on the critical issues (by eliminating the secondary ones), whether or not management consultants are involved in the problem-solving situation.

SETTING OBJECTIVES

Another essential step in problem definition, one that goes hand in hand with limiting the scope of a problem, is setting meaningful objectives. Consultants often probe a client's expectations in this area by asking questions like: "What do you want to accomplish in this program?"or "What do you see as the major purposes of this effort?"

Objectives are most effective in directing the course of a program if they are specific. For example, below are the objectives of a market-oriented acquisition analysis. (The company being analyzed was in the kitchen cabinet business.)

The objectives of this study were:

- To determine the size, structure, and growth potential for the residential kitchen cabinet market during the next five years
- To determine the competitive position and the strengths and weaknesses of Acme Manufacturing
- To define the market image, growth, and profit potential of Acme during the next five years
- To conclude whether Acme is a desirable acquisition candidate

Objectives should be designed to be attainable and realistic goals of the program. They not only define what is expected when the study is completed, but they are extremely useful in guiding the program during the execution of the study effort. New consultants are always advised to keep the objectives in mind. They are encouraged to look at them frequently to judge if what they are doing is leading to the objectives as stated. This may sound like simplistic advice, but you'd be surprised how far off course it's possible to get when drifting around in a sea of facts and opinions. Many problem solvers concentrate too much on what they know (or what they can easily grasp), rather than on the more nebulous, but often more important, issues.

LISTING QUESTIONS

It's important to make a list of specific questions that are to be answered during the study program. In preliminary meetings between consultants and clients, many of these questions will surface as the discussion progresses. Another major source of questions is the program objectives. Questions are developed by just listing the issues that must be addressed to meet the stated objectives.

Listed below are some of the questions that germinated in preliminary discussions of the kitchen cabinet acquisition study:

- What is the current size of the residential kitchen cabinet market (in dollars and units)? How is it segmented by price level? By material? What are the major end-use segments (builder, repair and remodeling businesses)? How important is the do-it-yourself market?

- What is the expected real growth rate for residential kitchen cabinets? What growth is expected in each product and market segment? Why?

- How does Acme's mix of product line and end market compare with that in the overall market? Are they in high-growth or low-growth segments?

- What is Acme's market share? Is it increasing or decreasing? Why? What is Acme's future growth rate?

- How do leading suppliers (including Acme) rate on marketplace image, product quality, service effectiveness, delivery, product innovation, etc.?

These are just some of the questions for which the client (the potential acquiring company) wanted answers. The total list was about three times as long. A single-spaced page to a page and a half of questions is average for most studies, although the number of questions can vary a great deal.

This brings up another important issue. There is a danger in too many questions: Then one doesn't see the forest for the trees.

I still remember when a good friend of mine in the consulting business sold his first study. He wanted so much to please the client that he agreed to answer a list of questions that would choke a horse. He then compounded his mistake by actually trying to answer all the questions. In fact, he was so busy trying to answer all the questions that the agreed-on final presentation date came and went without a meeting. The client's interests were not being served by this exhaustive attempt to answer obscure questions. The client needed a solution to a problem, not a list of answers to tangential or irrelevant questions.

One last point about questions. Some problem areas by their very nature don't really have a list of questions associated with them. Examples that come to mind include compensation and inventory-control problems. Lists of questions to be resolved are more frequently associated with strategic planning and market-related problems.

IDENTIFYING INFORMATION NEEDS

You may recall that the second step in the universal approach to business problem solving is to gather necessary information. An integral part of defining the problem is to determine what information will be required to solve the problem. Defining information needs early in the problem-solving cycle is essential because information gathering will consume one-third to one-half of the entire program.

A consultant who misjudges the type of information that will be needed or miscalculates the difficulty of gathering it, may end up with egg on the face. This is true because a miscalculation will either result in a budget overrun that must be absorbed by the consulting firm or a surprisingly high dollar figure on the client's final invoice (and clients don't like to be surprised that way). Underestimating the amount of effort or quantity of information needed may also result in program delays (clients don't like program delays either!). So it behooves a good consultant to estimate accurately the time and effort required to satisfy the program's information needs.

The best way to explain how consultants do this is with illustrations of a variety of actual client problems. But I won't get bogged down in a lot of that now—there'll be more on this topic in Part 2.

PREPARING A WORK PLAN

Many consulting firms have a standard form that is used to specifically lay out the work required to complete a program. The form is filled out as an integral part of preparing the proposal. The form is a simple matrix with levels in the organization going across the top and program activities going down the left side. It's used to calculate the total number of work days per firm employee that will be required to complete the program. Multiplying these numbers by daily billing rates of each project team member yields the cost of the professional effort part of the program.

The activities included in a work plan are basically those necessary to execute the four-step approach. Typically, work activities include client meetings, information gathering, analysis, report writing, etc. I should point out that the client is not privy to the contents of the work plan. It is basically an internal document.

PREPARING A SCHEDULE

Once the above steps in the problem definition phase are complete, the consultant will prepare a proposal to be submitted to the client. Proposals often take the form of fairly formal documents. A formal proposal, which is almost like a mini-report, is typically used on very large studies or for new clients. On smaller efforts, or for established clients, a letter format is often used. The main topics in a proposal, for either the formal or letter type, are:

- *Background:* A brief lead-in to demonstrate the consultant's understanding of the client situation
  - *Objectives and questions*
  - *Program approach:* A layout of the basic steps in the work plan
  - *Time, cost,* and *administration*
  - *Conclusion:* An enthusiastic statement about your role in the project

The proposal will also indicate that the study can be completed in some specific time period, which begins when authorization to go ahead is given. If and when the consultant gets such authorization, the first step is to prepare a time schedule. This schedule takes the activities in the work plan and details them in a time sequence. The specific "bodies" (consultants) to work on the program are also selected at this time. The purpose of the time schedule is to help ensure that the program will be completed by the date promised in the proposal.

After completing all the above steps in the problem definition phase, the consultant should have the problem definition clearly in mind. Unfortunately, this is not always the case. I've been involved in several studies for which we never did define the problem, let alone recommend a practical solution! Fortunately these cases are rare. But it isn't uncommon for problem definition work to carry over into the second phase of the effort (the information-gathering phase). In some situations, the early information-gathering efforts are specifically designed to contribute to identifying and defining the problem.

I want to make one last point before introducing the consulting assignment that I am currently working on. The steps in problem definition that I have just described are not the exclusive territory of management consultants. They are effective tools that can be applied by anyone who is interested in solving unstructured business problems.

AN "ALMOST TYPICAL" CONSULTING ASSIGNMENT (DARWIN INDUSTRIES)

I've chosen an example to illustrate the basic steps in business problem solving that involves company politics, complex strategic issues, multiple information-gathering techniques, a picky client, and a very challenging problem. The reason I've labeled it "almost typical" is that most consulting engagements are not this complicated. But because of the complicated nature of the situation it makes a beautiful example for illustrating almost everything.

My relationship with this client began almost three years ago. The company, which I will call Darwin Industries, is in the heavy industrial equipment business. One of their main products is heavy-duty transmissions. At the time I first contacted Darwin, I was pushing an unsolicited multiclient proposal for the study of the heavy truck aftermarket. ("Aftermarket" refers to the parts and service portion of the business—it comes after the original equipment is in use.) Heavy trucks were one of Darwin's major end markets, and so Darwin seemed like a natural prospect for the truck aftermarket study. I called Darwin at their headquarters in Minneapolis to tell them about the aftermarket study. Their parts marketing people were pleasant enough, but after considering sponsorship of the study, they decided to pass.

I must, however, have made a favorable impression on them, because about six months later Darwin's transmission parts marketing manager telephoned me to see if I'd be interested in preparing a proposal for them. They wanted a study of the practices of large trucking fleets with regard to the purchase of transmission parts. They suspected that they weren't getting the share of that market that they deserved. The study was to have two objectives: (1) to determine their market share, and (2) to recommend a program for improving it.

I gladly submitted a formal proposal and then crossed my fingers. I figured I had a good shot at getting the engagement because of my mechanical engineering background and because of my industrial experience in the transmission business with one of Darwin's competitors.

My hunch was right. About two weeks after submitting the proposal, I got a call informing me that my firm's proposal had been selected out of a total of five. I felt pretty good. A program kickoff meeting was scheduled for the following Friday. The day before the kickoff meeting my bubble burst. Darwin's budget for the program had been withdrawn because of a softening of new transmission sales.

During the two years after this program was withdrawn, I telephoned my prime contact at Darwin only once. Budgets for outside services continued to be nonexistent. I really wasn't too upset by this because I was getting more involved in my own writing, and success in selling consulting services for my firm didn't mean as much to me. In fact I took a leave of absence from the firm in the summer of 1976 to write my first book, and in the fall of 1976 I went back only to clean up some loose ends before I struck off totally on my own.

One day in November of that year I just happened to be in our firm's offices. I was busy cleaning out my office. To my complete surprise, I got a call from a guy at Darwin named Jim Harvey. I had never heard of him before. He said that he was the director of service and distribution for Darwin. Jim went on to say that he was calling to see if we'd be interested in submitting a proposal on a study of Darwin's North American service organization. It seemed that Darwin was concerned about the competitive posture of its service capability. Jim said they were interested in doing individual studies on each of the thirty distributor territories, with a possible study of the worldwide service system to follow. He said that four or five other consulting firms were being contacted, and that the planned service organization study was initiated by the president of Darwin. I could tell that Darwin was talking about spending a lot of money. A typical study of one territory usually costs $20,000 to $30,000. Multiply that by thirty and then add "worldwide," and they're talking about spending half a million dollars in the next couple of years. This was too big a study for me to handle myself, and it would siphon off too much of my time from writing, so I decided to turn the lead over to the head of my old firm.

After hanging up the phone, I casually strolled down the hall and into the chairman of the board's office. His name is Allen. I told him about the call. Dollar signs were twinkling in his eyes as he mentally multiplied $25,000 times thirty territories. Then he remembered that I was no longer a member of the firm! Allen said, "Do they know you've left us?"

"No," I replied, "They think I'm still on the staff. I was here when they called, wasn't I?"

"We're going to have to be very careful about how we handle this situation," Allen said. "You're going to have to be involved in the preliminary discussions with them and in the proposal preparations. After all you are the expert in this area. Arrange a date with your contact at Darwin for you and me to visit them on this study—O.K.?"

"O.K.," I said.

Our plan was to call on Darwin for preliminary discussions. Then I was to gradually shift the contact from myself to Allen, assuming we got the study. I was agreeable to this, and felt that Allen was right in protecting the long-term interest of the firm by getting involved right away in the Darwin relationship.

What turned out to be almost a day-long meeting with Darwin began with a 7 a.m. breakfast meeting in a motel near Darwin's corporate office building. In addition to Allen and myself, there were Jim Harvey and his boss, Bill Holty. Bill is the vice president in charge of distribution. A conflict had developed in his schedule for that day so he shared all his thoughts about the planned study with us as we ate. He rattled off a list of things that he wanted. Bill said they wanted to conduct a pilot study in the Seattle territory. This pilot would have two purposes: (1) to develop an approach that could measure service effectiveness in a quantitative and repeatable fashion, and (2) to decide how the Seattle distributor was doing (he was labled as a "problem" distributor).

Bill then went on to criticize past work that had been done by consulting firms for Darwin. He said, "Past studies have been too general. Nothing ever seems to happen as a result of them. There's no implementation. They're just read and forgotten. I don't want that to happen this time. We need actionable conclusions and recommendations."

After breakfast Jim, Allen, and I reconvened in Jim's office. We found out that a total of seven consulting firms were being invited to submit proposals. Darwin really believes in open competition! Jim handed Allen and me a two-page proposal request for the planned effort. It listed three objectives:

- To determine if Darwin outservices its competitors
- To determine the strengths and weaknesses of Darwin's service system
- To isolate specific problems for corrective action

The overview also stated that Darwin wanted to experiment with all possible means of gathering information in the Seattle territory. Darwin wanted to use personal, telephone, and mail interviews, and they wanted to include all of their end-market segments (trucks; logging, marine, mining, agricultural, and construction equipment; and generator sets).

Allen and I had no qualms about testing all the different approaches to information gathering, although we told Jim that we felt that personal interviews would probably yield the best results. Then we got into a long discussion about the end-market segments. A problem developed because although Darwin wanted quantitative results, they had no quantitative information about their own customers. They weren't really sure who owned their transmissions or how many transmissions were in use in the Seattle territory. Three or four experts were called into the meeting and none could contribute any meaningful insight. The reason it was important to Allen and me was that the total user population and the size of each end-user segment would determine the number of interviews required, and the number of interviews would influence the price quoted in the proposal.

Allen then questioned the wisdom of using a "problem" territory as the pilot study territory. Jim agreed that it probably wasn't a good idea, but he had no choice because it was dictated by the president of Darwin. Unable to change the pilot territory, we probed to get an understanding of exactly what the problems were with the Seattle distributor. Jim said something like, "We're really not at liberty to discuss that at this time." And the topic was dropped.

We ended up spending the whole morning, the lunch hour, and part of the afternoon with Jim and several of his people. But we had found out very little that would help us write a good proposal. We also found out little that would help us understand the problems that originally created the need for the study, and nothing about the specific problems in Seattle. Allen and I agreed that we would have to write a "boiler-plate" proposal (full of fluff and pleasantries) and then just cross our fingers.

I should emphasize that it's not at all uncommon for a potential client to state the objectives of a proposal study without specifically identifying the underlying problems. But face-to-face, open-ended questions are usually able to draw out the specific problem or problems. For some reason, we weren't able to accomplish this with Darwin. Therefore we had not defined the problem. That would have to wait until the preliminary information-gathering stage of the study (assuming we beat out the other six firms).

On our trip back to Chicago, Allen and I discussed the approach we would take in the proposal. We also discussed the scope of the study, the statement of program objectives, the questions we would address during the study (this was a difficult area since we had trouble coming up with meaty issues), the information needs we had, and the work plan.

Excerpts and highlights of the proposal that resulted from these discussions follow. (My former firm will be referred to as Tower Consultants from now on, for lack of a better alias.)

DARWIN PROPOSAL

I. *Introduction*

Darwin Industries is a leading supplier of transmissions and repair parts for both automotive and industrial applications. A North American service organization, composed of 30 distributors, 120 branches, and approximately 2500 dealers, provides aftermarket parts and service support for all end-use applications.

Darwin is interested in conducting a study of its service organization to determine its effectiveness and to strengthen its future position. Because of the complexity of the issues involved in a study of this type and because several different methodologies are available, it has been decided to begin the North American effort with a pilot study. The Seattle region has been chosen as the location for this pilot program, and this pilot will be used to test various approaches, as well as to analyze the Seattle region.

Darwin has requested that Tower Consultants propose an approach to conducting this study. This proposal, entitled "A Study of Darwin's North American Service Organization," represents the best thinking of Tower Consultants with respect to what has been requested by Darwin. It is designed to present Darwin's management with the specific information and conclusions necessary to plan future service activities most effectively.

Tower Consultants would like to emphasize that all personal and telephone interviews (in the pilot study and in the North American effort) will be conducted by professional staff members at Tower Consultants. These staff members have experience and background in the transmission, heavy truck, and heavy equipment markets. By utilizing this high-level interviewing approach, Tower Consultants will be able to develop detailed and actionable information and conclusions.

Darwin has indicated to Tower that this study at some future date could become international in scope. Tower has an extensive international capability, as described in the qualifications section of this proposal, and as such, would be fully prepared to undertake such an effort under the guidance of the same personnel who would be responsible for the North American effort.

II. *Study Objectives*

The basic objectives of this proposed study (both pilot and North American) are:

- To determine how Darwin's service compares with its competitors
- To determine the specific strengths and weaknesses of the current service system
- To develop specific conclusions and recommendations to strengthen the system at both the regional and national levels
- To develop a system to measure service effectiveness with the aim of monitoring changes and improvements from year to year

In order to meet the objectives indicated above, the following types of questions will have to be answered. These questions are meant to be indicative of the areas which must be explored and are not meant to constitute an exhaustive list. It is anticipated that the list will be modified by Tower Consultants and Darwin at the program planning meeting.

- What portion of service and parts expenditure for Darwin transmissions is being realized by the Darwin distributor in a region? By the Darwin dealers? How does this compare to the situation with Darwin's major competitors?
- What is the relationship between price and value for Darwin's service and parts as seen by end users? How do users view the relationships between price and value for independent repair shops and nongenuine parts? Do these relationships vary by end user? By type of part? By frequency of purchase?
- How does Darwin's service availability compare with that of its competitors? How important to users are service hours and location? Where are competitive branches, distributors, and dealers located?
- What is the image of the Darwin service organization as seen by customers, noncustomers, dealers, and independents? What changes have they perceived in Darwin's image?
- How does Darwin's service effectiveness vary by size of customer and by end-use segment (on-highway, marine, agricultural, etc.)? If differences exist, are they a result of user attitudes and practices, or are they due to the distributor's approach to service business? Are competitive outlets more effective in some segments? If so, why?

- How does Darwin's service compare with competition in the areas of responsiveness, reliability, fairness of warranty service, etc.? How important are these competitive differences?
- How does Darwin's dealer support compare with that of competitors? What types of programs are considered successful by competitive dealers? Why?
- How effective is the Darwin training program for Darwin distributors? What steps do they feel should be taken to improve these programs? How should these improvements be implemented?
- In what specific ways can Darwin improve its service effectiveness? What results would be anticipated from these improvements?
- What steps should Darwin and Tower undertake to further refine study methodology so that future efforts will be as effective as possible? What in-house data collection and refinement efforts should be undertaken?

III. *Study Approach*

As indicated in the introduction, Seattle had been selected as the location of the pilot study. The purpose of this pilot program is to develop the most appropriate approach for the North American program, in addition to determining the effectiveness of the service organization in the Seattle region.

To achieve these dual objectives, Tower Consultants proposes a five-phase study program.

Phase 1: Project Orientation

Tower Consultants believes that it is important to have its study team meet initially with appropriate Darwin personnel to ensure that the program is clearly defined and oriented. This meeting will allow Tower to become completely familiar with Darwin's service marketing approach. Also, the final list of questions and topics will be developed at this time. It is anticipated that the project start-up meeting at Darwin will require one day.

Tower Consultants will also, as a part of phase 1, review all available secondary sources and data bases to ensure that this information is noted prior to instituting the fieldwork in phase 2. The final step in this phase will be the preparation of the interview guides to be utilized in the field interview portion of the program. Darwin can review these guides at this time if it so desires.

Phase 2: District Office Interviews

Tower Consultants feels that it would be beneficial to meet with Darwin's personnel at the Western divisional district office. These one-on-one meetings would be helpful in understanding the service system, the relationship between the district office and the Seattle distributor, the types of communications that take place, etc. It also will be beneficial to meet with the Seattle distributor.

Phase 3: Field Information Effort

Tower Consultants recognizes three distinct alternative methodologies to obtaining field information: personal interviews, telephone interviews, and mail questionnaires.

In terms of a study of this type, we believe the personal, in-depth interview, which permits elaboration and challenge of the points made by the respondent, is unquestionably the most effective. Obvious responses as to the rationale for Darwin's position in the marketplace are probably well known to local personnel, but the subtleties of the respondent's feelings, which often are the *key* reasons for his or her actions, must be drawn out and evaluated through a personal meeting. Because of this need, we have emphasized the personal interview mode in the field information-gathering phase.

Telephone interviews can be used effectively to gain a broad exposure to interviewees if we sense a reasonable degree of consistency in terms of the responses from the personal interview effort. On the assumption this consistency will occur, we have included a telephone effort with both dealers and end users. The preponderance of these interviews will be with end users because they are probably the least difficult respondents to gain access to and to get information from. Dealer interviews will be aimed primarily at gaining geographic coverage and filling in competitive representation that might not be balanced as a result of the personal interviews.

Tower Consultants generally does not use or recommend mail surveys in industrial markets. However, mail surveys do lend themselves to the quantification of results, and since Darwin is interested in developing a system that can measure the change in service effectiveness from year to year, a mail survey of end users could be appropriate. We have presented this alternative methodology as an optional effort for Darwin.

The following three steps describe our present thoughts on the scope of each alternative methodology. Additional information needed to quantify the degree of fieldwork required must come from the Seattle distributor. Darwin has indicated to Tower Consultants that specific data relating to the Seattle distributor will not be available in time for it to be considered in the preparation of this proposal. Therefore, Darwin has directed Tower to prepare a proposal assuming two different levels of field effort. Further refinement of this approach will occur before the program authorization is accomplished.

Step One: Personal Field Interviews
Personal field interviews will be conducted with dealers and dealers' branches and end users. In order to quantify the number of interviews required in each category, Tower has collected the sales and service directories of Darwin's major competitors. Summarized below is the information that has been tabulated from these directories for the Seattle district (Washington and Oregon).

	Dealers	*Branches*
Darwin	120	1
Competitor A	60	12
Competitor B	2	20
Competitor C	9	1

Summarized below is our preliminary perspective for the personal field interview effort required for each level of respondent.

	Level I	Level II
Regional offices	12–14	12– 14
Dealers and dealer branches	12–14	30– 35
End users	25–30	55– 65
Totals	44–58 (50)	95–112 (100)

As indicated previously, the purpose of all personal interviews is to gather information, attitudes, and subjective feelings that can only be addressed in face-to-face, openended discussions. Image, pricing, reputation, responsiveness, dealer relations, and the strengths and weaknesses of the Darwin service organization will all be discussed in detail.

Step Two: Telephone Interviews
Tower Consultants feels that 50 to 60 telephone interviews during this phase will be adequate. These interviews by their very nature are normally shorter and less detailed than personal interviews, but they can be used to expand the personal end-user information base and to gather as much quanitative data as possible. Although both dealer and end-user interviews will be conducted, it is felt at this time that the end-user interviews will predominate.

Step Three: Mail Survey (Optional)
Tower could conduct a mail survey as part of the program, and at this time, a sample of 2000 medium and small users (in all end-use market segments) appears appropriate for the size and nature of the Seattle district. Several different questionnaires will be tested, and the offer of a premium can also be made to see if it will increase the response rate.

The questionnaires to be used will be reviewed in detail with Darwin personnel. Further, it is preferred that such an effort not be undertaken until a significant number of personal and telephone interviews have been completed. In this manner, the team will have sufficient market insight to structure an effective question sequence.

Phase 4: Analysis and Presentation of Findings
In the final phase of the study program, Tower will analyze the information previously gathered, put it into meaningful perspective, and prepare a flip-chart-style report. In this report, all pertinent information, tables, and data will be fully detailed and all conclusions and rationale will therefore be fully documented. The report will be presented orally to Darwin at its facilities. Copies of the final report will be available at this presentation.

Because of Darwin's interest in specific quantitative findings and conclusions, Tower will emphasize this aspect during the fieldwork and analysis portions of the program. End-user interviews will be tabulated and cross-tabulated to highlight specific information. Matrices will be generated wherever possible to illustrate important conclusions, and major effort will be undertaken to develop a reliable system of measuring service effectiveness on a year-to-year basis.

Specific actionable conclusions and recommendations to improve service performance will be an integral part of the report.

Phase 5: North American Study

The North American study will probably be initiated on a regional basis. By concentrating effort on one distributor territory at a time, maximum benefit will be derived.

Each regional study will be founded on three distinct and separate inputs. First, the methodology to be used will be selected based on the findings of the Seattle pilot study. Second, the data from the local Darwin distributor will be used to estimate the degree and nature of the fieldwork effort required. Finally, local data base information (for example, that obtained from the truck inventory and use survey) will be used to assist in the quantification of results.

The North American study report on any given region will follow the format developed in the Seattle pilot study.

IV. *Qualifications of Tower Consultants*

Tower Consultants is an independent, technically oriented management consulting organization specializing in assessing the impact of changing situations on markets, products, and companies. As an independent organization, our staff of professional consultants is able to work effectively at many levels within the technical and marketing groups of the various companies to be contacted during the course of this study program. Tower Consultants prides itself on offering experience-tested individuals to assign to a sponsor's program ... [This section was followed by resumes.]

V. *Pilot Phase Timing, Cost, and Administration*

Darwin's internal scheduling commitments require the pilot program to be completed by the end of the first quarter. Tower Consultants will be in a position to meet this schedule if an authorization to proceed is made in December.

One of the elements of the program that may take a long time to complete is the mail survey. Ideally, this mailing will not be undertaken until a substantial portion of the personal fieldwork is completed. If this is done, it is possible that the mail survey will not be finished by the March deadline. A decision on the timing of the mail survey can be made at the program planning meeting.

The cost of the professional effort for the study program will depend on the specific amount of personal study effort that is felt necessary (this decision is pending specific information on the Seattle region). Pricing at the two levels of effort suggested earlier in this proposal is presented in the table below.

	Personal Interviews	*Phone Interviews*	*Professional Effort**
Level I	44– 58 (50)	50–60	$21,800
Level II	95–112 (100)	50–60	$32,900

*Out-of-pocket expenses, which include such items as travel, telephone, photocopying, etc., will be invoiced as incurred; these normally run in the range of 40 percent of professional effort.

In addition, the cost of the mail survey will be $2200 to $3000 plus duplicating, envelope, and postage expenses. A range is required because the tabulation expense depends on the response rate.

In order to maintain a close liaison between the Tower study team and Darwin, informal communications will be encouraged throughout the course of the study to provide Darwin with the maximum flow of information, and Tower with Darwin's current thinking. Darwin's personnel are also invited to take part in portions of the fieldwork if they so desire.

VI. *Conclusion*

The program outlined in this proposal represents a comprehensive approach to assisting Darwin in making decisions regarding service effectiveness. We feel that the approach represents a practical program that will yield meaningful results.

Tower Consultants is well qualified to conduct this program. We have had significant experience in the transmission and heavy truck markets, and we have performed many planning and consulting programs posing the same basic questions in areas related to the interests of Darwin.

The program outlined in this proposal represents the experienced judgment of our staff, but is not meant to be inflexible. Its scope and approach can be modified to make it fit more closely the requirements of Darwin.

We look forward to initiating a professional relationship between our organizations.

Respectfully submitted,
Tower Consultants

Kenneth J. Albert

You may have noticed that nowhere does the proposal directly address the issue of how we were going to quantify the results. That's because we didn't know how we were going to do it! Two interviewing levels were included because we weren't able to determine accurately Darwin's price sensitivity. So we gave them two prices to choose from. We also did it because we knew nothing about the Seattle situation (that is, the specific problem, the population of customers and noncustomers, etc.), and we didn't want to be too specific.

3
Gathering the Necessary Information

A prudent question is one-half of wisdom.
— FRANCIS BACON

No man really becomes a fool until he stops asking questions.
— CHARLES P. STEINMETZ

When I wrote this section, I was up to my ears in the information-gathering phase of the Darwin study. I had subcontracted with my old firm to do a part of the project. Not only were the questionnaires a complicated mess (because of all the quantification), but Jim Harvey literally shadowed us as we did the field interviewing. He had dinner with us every night for a debriefing session.

Before I get involved with describing the second step of the Darwin study, it's probably a good idea to present the basics of all types of information gathering.

SOURCES OF INFORMATION

There are at least six different basic sources of information. Not all are applicable to every study, but in most studies, at least two of these sources are investigated. I'd like to touch briefly on each of these sources and indicate in which type of problem-solving situation each is most appropriate.

Client Records and Files

Client records and files include anything a client has on paper that can contribute to understanding or solving the problem at hand. Five-year plans, financial records, interoffice memos, sales records, inventory records, and product literature are just a sampling of valuable and meaningful information in this category.

Gathering information from clients seems as if it should be as easy as falling off a log. But to overwork another trite expression, in many cases it's more like pulling teeth. The ultimate frustration results when there aren't any teeth to pull. Frequently even sophisticated Fortune 500 companies don't have records of some fundamental information.

Recently I was involved in a study for a major manufacturer in the transportation business. One of their divisions was losing money at a rate of $7 million a year. At our initial meeting with the division general manager and his staff, we requested some basic sales information. The marketing manager said they were just putting in a system to collect what we wanted. I couldn't understand how they could function without it. This lack of basic data was one of the reasons for the losses in the division.

Client Personnel

An obvious extension of a client's records and files as a source of information are the people who work in the client company. These people are invaluable and essential sources of information for studies that are aimed at solving problems inside the company itself. For example, facts, opinions, and even gripes are extremely useful in solving problems in the areas of executive compensation, reorganization, and productivity.

This type of information is generally gathered in one-on-one, face-to-face, open-ended, confidential interviews. Specialized interview guides and reams of lined note pads are the primary tools used to record the substance of these meetings.

Interviews with client personnel also are very useful in solving business problems that are external to the organization. Typical external problem areas include strategic planning, new product potential analysis, and corporate growth planning. Even though the key information sources for these types of studies are outside the company, employees can contribute significantly to understanding of the problem.

I'm sure you're familiar with this classic complaint about management consultants: "All they do is come in and pump us, boil it all down, and then tell it all back to us at the end of the study." Employee interviews are largely responsible for this complaint. In some instances the complaint is valid. Sometimes all the client needs to solve the problem is to have an impartial party "tell it like it is." Consultants always run the risk of this form of criticism if they rely too heavily on employees as a source of information.

The Government

Depending on the particular information needs, the government can be an excellent source of information. The federal government publishes tons of information every day. Meaningful federal data include such sources as current industrial reports, research reports, and regulatory agency publications. State and local governments can also be very useful. For example, if you're doing some site selection work, for anything from a restaurant chain to a new manufacturing plant, information on demographics, traffic patterns, and local labor rates can be very helpful.

Another good example of meaty information is the financial disclosure data that are published by companies in compliance with Securities and Exchange Commission (SEC) regulations. Detailed financial data, far more inclusive than can be found in annual reports, are available on any publicly held company. All you do is walk into the regional SEC office and ask for a 10K report on XYZ company. I've always been amazed at how many knowledgeable people in industry are not aware of 10K reports. They're very useful in any acquisition screening or market analysis work. They may also be more useful, especially in making credit decisions, than Dun and Bradstreet (D&B) reports.

Trade Associations, Publications, and Other Data Sources

Consulting firms probably account for more than half of all phone calls placed to trade associations! At the beginning of every study, a consultant will get in touch with every trade association that is even remotely involved in the areas that the consultant is interested in. Trade associations are most appropriate for studies that require information external to the client company.

It's not uncommon for a consultant to interview the managing directors of trade associations that the client belongs to. They are potentially very good sources of information about industry trends and competitors. They are also very good at explaining how they manipulate and categorize the data they collect from member companies.

Publishers and publications, primarily magazines, are great sources of background information if the client assignment involves a new market, an acquisition candidate, or some other topic that is new to the experience base of the consultant, the company, or both. I brought it up, so I might as well address the issue of consultants' lack of knowledge in particular areas. Companies quite frequently hire consultants who have no experience in a particular industry. I've done work in more industries that I knew nothing about than in industries where I had meaningful experience! Publishers and their magazines are a great way to pick up the right buzz words quickly. One study involving deciding which system of warehouse order picking would be best for a client was driving me crazy because I couldn't figure out a good system to recommend to the client. But I discovered the perfect system in a magazine article. I was hoping against hope, at the final presentation, that the client had not read the same magazine!

"Other data sources" is a caption to describe anything and everything else. There are people and organizations in the business of putting together, and then selling, low-priced information. Dun and Bradstreet's credit reports are probably the best known. But there are others, for example, R. L. Polk, which publishes statistics about the automotive industry. There are organizations like Predicast that publish reports on new products and high growth markets. Consultants have been known to buy Predicast reports and even attend seminars in order to quickly learn what is needed to relate to a client's problem.

The Marketplace

The marketplace and client personnel are the two most important information sources. Marketplace information sources include any individual or company that is involved in the market area of interest. Vendors, customers, noncustomers, distributors, dealers, competitors, and former executives of competitors are all likely prospects.

Marketplace information is obviously useful in any problem-solving situation that is market related (new product studies, acquisition screening and analysis, client image problems, marketing strategy, etc.). Marketplace information is also extremely useful in apparently internal problem areas like sales forecasting, salesperson compensation, and even organization planning. Let's take sales compensation. It's fine to redesign a sales incentive system to increase the motivation of sales personnel. But to make this type of change without understanding the incentive systems that are used by similar industries and competitors is to do an injustice to the client.

I once worked with a consultant who made just that mistake. He managed an $80,000 sales forecasting study for a client in the consumer electronics business. But he was too lazy to find out what successes and failures other consumer electronics companies had experienced in their sales forecasting techniques. He could have gotten this type of information very readily, and without it, he might have been "inventing" a wheel that had been invented by some other company years ago, and had failed!

WAYS OF GATHERING INFORMATION

There are basically four ways of gathering information, and each way has its particular uses. This section introduces each method and describes primary applications.

Personal Interviews

Personal interviews are the backbone of almost all management consulting firms' approach to information gathering, because they are the most useful approach. The personal interview allows for direct, private interchange of thoughts and ideas. It allows the consultant to ask follow-up questions and to probe for additional understanding. It permits the interviewer to ask a series of searching, open-ended questions. There are disadvantages associated with personal interviews, however. The main disadvantages are cost and time. Personal interviews typically cost between $100 and $150 each after all professional effort and related expenses are tallied up. Furthermore, a consultant can only do three to five personal interviews a day. Sometimes, if there is a great distance between interviews, a consultant is lucky to do two in a day. It took all the energy I had and about fourteen hours for me to do two interviews on a marketing study I did several years ago. One competitor was located an hour's drive from Atlanta's airport, and the other was an hour and a half from downtown Houston. Because of bad weather and delayed flights, I ended up doing the Atlanta interview at 10:00 a.m. and the Houston interview at 5:30 p.m. that same day. Those two interviews ended up costing the client about $400 each. (In this case they were probably worth it because of the insight that was gained.)

Personal interviews also require time for the consultant to set up his appointments and make travel arrangements. Fortunately for the client's pocketbook, consultants rarely fly during business hours. Once appointments have been arranged, personal interviews follow a fairly set pattern. After the handshake and greetings are completed, consultants first try to establish a pleasant working relationship with the interviewee. A consultant may ask, "What do you think about this weather?" or "Have you lived in this area very long?" Then comes the easy question phase. This is when all the nonthreatening questions are asked. Finally, there's the hard question phase. That's where, if a consultant is doing an interview with a client's leading competitor, he asks questions like, "What was your dollar volume in product X last year?" If the interviewee is offended by this hard question and decides to become politely uncooperative, the consultant has lost nothing, since he has already obtained answers to the easier questions.

Personal interviews done in the marketplace, and especially interviews with client competitors, are frequently arranged by promising the interviewees some form of reciprocity. A consultant might say, "We've done a great deal of research in this area, and I'd like to stop in and bounce it off of you to get your reaction." If necessary, a consultant may encourage cooperation by inviting an interviewee to "call me back after our analysis is completed and we can discuss some of our nonproprietary findings."

Personal interviews with employees of the client company are often done with specialized interview forms. For example, some firms have questionnaires specifically designed for organization studies. One organization study questionnaire that I'm aware of has seven pages, and each page is dedicated to a specific topic. I'll get into this subject in more detail later, but just to give you an idea here are the seven topics:

1. Organization chart
2. Duties, functions, and responsibilities
3. Departmental operations
4. Duties and functions of subordinates
5. Authority and relationships
6. Problems and suggestions
7. Personal background and experience

Notice how the topics progress from the easy, concrete subjects to the more complex issues.

Telephone Interviews

Most consulting firms consider telephone interviews an inferior substitute for personal interviews. Telephone interviews are typically used to develop a broad base of fairly straightforward information. For example, I once did a distribution strategy study for a client concerning a new product they were considering introducing. A competing company was just in the process of introducing a similar product. We wanted to know how far along this competitor had gotten in establishing distribution. So it was quite easy and inexpensive to sample fifty distributors across the country by telephone. These distributors were more than willing to tell us if they were carrying this new product and what chance they felt it had in their particular market. But key marketplace interviews are rarely done by telephone, since it's impossible to keep someone on the phone long enough to obtain more than a few straightforward facts. Also, it's too easy for the source to terminate the discussion by hanging up.

Focus Groups

The focus group can be a very useful specialized tool. Say, for example, a company has a new frozen-food concept that is designed to be sold through supermarkets. The company's consultant might recommend testing and refining the concept by getting together a group of frozen-food buyers and merchandisers. These get-togethers are typically held at a convenient hotel, with dinner and cocktails used to encourage participation. When the actual focus group session is convened, a discussion leader from the consulting firm will briefly describe the concept and then guide the discussion among the participants by asking a series of open-ended questions. Focus groups are very effective for this type of information gathering because the group seems to feed on itself and frequently generates a lot of creative, original thought. It's also relatively inexpensive; as many as eight interviews can be had for the cost of a meeting room, food, and drinks.

Mail Surveys

Mail surveys are a last resort for most consulting firms because they limit the types of meaningful information that can be obtained. Effective mail questionnaires are, by their very nature, highly structured, short, and direct. They're great for generating a lot of specific data, but it is often impossible to develop, with confidence, any actionable conclusions from them. Take the Darwin study, for example. We may find that 62 percent of users returning the mail survey questionnaire feel that Darwin's service is adequate or above average. But, so what? Finding out what's wrong in the minds of the other 38 percent is impossible with a mail questionnaire. Highly structured mail and telephone surveys are fine for consumer market research and political pollsters, but business problem solving is another ball game.

DARWIN INFORMATION GATHERING

The information-gathering work on the Darwin study began with a day-long project orientation at Darwin's headquarters in Minneapolis. Allen, a consultant named Joe Kosner, and I attended this meeting. Joe was going to work on the pilot program. In fact, he was scheduled to put in most of the effort.

This is probably an appropriate point to introduce the work plan that was prepared for the program. This plan, Exhibit 1, outlined the proposed tasks and the number of days that were to be devoted by each person to each task. It included estimates for the work of four people: Allen, Joe, a research assistant, and me. (The research assistant was to do most of the telephone interviewing because research assistants have low billing rates and therefore help keep us in budget.) Remember that this work plan was an internal document and had never been seen by Darwin.

EXHIBIT 1   Darwin Work Plan

	Number of days devoted to task			
Task	Allen	Ken	Joe	Assistant
Project orientation meeting	1	1	1	. . .
Program planning	. . .	1	2	. . .
Internal information gathering*	2	2	4	. . .
Personal field interviews	. . .	6	15	. . .
Telephone interviews	. . .	1	1	7
Interim meeting	1	1	1	. . .
Mail survey	. . .	. . .	3	3
Analysis and report writing	1	3	7	5
Final presentation	1	1	1	. . .
Totals	6	16	35	15

*These days were added by Darwin after reviewing our initial proposal.

The morning session of the project orientation meeting was devoted to reviewing the questions in the proposal and to working on a draft of the end-use and dealer interview guides. Jim Harvey, my main contact at Darwin on this study, complicated this session immensely by inviting everybody and his brother to the meeting. There were marine marketing people, logging marketing people, and on and on. All told there were about a dozen Darwin representatives there, and everyone had some questions to include in the interview guides. Darwin's insistence on quantification of the findings made things even more complex.

It was at this meeting that some of the unexplained problems in the Seattle distributorship began to surface. Three or four of the Darwin people made caustic remarks about the Seattle distributor, Gregg Wilson. It was obvious that some strong personal animosity existed between these people and Mr. Wilson.

The afternoon session that day was consumed in short sessions that were designed to explain various facets of Darwin's distribution and service system to us. We were briefed on distributor policy, pricing strategy, warranty policy, and current transmission deficiencies (like gear failures and excessive oil leaks).

The next step in the initial information gathering was a meeting at Darwin's San Francisco divisional office. Allen, Joe, and I met with the Darwin division vice president, Dave Freeman, and Jim Harvey. It was Freeman's responsibility to supervise the Darwin distributors that were located in the Western states.

It became obvious that his main purpose for this meeting was to brief us about Gregg Wilson, the Seattle distributor. Wilson and his operation presented a fascinating problem—on one hand the distributorship was burdened with problems, but on the other hand it was very successful financially.

There were five primary problem areas. The new transmission market share in Wilson's territory had slipped by 10 percent in the last three years. It was surmised that Wilson's service performance (or lack of it) was contributing to the market share decline. The vice president felt that Wilson was too harsh in his relationships with customers. This harshness was exemplified by tight credit policies and occasional reports of overpricing. Wilson's dealer relations were also criticized. He was characterized as having two classes of distributors. Those who were close by were treated as competitors, and those in remote locations were treated as full partners. Another problem area cited by Dave Freeman was Wilson's outside business activities—outside the distributorship, that is. He was involved in all kinds of things like investing in ski resorts and restaurants. This dilution of effort was frowned upon by Darwin. Darwin wanted all distributors to devote full time to transmissions. One last problem area was Wilson's purchase of a small company, Crocker Parts, which specialized in making nongenuine replacement parts for the transmissions of Darwin's major competitor. The parts are called gypoparts in the trade. Wilson's independent spirit obviously did not sit well with Darwin. I can still recall Freeman saying, "That's just not the kind of thing that's done by a responsible member of the Darwin family." This reference to family typifies Darwin's paternalistic distributor attitude. In an attempt to smooth over relations with headquarters, Wilson had recently indicated that he would give added effort to the Darwin distributorship in the future.

At the end of our session, Dave Freeman emphasized that all the information that we heard was to remain completely confidential. Wilson was not to find out that we had been made privy to these matters.

Now to the other side of the coin. Wilson's operation had performed exceptionally well in the financial area. Sales (about $30 million) and profits were both steadily increasing. But because of Wilson's maverick attitude and his somewhat unorthodox life-style (he had recently divorced his wife and frequently dated women young enough to be his daughter), Freeman said that Darwin was seriously considering cancelling Wilson's distributor contract. Freeman felt that a prime purpose of the study should be to decide if Wilson's contract should be terminated.

Early that evening we five flew up to Seattle. Gregg Wilson had arranged to take us to dinner at a famous seafood restaurant. There was only one hitch: Gregg couldn't make it until 9 p.m. because he was taking French lessons. So we all waited in the cocktail lounge and had several drinks.

At about 9:15, Gregg Wilson showed up. He was obviously a regular customer; the hostess greeted him by name. Wilson turned out to be a most charming and interesting man. Although he knew he was under the microscope, so to speak, he conducted himself in a relaxed and totally appealing manner. He was articulate and well versed in everything from world politics to fine wines.

The six of us had a wonderful dinner that included two wines selected by Wilson. If he was trying to charm us, he couldn't have gone about it more superbly.

Unlike most client-consultant get-togethers, our dinner developed into quite a relaxed affair. Almost too relaxed, as it turned out. I almost inadvertently let on to Wilson that we knew about his dirty linen. Freeman, the vice president, had casually said, "You know Ken, I really enjoy the West Coast. I don't know if I'll ever be able to go back to the Midwest."

I lightheartedly (and lightheadedly) replied, "Well, maybe you can buy Gregg's Crocker Parts business."

I didn't believe what I had just said. Gregg wasn't supposed to know that we knew about Crocker. I looked at him to see what he was going to do.

Fortunately Gregg was saying something to Allen when I made my slip. We instantly changed the subject!

The next morning we reconvened in the conference room at Wilson's distributorship to get our information gathering in gear again. We had a whole series of things we wanted to get from Wilson. We needed dealer lists, customer lists, financial information, sales data, etc. Wilson was very cooperative and very well prepared. When we left him that afternoon, we had all the information and understanding we needed to begin the market interviewing.

Two weeks later, Joe and I flew back to Seattle go begin the personal interviewing. Jim Harvey also came along and pumped us every evening at dinner to see how things were coming. He was like a brooding mother hen. Overall, this part of the work went smoothly, although the quantification of findings was not working out quite as well as Jim had hoped. We ended up using a lot of matrixes to satisfy Darwin's craving for numbers. A typical matrix looked like this:

Quality of repair work	Rating			
	Excellent	Good	Fair	Poor
Competitor A				
Darwin				
Competitor B				
Competitor C				

We got users to rate each competitor, but Joe and I both found the responses to the "why" questions that we also asked to be much more meaningful. We did interviews with users and dealers all that week in Seattle, Spokane, and Portland.

Upon our return to Chicago, Joe prepared an informal interim report that dealt with both the pilot phase methodology and our preliminary findings. No conclusions were included because we felt that it was too early to firm anything up at this point in the marketplace fieldwork.

Before the interim meeting in Minneapolis, Joe also prepared the telephone and mail questionnaires. We reviewed them with Jim on the afternoon following the interim meeting. To our surprise, he passed on them without much alteration. I wondered if he was beginning to realize the relative meaninglessness of telephone and mail information gathering, compared to personal interviews.

After the interim meeting, Joe took two more trips to Seattle—one to finish the user and dealer personal interviews and the other to interview the Darwin district office people and Darwin's competitive distributors and district office people. These competitive interviews were critical because they were the major source of insight into the new transmission market share slippage issue. It was important to know if the competitor had perceived a slippage in Darwin's position, and, if so, why they thought it had occurred. Was it the way Wilson had run his operation, or was it something else? We knew, for example, that one of Darwin's major competitors had recently made some significant improvements in the reliability of their products. Could these product improvements, which resulted in a more viable competitor, coupled with Wilson's supposedly harsh customer relations approach, have caused the market share slippage? That's what Joe went to Seattle to find out.

4
Analysis and Conclusions

Statistics are no substitute for judgment.
— Henry Clay

*Common sense is the knack of seeing things as they
are, and doing things as they ought to be done.*
— Stowe

Part of the *Webster's New Collegiate Dictionary* definition of the word
"analyze" is: "to study or determine the nature and relationship of the parts
of a problem by analysis." This definition is O.K. for most purposes, but I'd
like to suggest a definition specifically for business problem solving: Analysis is doing whatever you have to do with the information you've gathered
to reach a timely, practical, and acceptable solution.

"Doing whatever you have to do" can mean nothing more than a simple
and straightforward review of the information; it can also mean tedious
numerical calculations, exhaustive written explanations, and seemingly
countless hours in strategy review meetings.

Effective analysis must be appropriate to both the problem at hand and
to the existing situation. There is no "right" analysis for a specific type of
problem. Therefore a good deal of judgment is necessary to choose the type
and the extent of the analysis required. For example, if you own a small
business, and you're solving one of your own problems, the analysis need
only be thorough and extensive enough to convince yourself that you're
making a sound decision. However, if your analysis will be reviewed and
either accepted or rejected by others (be they superiors, fellow managers,
partners, or whoever), then a comprehensive and professional job is essential.

Approaches to business problem analysis fall into two categories: quantitative analysis and qualitative analysis. In some business problem-solving
situations, for instance, in a lot of facilities planning work, a strictly quantitative approach is most appropriate. In other situations, like many organization planning and analysis problems, only a qualitative evaluation pro-

duces meaningful results. But quantitative and qualitative approaches are not mutually exclusive. In the majority of cases a combination of these approaches is the most appropriate and effective method.

I'd like to discuss quantitative analysis first, because it's more straightforward and less subjective. Several examples will be presented to illustrate key points, followed by a companion section on qualitative analysis. Then we'll get back to the Darwin Industries study, to examine both the quantitative and the qualitative approaches used in this engagement.

You may have noticed that I haven't written anything yet about the word that shares half the billing of this chapter—"conclusions." This isn't because I believe that conclusions are unimportant. On the contrary, reaching conclusions is the purpose for doing the analysis in the first place. It's just that I've found you don't consciously pursue conclusions separately from the analysis. In most cases, conclusions are an integral part and an inseparable result of the proper analysis process. That is, if the analysis is appropriately selected and conscientiously carried out, the conclusions will be there when the work is completed.

QUANTITATIVE ANALYSIS

Quantitative analysis is, of course, a process of manipulating the quantitative information that had been gathered in the previous step of the universal approach to business problem solving. It follows that quantitative analysis is dependent upon quantitative information. But don't make the mistake of believing that complete and accurate quantitative information is necessarily required to do a meaningful quantitative analysis.

There are two types of quantitative information: (1) that which is known to be accurate (prices, sales figures, distributor margins, etc.) and (2) that which must be estimated (future sales volume, competitors' market shares, escalation in factory labor rates, salvage value of equipment, etc.). Often the most critical information is of the second type. Do your best to estimate all that you don't know. Guess at it if you have to. Take your best shot at it and then charge right ahead into the analysis.

When the analysis is completed and the conclusions are arrived at, it's time to remember all your *estimated* bits and pieces of information. Then ask yourself the question, "If my estimates were different, would it change the overall conclusion?" My experience suggests to me that usually the answer is "no." If you're unsure of the answer, go back and repeat the analysis with different estimates and see what happens. Usually, running a new number through an already completed analysis takes 10 percent or less of the time the original analysis took. By repeating it, you learn much about the sensitivity of your conclusion to changes in information. If you are dealing with a highly sensitive situation, you may need to develop more faith in the accuracy of your information-estimating procedures.

Early in my consulting career, I was doing part of a study that required estimates of the annual domestic usage of hardwood veneer in four end markets. The purpose of the study was to evaluate the wisdom of one of the client divisions (a veneer producer) expanding its production capacity to meet anticipated future demand. I was handling the kitchen cabinet, wall paneling, and flush door end-use markets. My associate who was directing the study was doing the furniture end-use market. I did interviews with all the right people in each of my end markets and had no trouble with the estimates for kitchen cabinet and wall paneling veneer usage. Industry sources knew the number of wooden kitchen cabinets sold each year and the average amount of veneer used on each cabinet. The size of the wall paneling market was also readily available. But the flush wood door market was giving me problems. There were dozens of door producers and I couldn't possibly interview all of them and stay within my budget. There were no reliable industry statistics on flush doors, and the statistics that were available included metal, vinyl, high-pressure laminate, hardboard, and painted flush doors. Finally, I had an import consideration (Asian lauan door skins) and multiple end markets (commercial, new residential, residential repair and remodeling, mobile homes) to sort out.

The project manager repeatedly suggested that I make a wood flush door market-size estimate so we could add up all four end markets and complete the analysis. I balked. I stalled for more time. I made phone calls and reviewed government statistics in hope of finding a believable method of estimating. Finally, when we were almost out of time, I was forced by the project manager to make my best *guess* "based on what you now know." I did it, and the analysis went ahead. This is when I began to realize that the accuracy of my guess probably wouldn't have any impact on the conclusion we were developing. Veneer used in wood flush doors only accounted for about 10 percent of the total veneer market, so even if my guess was off by 100 percent, it would have very little impact on the overall veneer market size and projected future market growth rate. We concluded in the report that hardwood face veneer would only experience an average annual growth rate for the next ten-year period of about 1½ to 2 percent a year, and that capital investment in veneer plants and equipment was probably not merited. That's when I looked back on my wood flush door market-size guess and realized that it had no impact whatsoever on the only important output of the study, namely, "Don't invest capital in the veneer business."

A Typical Quantitative Analysis

Actually the title of this section is somewhat deceiving, because there probably is no such thing as a typical quantitative analysis. Each analysis is unique in approach, detail, procedure, and complexity. However, the example I'm about to present is typical in one important way—it illustrates the blending of known and estimated information and the considerations of options that are usually an integral part of quantitative analysis in an unstructured business problem-solving situation.

This example concerns a small company (call it Triangle Manufacturing) that had an unusually pleasant problem: Taxes were becoming an excessive burden because of the company's much improved earnings situation. Triangle Manufacturing had been in business for almost thirty years before they became a client in 1976. The business had always been family-owned, and it was organized as a sole proprietorship at the time of the founder's death in 1974. The business was left by the founder's will to his wife and children in the form of a life estate. The oldest son, Tommie Wilbur, was running the operation. Triangle had never made much money. In fact, after Tommie's father took out a modest salary for himself, the bottom-line profit was almost nonexistent.

However, Tommie had breathed new life into the business during his two years of leadership. A series of successful new product introductions and the expansion of Triangle's geographical territory had increased pretax profit to almost 18 percent of company sales. And the future looked even brighter.

The business's new-found prosperity, of course, increased all the family members' tax obligations. The business itself, since it was being taxed as a sole proprietorship, was paying taxes according to the personal income tax schedule. As you may have guessed, the apparently obvious corrective action was to convert the sole proprietorship into a corporation, thus limiting the business tax obligation to about 48 percent of pretax profit. But incorporation was not "apparent" or "obvious" to Tommie or his two brothers. They had apprehensions concerning the procedures and legal implications of administering a corporate business. Their long-time business (and family) lawyer was extremely indecisive and noncommittal. He talked of advantages and disadvantages and of implications and ramifications, but he made no recommendation.

But Triangle's auditor and financial advisor was not lacking in opinions and advice. He was dead set against incorporation. He felt that it would force the family to unduly disclose confidential financial information. He also expounded on gift and inheritance tax considerations to support his position.

Any change in ownership structure was also complicated by several other business operations which were subsidiaries to Triangle's manufacturing operation. Triangle had extensive timber holdings, conducted logging operations to supply the manufacturing business, owned and operated several farms, and produced and sold wood extracts. Each family member had a large stake in "who would get what" and "what would go where" in any possible change in business structure.

Tommie Wilbur requested that our firm come in to try to make some sense out of the situation. We visited with Tommie and his brother for almost a full day in the early spring of 1976. Then I spent the next morning with Triangle's lawyer in Atlanta. That afternoon, after almost a two-hour drive, I sat down to discuss the situation with the company's hospitable but stubborn accountant.

I came away from these meetings with one firm conviction. It was clear to me that the only way we were going to be able to demonstrate the advantages of a corporate business form was with a solid quantitative analysis. Numbers would have to do the talking, because words (especially those that came out of the mouths of northern city slickers) were not going to carry any weight at all!

We reached an agreement with Tommie to proceed with the analysis. Possible alternative business forms, including partnership, incorporation, and combinations of the two, were to be considered. It was further agreed that any legal input required in the analysis would come from our firm's lawyer. We felt this step was necessary to guarantee fresh, unbiased opinions. Finally, it was agreed that any change in corporate form must strike a balance among the following objectives:

- A fair and equitable business income for each member of the family
- A fair and equitable ownership position for each member of the family, at that time and in the future
- Sufficient flexibility for the business to meet the challenges and opportunities ahead in the areas of finance, production, and marketing
- Minimum business tax burden
- Minimum personal tax burden
- An independent income for Mrs. Wilbur (the founder's widow)
- Transfer of Mrs. Wilbur's ownership to her children over time, to minimize taxes.

The analysis was begun by organizing all the assets of the existing sole proprietorship into four functional groups. (This was done so that it would be possible to superimpose a business form on each asset grouping and examine the resulting situation):

- Triangle Manufacturing
- Wood extract business
- Logging operations
- Real estate investments (farms and timberland)

The structure of each alternative business form was defined by using the four functional or operating groupings. Upon initial examination it appeared that there would be an almost endless variety of combinations of business forms and business functional groups to analyze. For example, with a partnership form, each functional activity could be set up as a separate partnership, or combinations of two or more could be grouped into separate partnerships. Fortunately, several criteria emerged which limited the acceptable combinations.

1. The family preferred that the real estate investment activity be organized as a separate entity (either as a partnership or as a subchapter S corporation).

2. The wood extract business and the logging business, which constituted minimal income but had high liability potential, should be incorporated.

3. The wood extract business and the logging business should be separate entities from the Triangle Manufacturing operation.

With these criteria, we were able to boil all the alternatives down to only five distinct possibilities. These five alternatives are summarized in Exhibit 2.

A financial projection was required to estimate the tax burden associated with each alternative business form. Triangle's income statement was projected for each of the next five years. This process naturally entailed making estimates (or assumptions) in all revenue and cost categories. Sales, for example, were forecasted to increase at 13 percent per year based on input from Tommie, the sales manager, and the advertising agency's account executive. Fixed and variable costs were projected primarily on judgments of appropriate individuals within the client company.

Now that the five alternative business options and a pretax net income forecast were in hand, it was possible to begin the actual analysis work. The

EXHIBIT 2   Structure of Each Alternative Business Form

Alternative	Triangle manufacturing	Wood extract	Logging	Real estate
1. General partnership	Partnership	Corporation	Corporation	Partnership or subchapter S corp.
2. Limited partnership	At least one limited partner	Corporation	Corporation	Partnership or subchapter S corp.
3. Corporation	Corporation	Corporation	Corporation	Partnership or subchapter S corp.
4. Combination partnership/ corporation	Partnership owns assets: these are leased to manufacturing corporation	Corporation	Corporation	Partnership or subchapter S corp.
5. Partnership converting to a corporation	Partnership converting to a corporation after two years	Corporation	Corporation	Partnership or subchapter S corp.

first issue to be confronted was the transfer of assets from Mrs. Wilbur to her three children. The will had left her with one-half of all assets outright in fee simple ownership, and the other half in the form of a life estate (to be divided equally among the children upon her death). Mrs. Wilbur had the option of transferring all assets through her will when she died, or giving them away while she was living. The major criterion for making this decision was the impact of gift and estate taxes.

I'm raising this issue because it compounded our quantitative analysis work. It was decided to select two "most appropriate" asset transfer possibilities and carry each through the entire tax calculation for each of the five alternative business forms.

First, both federal and state income taxes were calculated for each alternative for each of the five years in the forecast period. These were summarized in a table like the one shown in Exhibit 3.

Next, personal taxes (both federal and state) were calculated for Mrs. Wilbur and the three children for each of the five alternative business forms and for each of the years. This required the calculation of over 1000 individual tax computations, but the results were well worth the exercise. The summarization of business taxes, personal taxes, and miscellaneous taxes clearly showed that the corporate alternative (3) yielded the lowest tax burden. In fact, the estimated total tax obligation for the business and all members of the family for the corporate alternative was 16 percent lower than the present form of business organization. Conversion to the corporate form would result in an estimated tax savings over the five-year period of almost $500,000.

We now had hard numbers to demonstrate the tax obligation advantages of incorporation, but there were still all the nonquantitative considerations. We felt a need to address these issues in a quantitative format, if possible. The first step in this quantification process was to assign an importance rating to each issue (including the tax burden issue) as shown in Exhibit 4.

Now it was possible to construct a table that would compare each alternative business form in each of the key decision categories. In the table

EXHIBIT 3   Tax Summary Table

Business alternative	1977		1978			Five-year total
	Fed	State	Fed	State	. . . .	Federal and state total
1						
2						
3						
4						
5						
Present situation						

EXHIBIT 4   Importance Rating for Key Decision Issues

Issue	Importance rating
Public disclosure of information	10
Limiting liability	10
Flexibility in financial structure	15
Ease of formation and start-up	5
Fringe benefits for family members	10
Complexity in administering business	10
Tax burden	20

each issue for each alternative was ranked on a scale of one to ten, with ten indicating full satisfaction of the issue. Summation of these seven rankings for a given business form alternative resulted in an unweighted total score. By multiplying each ranking by its respective importance rating, a weighted total score was also determined. An abbreviated version (showing only two of the five alternatives) of the table which appeared in our report is shown in Exhibit 5.

The corporation outscores the partnership in both the unweighted and weighted columns, and the weighted comparison clearly shows the advantage of incorporation.

The approach illustrated in Exhibit 5 is one of the most powerful tools in quantitative business problem-solving analysis work. Once you master its use, it becomes an invaluable decision tool. It can be, and is, used (as you'll see later on) even in such qualitative areas as candidate appraisal in the executive search process.

The Triangle case illustrates almost total reliance on quantitative analysis. Now let's look at qualitative analysis.

EXHIBIT 5   Summary Comparison Table

		Scoring			
		1. Partnership		3. Corporation	
Key issue	Importance rating	Unweighted	Weighted	Unweighted	Weighted
Public disclosure	2	10	20	8	16
Liability	2	5	10	10	20
Financial flexibility	3	5	15	10	30
Ease of formation	1	10	10	7	7
Fringe benefits	2	7	14	10	20
Complexity	2	10	20	8	16
Tax burden	4	9	36	10	40
Totals		56	125	63	149

QUALITATIVE ANALYSIS

If you felt that some of the material in the quantitative analysis section was too complicated, you're in for a pleasant surprise. Qualitative analysis, as applied to unstructured business problem-solving situations, is extremely straightforward. In most instances, it involves only these three steps:
1. Organizing gathered information
2. Examination of the resulting displays
3. Drawing conclusions

Let's briefly examine each of these steps.

Organizing gathered information means literally taking all the relevant information that has been gathered and displaying it in some appropriate and logical fashion. The most common display is probably that which lists advantages in one column and disadvantages in an adjacent column. Another useful approach is to group findings into categories by importance, listing key findings first.

Examination of the resulting displays is the next step. I'm afraid I'll have to use clichéd phrases to describe this process, but I have no choice. Effective examination does require "sound judgment," "appropriate experience," and, probably most important, "good common sense." In qualitative analysis, the implications of the information in hand are seldom obvious. There is often no black or white—only shades of gray. So judgment, experience, and common sense go a long way toward effective interpolation and extrapolation.

Drawing conclusions in qualitative analysis, as in any analysis, is the "fallout" of the analysis process itself. Organization and examination of the information will produce conclusions. Confirmation or rejection of hypotheses will begin as soon as the information starts to appear in an organized form. (Since qualitative analysis is so subjective, a conclusion that is crystal clear to one person may not be at all apparent to another. That's why partnerships with an odd number of partners are more effective decision-making bodies than partnerships with an even number. There is always someone to cast the tie-breaking vote! That's also why the autocratic system is essential in business. There's always a boss to make the decision!)

It doesn't seem that the qualitative analysis process has changed much in the last two centuries. Benjamin Franklin described it this way:

> When confronted with two courses of action, I jot down on a piece of paper the arguments in favor of each one—then on the opposite side I write the arguments against each one. Then by weighing the arguments pro and con and cancelling them out, one against the other, I take the course indicated by what remains.

There are many real business problems where, in the final judgment, qualitative analysis is the only way to make a relevant decision. One consulting assignment I did in the early 1970s is representative of this class of problems. A client came to us with a request to analyze a new business opportunity. They had developed a process to make an ultrasweet corn syrup. They felt that it might be used in many food products that currently were using sugar. This corn sweetener, called high-fructose corn syrup, could be marketed very profitably at 10 to 20 percent below the price of sugar.

At an initial discussion of the study with our client, they indicated that two corn processing companies were just introducing similar high-fructose products. These companies, A. E. Staley and Clinton Corn Processing, were using a licensed Japanese production technology and were marketing the product in small quantities. The objective of our study efforts was to recommend whether or not to proceed with a commitment to produce and market high-fructose corn syrup by evaluating the business opportunity that existed.

Since the syrup could only be produced as a liquid, it was not an appropriate product for the retail consumer market. The success of a high-fructose corn sweetener was therefore dependent on the willingness of food processors to substitute it for more expensive sugar. Our interview program included discussions with:

- Sugar refiners
- Sugar brokers
- Food processors in these areas:
  - Soft drinks
  - Baking
  - Wine
  - Salad dressing
  - Pickles and relishes
  - Candy
  - Table syrups
  - Ice cream
  - Catsup
  - Jellies and jams
- Corn processors (including Staley and Clinton)

The information we gathered was mixed concerning the outlook for high-fructose corn syrup. Obviously, the sugar people gave it no chance at all of succeeding ("It has an aftertaste." "It's not really as sweet as sugar."). On the other hand, Staley and Clinton said that high-fructose corn sweetener was directly substitutable for sugar, gave the final food product identical characteristics, and saved the food processor money. As you might suspect, the food processors were in both camps. For example, soft drink bottlers were against it, as were wine producers. Basing their opinions on brief preliminary evaluations, some of the syrup, baking, and other food producers felt that it could be substituted for a portion of the sugar in their products.

The attractiveness of this project to our client depended primarily on the eventual size of the high-fructose corn syrup market. After all, two companies were already committed to production. Would there be enough of a market for three producers? We could not reliably quantify an answer to this question since there were too many unknowns, too many ifs and buts. We developed a market-size forecast, but had to tell our client that our confidence level in the forecast was low. The numbers did suggest that there would be enough business for three or even four high-fructose corn syrup producers, but the numbers were not based on solid findings.

In the end, the decision had to be made on the basis of a qualitative analysis. The analysis we developed clearly suggested that our client should proceed with the project, and we made that recommendation. However, much of this recommendation was based only on a "feel" we got in our field interviews. The sugar refiners were obviously worried about high-fructose corn syrup and were defensive in their response to probing questions. Some of the leading food producers were open-minded and optimistic about the new high-sweetness corn syrup.

We, as consultants, felt "Yes, it's a good opportunity." Unfortunately, our client was not privy to what produced our "feel." The interviews were done by us—not the client. It was difficult for us, as intermediaries, to convey our positive impression without appearing to be optimistic without sufficient reason. Our client rejected our recommendation, and decided to pass on high-fructose corn syrup. In retrospect, that turned out to be a mistake. High-fructose corn syrup is now used in all kinds of food products, including soft drinks, where everybody had thought that it had absolutely no chance.

Maybe the moral of this story is that to gain a first-hand feel for a new market, a company should interview potential users themselves instead of hiring consultants to do it for them.

DARWIN INDUSTRIES

The analysis in the Darwin engagement used both quantitative and qualitative approaches. You may recall that Darwin put a great deal of emphasis on the need for quantification of findings. Early in the information-gathering stage, we realized that we were not going to be able to develop solid quantitative findings from personal interviews. So these interviews were used to develop an understanding of the problems in Seattle and to suggest possible recommendations for improvement. Quantitative support for the personal interview findings was generated in the telephone and mail survey phases of the information-gathering work.

We began our analysis by organizing all the personal interview information we had gathered. In almost all cases it was organized by specific issues. For example, take the issue of service parts availability. Information on this

EXHIBIT 6   Qualitative Analysis Process

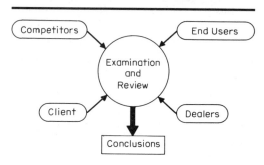

issue was gathered from internal, dealer, end-user, and competitive interviews. All this information on parts availability was tabulated. Then the tabulation was examined and reviewed for completeness, consistency, and implications. A diagram of this process is shown in Exhibit 6.

The analysis process determined that Darwin's parts availability in the Seattle territory was unsatisfactory, and poorer than competition. We further concluded that the reason for this deficiency was not Gregg Wilson's distributorship, but the Darwin service parts operations in Minneapolis. Sufficient service parts, especially for new products, were simply not available from the factory. This situation was creating excessive delays in transmission repairs and a credibility gap with Darwin's customers. The parts manager in Darwin's Seattle distributorship was unable to maintain satisfactory parts inventories despite anticipatory ordering practices and frequent follow-up on unfilled orders.

Organization of all other information by specific issue resulted in a series of other major conclusions:

• *Warranty:* Darwin's new transmission warranty was being administered too rigidly. No allowances were being made for extenuating circumstances and product deficiencies. For example, if a transmission with a warranty of 100,000 miles or one year failed at 103,000 miles eight months after being put into service, no warranty adjustment was being given to the customer. This inflexible stance was hurting Darwin's position because its major competitors in the Seattle territory were consistently making liberal warranty adjustments. The responsibility for Darwin's warranty problem was shared by the Seattle distributor and by the warranty administration group at company headquarters. Most of the difficulty appeared to be associated with a lack of communication and cooperation between Seattle and Minneapolis.

• *Product Dependability:* In the last two years Darwin had introduced a series of high-performance transmissions to match the new high-horsepower diesel engines being used in large on-highway tractor-trailer trucks.

The new Darwin products were experiencing severe reliability problems in the Seattle territory. It appeared that premature failure problems were more severe in the Seattle territory than in most other Darwin territories, primarily because of the mountainous terrain on the West Coast.

■ *Gregg Wilson's Image:* Wilson, the owner of the Darwin Seattle distributorship, was viewed by customers and dealers as a fair, but firm businessman. Most sources in the marketplace felt that his distributorship was providing good service, and that his business was well run and efficient.

However, we did sense that his non-Darwin business activities were interfering with his responsibilities to Darwin. Frequently, in personal interview situations, people would say something like, "He's never in when I call" or "It's impossible to talk to Gregg personally when I call."

You may remember that Darwin's management was concerned about the impact that Wilson's swinging-singles life-style was having in the territory. We found that it was not a problem. Most interviewees felt that Wilson should be able to follow the personal life-style that he chose. In fact, it was apparent that some envied him!

■ *Market Share Decline:* We concluded that the decline in the sales of new transmissions in the Seattle territory was caused by several problem areas. First, new products were not living up to expectations. Second, service parts were not available in many cases so that prompt repairs could be made. Third, the rigid and inflexible warranty policy was alienating some customers.

The total response to the mail survey that was sent to 2000 transmission users in the Seattle territory was 20 percent, or 400. Of the 1000 sent with only a cover letter, 150 were filled in and sent back. A $1 premium ("for your favorite child") was put in with the other 1000 questionnaires, and 250 of these were returned. We subcontracted the tabulation of the mail survey responses to a computer data tabulating house.

Use of the computer allowed us to readily display the results in specific categories. These categories were end-use industry, type of equipment the transmissions were being used in, and brand of transmission owned. Overall, the results of this analysis paralleled the results of the personal and telephone interview work, but these results were entirely quantitative. For example, we found that 72 percent of all respondents rated Darwin's parts availability as either poor or unsatisfactory.

We concluded that the mail questionnaire was the only way of quantitatively measuring the service effectiveness in a given territory. Mail was the only way to develop repeatable quantitative findings and the only way to totally eliminate subjective human judgments.

In the next chapter you'll see how the analysis and conclusions just presented were used to develop a series of recommendations for Darwin.

5
Recommendations and Implementation

Thinking well is wise; planning well, wiser; doing well wisest and best of all. — PERSIAN PROVERB

This chapter covers the fourth and last step in the universal approach to business problem solving—recommending and implementing. This step is often the most difficult to accomplish successfully, for it involves people and change. It is a part of human nature to dislike and avoid change even when the change is for the better. This step is usually the most time consuming as well. Frequently, it takes six months to a year to completely implement the recommendations of a study. During a long implementation period, patience and perseverance become the most important attributes of success.

RECOMMENDATIONS

Once a series of conclusions for a particular problem-solving situation have been established, it's time to develop meaningful and actionable recommendations. The first step in this process is to make a comprehensive list of possible recommendations. Entries on this list should be detailed enough to differentiate among alternatives, but not so detailed as to be tedious. Only distinctly different courses of action should be listed at this stage. Sometimes as few as two distinct alternatives will comprise the entire list. In other situations, as many as six or eight possibilities can be generated.

Once the list of possible recommendations has been developed, a comparison and weeding-out process should be undertaken. This can be done in several ways. One possibility is to develop charts or tables comparing the advantages and disadvantages of distinctive sets of recommendations. Laying out this type of information may make the best course of action obvious. Another approach is to prepare a quantitative comparison table. In this

EXHIBIT 7   Quantitative Ranking Table

Alternative recommendations	Sample comparison criteria				Total ranking (out of a possible 34)
	Quickness (10)	Flexibility (6)	Expense (8)	Accuracy (10)	
1	9	5	5	6	25
2	6	6	5	7	24
3	10	5	7	10	32
4	5	6	8	8	27

type of table the alternative recommendations are usually listed in a column down the left-hand side of the page and all important comparison criteria are listed across the top. Then numerical importance factors are assigned to each criterion. Finally, each recommendation is scored for each criterion and a total ranking is accumulated across the table for each alternative. An example of this ranking process is presented in Exhibit 7. Note that alternative 3 got the highest score because it ranked high on the comparison criteria that were assigned the highest numerical importance factors (quickness and accuracy).

After the comparison and weeding-out processes are completed, a choice of the most practical and acceptable set of recommendations should be possible. This final choice must often be based on judgment and common sense, despite the use of advantage and disadvantage comparisons and quantitative ranking tables. These techniques may point the way, or substantiate personal judgment, but in the end the right course of action is usually chosen because it simply seems like the best thing to do.

The last step in the recommendation process is to concisely and simply state the recommendations that have been chosen. Make sure this statement is specific enough to actually function as an action plan. Liberal use of words that convey the feeling of action—words like begin, revise, develop, design, build, initiate—is suggested.

DARWIN INDUSTRIES

Darwin's distributor contracts are renewed every three years. At each of these renewals, Darwin has the option of purchasing back the franchise from the assigned distributor. The distributor is obligated to sell the distributorship to Darwin at a price based on a prescribed asset valuation procedure. Darwin's normal procedure is to renew for another three-year period, but automatic renewal was not the case with Gregg Wilson in Seattle. You may recall that Seattle was chosen as the pilot territory for the study because of a special situation that existed there—that special situation being Gregg Wilson.

Wilson's current three-year contract was due to expire two months after we made our final presentation. Before developing a series of recommendations to improve Darwin's service in the Seattle territory, we had to address the contract renewal issue.

We knew to begin with that Wilson's contract would not even be *considered* for renewal under a status quo situation. Consideration of renewal would require that some changes be made in his business practices and in his personal life. Specifically, Wilson would have to agree to dispose of most of his outside business (especially Crocker Parts—the gypoparts line for competitors' transmissions), and he would have to entirely separate his flamboyant personal life from his Darwin distributorship. (At the last annual distributorship meeting at company headquarters, for example, he brought along a beautiful young female traveling companion. Other distributors brought their spouses, or came alone.) This type of thing would have to stop if Wilson's contract was to be considered for renewal.

The Darwin Western divisional vice president, Dave Freeman, had possibly the closest personal relationship to Wilson. So we decided to request that Dave have a heart-to-heart talk with Wilson. Freeman diplomatically explained to Wilson that in the future he would have to devote full time to the Darwin distributorship and stop flaunting his personal life-style if he wanted to be considered for contract renewal. Fortunately, we made it over this first hurdle; Wilson agreed to these stipulations. Darwin indicated that if his contract were renewed, Wilson would be given one year to dispose of Crocker Parts.

If a decision were made to replace Wilson, finding a replacement would not be a problem. It was Darwin's practice in these situations to bankroll bright corporate executives so that they could purchase available distributorships. I had the feeling that several Darwin executives anxiously awaited the chance to become the Seattle distributor.

With an understanding reached on Gregg Wilson's position, it was possible to proceed with the choice of our recommendation regarding the franchise renewal issue. We had two choices:

1. Recommend that Wilson be retained
2. Recommend that he be replaced by an unspecified Darwin executive

The advantages and disadvantages of each choice were developed in the table shown in Exhibit 8. A review of this information strongly suggested that the advantages of retaining Wilson were much more important than the advantages associated with replacing him. However, there were some definite advantages to replacing Wilson. Ultimately, we felt that Darwin had much more to gain by constructively trying to change Wilson than replacing him with someone who would be an unknown quantity.

We recommended to Darwin that it renew Wilson's contract for a period of eighteen months, rather than three years. During this period Wilson would be able to demonstrate his willingness to give full effort to the distributorship, and to separate his personal life from it. This recommendation was accepted and implemented by Darwin.

Now we could submit the recommendations we felt were necessary to improve service and increase the market share in the Seattle territory. The recommendations were straightforward and came directly from the conclusions presented at the end of the last chapter. Here is a summary of the basic recommendations:

- *Parts Availability:* The supply of parts, especially for the newer high-failure-rate transmissions, must be improved. This would require larger inventories in the parts warehouse in Minneapolis, holding parts suppliers to delivery commitments, prompt filling of distributors' parts orders, and minimizing the practice of "robbing" the service parts warehouse to keep the new transmission production line going.

- *Warranty:* Recommendations related to warranty were divided into three categories.

First, it was recommended that an unbiased committee be established to review the procedures and communications channels between the distributors and the warranty administration group at headquarters. This committee was to develop recommendations to streamline procedures and improve communications within eight weeks of convening. This recommendation was made because our study did not allow us to review headquarters operations.

EXHIBIT 8   Advantages and Disadvantages Associated with the Choice of a Distributor in Seattle Territory

Retain Wilson	Replace Wilson
Advantages	*Advantages*
■ Retain his experience in running a distributorship.	■ This step would surely put an end to the problem that Darwin is having with Wilson.
■ Retain his knowledge of the Seattle market area.	■ Replacement may signal a fresh start to customers in Seattle territory.
■ Wilson's business is now basically sound and well run.	
Disadvantages	*Disadvantages*
■ He may not, in fact, devote full time in the future to Darwin.	■ Loss of marketing momentum.
■ People at headquarters who dislike Wilson may try to sabotage this choice.	■ Need for training and orientation of replacement.
	■ Replacement may be too busy learning and won't properly attack current Seattle service problems (warranty, new product failures).
	■ Replacement may also have idiosyncrasies.

Second, we recommended that Darwin assign a local warranty adjuster to the Seattle territory on a trial basis. Darwin's major competitors had local warranty administrators and it appeared to streamline and expedite warranty administration.

Third, we recommended that Darwin consider informal extension of warranties beyond the specified mileage and time limits. We felt this was especially important on the newer transmissions that were experiencing excessive failures.

▪ *Products:* We recommended that Darwin expedite product improvements to correct new product deficiencies. Darwin should own up to its current product problems and do its best to communicate specific measures being taken to correct deficiencies.

▪ *Gregg Wilson:* We recommended that Darwin should monitor Wilson's progress toward meeting his personal commitments to Darwin's management and take corrective actions as needed.

▪ *Measuring Service Effectiveness:* We stated that the only repeatable quantitative approach was to utilize the mail questionnaire developed in the Seattle pilot study, but that it could not be relied upon for identifying appropriate actions for improvement. Furthermore, we felt that personal interviews with users, dealers, and competitors were the only appropriate means of identifying actionable improvements.

This completed the initial study effort for Darwin. They must have liked it. We're beginning a study of their Cleveland territory next month.

IMPLEMENTATION

As I said at the beginning of this chapter, effective implementation takes patience and perseverance. It also takes method. There are six steps that should be followed in implementing recommendations. These steps apply to almost all problem-solving situations. A brief description of each is presented in Exhibit 9. More detail on implementation in specific problem-solving situations is presented in Part 2.

EXHIBIT 9 Steps to Successful Implementation

1. Define and list all the essential steps involved in the implementation.
2. Establish a tight but realistic schedule with built-in review points at significant milestones.
3. Assign overall implementation responsibility to one individual.
4. Monitor and review progress frequently.
5. Make adjustments and refinements wherever and whenever appropriate.
6. Instill in employees confidence in the implementation plan by supporting it and standing firm.

part 2

Putting the Management Consulting Approach to Work

6

Planning for Future Success

(CORPORATE GROWTH PLANNING)

*We judge ourselves by what we feel capable of doing
while others judge us by what we have already done.*
— HENRY WADSWORTH LONGFELLOW

This is the first of a series of chapters designed to show you how to put the management consulting approach to business problem solving to work on your problems. In each chapter, a specific problem area is addressed, and the application of the four-step approach is illustrated.

In several of the illustrations the problem was solved internally (without the use of consultants) or through the use of consultants on only a designated portion of the problem. However, in most of the examples, outside consultants were used to solve the problem as a whole, not because this was the only way to solve the problem, but because it was the way the client company chose to handle it. In many of the problems that were handled by outside consultants, I'm going to point out alternate approaches that could have used internal capabilities to solve the entire problem or a major portion of it. And in some situations I'm going to maintain that the use of outside consultants would have been the only sound approach— even if you had to borrow money from your in-laws to pay the bill!

CORPORATE GROWTH PLANNING

Many books and articles have been written on the topic of corporate growth planning. As an author I feel a responsibility to investigate, review, and digest what has been written before I put down my own message. As a management consultant I feel much less responsibility in this area. Sure, management consultants are expected to keep up on new ideas presented in the literature, and they usually do. But most information in books and articles leans too much toward the theoretical and too far away from the pragmatic to be actionable. So when a corporate planning study comes along, most consultants will rely on their basic approach to business problem solving, and that's what I've decided to do in this chapter. I'm going to present a simple, proven approach to corporate growth planning (a multitude of others exist) and illustrate it with real case histories. If I err, it will be on the side of the practical and pragmatic rather than on the side of the theoretical.

Corporate growth planning is one of a number of consulting specialties that is not directly problem-oriented. This is because in a corporate growth planning assignment there really isn't any specific problem, except perhaps some recognition or vague feelings on the part of management that future growth isn't likely to be as good as it should be. This is probably why full-blown corporate growth planning studies don't come along as often as consultants would like them to. Often prospective clients have to be sold on the need for and benefits of formalized corporate growth planning. This need for prodding may suggest a deficiency on the part of top management, because planning for future growth is one of the prime responsibilities of management. This responsibility should be addressed in a logical, organized manner, whether it is done internally or with the assistance of outside consultants.

BASIC STEPS IN
GROWTH PLANNING

There are essentially two types of corporate growth planning. The first is the full-blown corporate planning study, which involves a total examination, review, and analysis of the organization, its outlook, and its options. The second type of corporate planning study is more directed and narrower. Sometimes these narrower efforts are called strategic planning studies because they involve strategic decisions with a finite number of options. In many instances, a strategic planning study is done because only limited objectives (or specific products) are to be addressed.

Both types of corporate planning effort are covered in this chapter. The full-blown version will be introduced and explained first because it encompasses all possible situations. Then the strategic type of study will be illustrated.

The full-blown corporate growth planning study is composed of five distinct steps:
1. Internal audit and setting objections
2. Market audit
3. Screening and ranking of growth alternatives

4. Intensive evaluation of selected opportunities.
5. Formalizing the growth plan

In actuality, each of the first four steps is a separate mini-study. Each mini-study has its own problem definition, information-gathering phase, analysis and conclusions, and implementation. The implementation phase of each is the action required to initiate the next mini-study.

Internal Audit and Setting Objectives

The primary purpose of the internal audit of operations is to define the strengths and limitations of the organization. A further purpose of this step is to establish corporate objectives for the planning period (usually five years). Establishing corporate objectives means reaching agreement among the executives of the company on the rate of growth that is desired and that can be attained within financial, physical, and management limitations. A 15 percent compound growth rate, which would mean doubling the company's sales in five years, is a typical growth rate agreed upon as a result of this type of interplay. A preliminary consensus is also sought on issues such as the desirable rate of return on investment and the merits of acquisition versus internal development.

Phase 1 in the first mini-study is to agree that an internal audit of operations and establishment of corporate objectives are an essential beginning to meaningful corporate planning. It may also be appropriate to define the scope of the overall effort at the same time. For example, a company may decide that diversification should concentrate upon compatible, logical extensions of the existing operations.

Phase 2 is to conduct several internal interviews with each key executive. This is the primary information-gathering technique used in defining strengths and limitations and setting objectives. These interviews are usually conducted on a one-to-one basis and last up to two hours. Their main purpose is to guarantee an honest, frank exchange of ideas and opinions. Often ten to twelve top executives in a company are included in this series of interviews. Emphasis is placed on discussing specific areas where internal viewpoints may differ. Sometimes an initial group executive meeting is held both to communicate the objective and methodology of the study and to elicit areas of broad general agreement of goals, objectives, and resources. Then the individual meetings (or interviews) are used to gather details and understanding of the strengths and limitations of various functional areas.

In some instances, it is also necessary for the consulting team to interview managers of operational units. Quite often these people have an understanding of problem areas that is markedly different from top management's.

A secondary source of information during the audit are internal company records and documents. Sales data, profit by product-line data, five-year plans, and one-year plans are all analyzed by the consultants for whatever insight may be available.

After the information gathering is concluded, the consultants have a good understanding, as seen by the client, of the strengths, limitations, and objectives of the company. Of course, this understanding is something that any well-run company should already possess, or be able to generate internally. Recently, I was looking over a promotional brochure of a famous consulting firm that does a lot of strategic planning work. It says, in part, "We interview the top executive groups one at a time. We learn to look at the company, the competition, and the market *through their eyes.*" This suggests to me that the entire internal audit is not much more than a high-priced orientation and training program for the consultants. In some circumstances it can probably be done much more efficiently by company personnel.

Market Audit

The second mini-study involves an analysis of the company's position in their market, and an identification and analysis of relevant trends in that market.

There is a divergence of opinion among consulting firms as to who should be responsible for doing the bulk of the information gathering and analysis in the market audit step of the corporate planning study. Surprisingly, some consulting firms are willing to sacrifice their own billings by insisting that prime responsibility for the market audit lie with the marketing department of the client company. These consulting firms see their role as a coordinator, or at best as an auxiliary staff, in gathering, interpreting, and analyzing relevant information. The logic behind this line of thought is that the client company is more capable than the consulting firm of analyzing the markets it competes in every day.

Other consulting firms take the position that *they* are best able to make an assessment of the client company's market position because of their position as an independent observer. "Insiders can't help but see the market through rose-colored glasses," they might say. Consulting firms have one other advantage in market audit work. They can interview people in the marketplace that the client company cannot approach, namely, the client's competitors—who also happen to be the single most important source of market insight. Personally, I have to agree with the consultants who say that they can best analyze the position and trends in a given market. I take this position because I've done hundreds of interviews with client competitors, and I know how valuable they can be.

Information gathering in most market audits relies heavily on personal field interviews. A balance of interviews with competitors, suppliers, customers, noncustomers, and distributors is sought. Typically, thirty to forty interviews are involved. If the client company is in the consumer products area, consumer market research techniques may also be used to sample a broad group of users and nonusers.

This mini-study should include market share estimates, market and individual company growth rates, geographical strengths and weaknesses, client and competitor image data, technological trends, and customer use patterns.

At the end of the market audit, a meeting is usually held with the client to discuss the results of steps 1 and 2. This first interim meeting is used to provide a clear understanding and evaluation of the company's current overall position relative to its industry, and to review a summary of the relevant trends that are occurring in the marketplace.

Final decisions are also made at this meeting on corporate growth objectives, capabilities, and limitations. These decisions are then translated into new criteria for deciding among various growth options for use in the next step of the study. Finally, the consulting firm will usually present an assessment of current company operations and make recommendations for improvement, where appropriate.

Screening and Ranking of Growth Alternatives

In this step of the study, the consulting firm will concentrate on identifying profit and growth opportunities available to the client company, either through expansion of existing products, internal development of new products, or acquisition of other companies.

The first step in the identification process is to measure a wide variety of opportunities against the screening criteria established at the interim meeting. These criteria can include minimum size of business (for example, business potential must be greater than $10 million), return on investment guidelines, geographical limitation, risk/reward factors, and management expertise requirements. Basically these criteria define the kinds of businesses that the client company would like to be involved in.

One danger is to set overly stringent criteria. I was once involved in a corporate planning study where the criteria not only were too stringent, but also verged on being internally inconsistent. The company wanted to find new product opportunities that not only produced high profits, but also offered low capital investment and ease of entry. It was almost impossible for us to convince them that any opportunity that had low investment requirements, high profits, and ease of entry would attract competitors like honey attracts bees, and that all these new competitors would surely drive profits below acceptable levels. The study ended in a standoff; we were frustrated and the client was unhappy.

Once all possible business opportunities have been screened, those remaining are ranked in order of attractiveness. Ranking factors include size of market, expected growth, anticipated competition, return on investment, and operating margins. These factors and any others that are appropriate are assigned weights in order of relative importance.

The one asset that consulting firms claim to bring to this ranking process is their ability to develop enough information on each alternative to rank them properly. This information is typically developed through personal field interviews with appropriate trade and business sources. Depending on the specific information needed and the availability of this information, consultants may or may not be necessary in this step of the growth planning process. If consultants are necessary, there is no reason why they can't be hired for this task alone.

A consulting company can be called in and asked to prepare a proposal to study briefly eight or ten specific markets. A list of the information needed on each market can be supplied to them. The consulting firm will report back with their findings, and then client company personnel can do the necessary ranking.

At the end of this information-gathering and ranking process, a second interim meeting is usually held. At this meeting, the consulting team presents its business opportunity rankings along with the supportive data that have been collected. Generally, one to four of the top-ranking opportunities are then chosen for further evaluation in the next step.

Intensive Evaluation of Selected Opportunities

At this point in most corporate growth planning studies, the program has been transformed from a broad-based search for growth and profitability to the evaluation of one or two specific business opportunities. These opportunities take the form of acquisition possibilities, expansion of existing profit centers, or new ventures suitable for internal development. Acquisition and new venture work are the subjects of the next two chapters.

Formalizing the Growth Plan

The final step in the corporate growth planning cycle usually takes on a highly individual character. The content of the formal plan depends a great deal on the nature of the client company and on the nature of the business opportunities that are an integral part of the growth plan.

However, most consulting reports presented at the culmination of a corporate growth planning study will include recommendations concerning present company businesses, a summary of trends in the client's marketplace expected to affect the client's businesses, a discussion of identified opportunities, the needed financial and management commitments required, the projected return, a timetable for accomplishment, and the consulting firm's recommended strategy.

Full-blown corporate growth planning studies are usually expensive and lengthy. A typical effort for a single-industry company may cost between $50,000 and $100,000. The cost of multiple-industry efforts goes up from there. The time between initiation of the first step and presentation of the formal plan is usually about six months, although it could stretch out to as much as nine months, depending on the complexity of the effort. Obviously, if internal effort can be substituted for consultant effort in some areas, it is quite possible to save a good deal of the cost of a growth planning study.

STRATEGIC PLANNING

As mentioned earlier, strategic planning is a shortened, more concentrated vision of corporate growth planning. It also usually involves less company analysis and a limited number of options for growth. Strategic planning efforts are also initiated for different reasons than are corporate growth planning studies. You may recall that growth planning studies are usually the result of a feeling that growth and profitability are probably not going to be all that is hoped for. This sensitivity to a subpar performance level may be based on a maturing market, increased competition, or some other observation. Whatever the impetus, it's usually a generalized concern for a lackluster future. On the other hand, the need for strategic planning usually results from a specific threat or opportunity that calls for decisive action. The major question in strategic planning is not "What do you think we should be doing five years from now?" but, rather, "What are we going to do about *this* situation?"

Because strategic planning is problem-oriented (unlike corporate growth planning), there is no specific recipe for reaching a decision. Most strategic planning involves healthy measures of unstructured business problem solving. Because there is no recipe, it's impossible to describe the process in generalized terms, so I'm going to use two examples to do it. The first example concerns a company that fumbled the strategic planning ball, so to speak. The second example illustrates how to go about meaningful strategic planning. Ironically, the fumbling company is a sophisticated Fortune 500 member, and the more successful planner just a smallish unknown.

An Example of Poor Strategic Planning

Peterson Corporation is a company that grew and got rich on a single-product concept—air filtration. Their largest and most profitable product line is air filters for use in diesel and gasoline engines. Simple products in this category include carburetor air filters for passenger cars. Larger and more sophisticated filters are offered for industrial and construction equipment and heavy truck diesel engines. All these filters operate on the same simple principle: the unfiltered air is directed through small passageways which separate out the dirt. When the filter is filled with dirt, it is discarded and replaced.

In the mid-1960s, Peterson saw looming on the horizon a threat to its filter business, namely, the gas turbine engine. You remember the gas turbine engine. In the mid-1960s it was the heir apparent to the piston engine. Ford and Chrysler were touting it as the power plant of the future.

Gas turbines, of course, were well established in specialized markets. The jet engine revolution in commercial aviation proved its merits for aircraft application. Jet engines needed no filters, but the turbines that were expected to replace gasoline and diesel engines in ground applications did need filters. Peterson's filters for conventional gasoline and diesel engines did not work on gas turbine engines. A typical gas turbine engine requires five to ten times as much air as a gasoline engine of comparable horsepower, and the disposable filters that Peterson made, if put on a gas turbine engine, would have required replacement five or ten times more frequently than on a gasoline engine. The need for such frequent replacement would make disposable filters uneconomical.

Peterson executives decided to initiate a crash research and development (R&D) program to develop a permanent, reusable filter for gas turbine engines. In retrospect, this was a strategic mistake, because, as we all know, the turbine engine has fallen by the wayside. A thorough analysis of the problems that were to block commercial success of the gas turbine could have saved Peterson a lot of R&D money. I made such an analysis for another client at about the same time and correctly concluded that the turbine engine was not going to make it. I'm not saying this to boast, but to point out that an accurate judgment was possible.

I guess Peterson can be excused for this mistake, since they were going along with the tide and trying to protect their flank at the same time. Unfortunately, the R&D gas turbine filter program was only the beginning of Peterson's errors. The R&D group, in its efforts to develop a filter, ended up developing a centrifugal particle classifier because the turbine threat was subsiding. This air classifier was so sophisticated that it outperformed all known air classifiers. It could sort fine particles in very close tolerance size groups. A brief search of secondary source information indicated that the total market for air classification equipment was $20 million. Peterson decided to commercialize its air classifier and begin marketing efforts. The markets for classification equipment were totally foreign to Peterson. Two years later Peterson's air classifier sales had reached only $250,000. In the meantime, Peterson discovered that air classifiers were frequently sold in conjunction with particle pulverizing equipment. So what did they do? You guessed it. Peterson went out and acquired a small pulverizing equipment supplier. This acquisition was based on published government data which said that the pulverizer market was about $90 million. Despite this large market, Peterson's pulverizer sales were unaccountably stagnant at about $500,000.

That's when we were called in. Our consulting firm was asked to prepare a strategic plan for Peterson's air classifier and pulverizer product lines. It didn't take us long to find out why Peterson's products were not gaining a fair share of this $100 million plus market. Of the entire market of $110 million, only about $2 million was available to Peterson because of their specialized and highly sophisticated product line. The bulk of the sales in this industry were in big, heavy, relatively unsophisticated pieces of equipment. Peterson's sales had not grown because they already had captured about 35 percent of the $2 million market segment available to them. Great penetration but not much potential for future growth!

Peterson's management made two strategic mistakes. They never should have commercialized the air classifier without a thorough understanding of its market potential, and they should have never acquired a complementary company. That was just adding insult to injury. We found it difficult to find a polite way to tell Peterson's management that they had made such serious strategic errors. How could we prepare a plan to exploit a $2 million market that was growing at only 5 to 6 percent a year? We decided to show them the bad news and let them decide on their own to get out of the business.

One last point about this Peterson situation. There was no reason why Peterson couldn't have determined the market potential for their air classification product on their own. They knew the names of their competitors in this marketplace. All they had to do was order Dun and Bradstreet reports on them. They would have seen that almost all of them were little, privately held companies with sales of less than $300,000. Interviews with the major users would also have revealed that there was nothing on the horizon that would greatly increase demand for Peterson's type of product.

An Example of Good Strategic Planning

Wilson Brass and Copper Company is the small unknown company that I referred to earlier as doing a good job of strategic planning. Here's their story. Wilson, whose headquarters were in Chicago, marketed brass and copper strip products throughout the industrial Midwest. Sales had been increasing at an impressive rate of 15 percent a year, and the company was approaching the $50 million mark with a good profit. The basic business activity involved purchasing nonferrous strip products from an Eastern brass mill. Some of these products were warehoused and redistributed as is. The rest of it was slit (narrowed down to one-half inch or less) on a custom basis for delivery to customers.

Although business was good, Wilson foresaw a situation developing which could create a long-term vulnerability. Some brass and copper mills were diversifying by moving into the distribution and slitting business in major local markets. In fact, Wilson's major supplier had set up six warehouse distribution centers, and some competed directly with Wilson. The owners and founders of Wilson, the Wilson brothers, felt that they had to do something to guarantee a supply of mill products for slitting or redistribution. Their concept was to integrate backward by getting into the mill business themselves, but they didn't have the capital necessary to build a mill. So they decided their best bet was to form a joint venture with a Japanese company interested in penetrating the United States market. They felt that they could supply the marketing expertise, and their partner in the joint venture could supply the mill manufacturing expertise and most of the capital.

That's when our consulting firm was called in—not to weigh the merits of their strategy, but to provide an independent positive opinion on the value of their concept. However, we refused to rubber-stamp the plan. Instead we suggested a strategic planning study that would weigh the merits of the joint partnership idea along with several other possible options.

Other options to be evaluated included: (1) importing European or Japanese mill products, (2) forming a partnership with a smallish American mill that had no designs on entering the local warehouse distribution business, and (3) diversifying into the distribution of other copper and brass products, steel strip products, or even into nonmetallic products like engineered plastics.

At the program planning meeting which initiated the study, Wilson expressed several feelings about their business. They said that the only really profitable copper and brass strip mill, Trigger Corporation, was successful because they concentrated on extremely close tolerance products. Wilson said that Trigger was the only mill capable of supplying this type of product. Wilson also indicated that there was a major trend among customers to use close tolerance stripping, and that if Wilson and partner built a close tolerance mill they could successfully exploit this trend.

The consulting engagement was divided into two separate stages. The first stage was designed to weigh the options and make a decision. The second stage would then develop a strategic plan for implementing the chosen course of action.

To the surprise of the Wilson brothers and the rest of the board of directors, our finding did not support the plan to form a joint venture to build a copper and brass mill in the United States. After conducting interviews with major customers, copper and brass distributors, and domestic mills, we concluded that:

1. Excessive mill capacity existed in the domestic market. One mill had gone bankrupt because of lack of business and another was being propped up by a state guaranteed loan.

2. All United States mills were capable of producing, and actually did produce, close tolerance strips.

3. Trigger Corporation's success was not based on close tolerance strips, but rather on munitions and coinage contracts, emphasis on direct selling to large industrial accounts, consistently good quality control, and good customer service.

4. There was no discernible trend to the use of close tolerance strips. At best it represented only 10 to 15 percent of the total strip market.

5. Most mills had learned through first-hand experience that forward integration into local distribution and slitting operations was unprofitable. Plans to further expand in this area had been shelved by most mills.

6. Most customers had serious reservations about using foreign-made stripping because of poor quality control and lack of guaranteed availability.

7. Most distributors (in product categories similar to Wilson's) had diversified successfully into other product categories.

Basing our conclusions on these findings, we recommended the following course of action to Wilson's board of directors. First, develop a supply relationship with a smallish mill that needed Wilson as much as Wilson needed them (several such mills were identified). Second, develop and implement a plan to diversify into new product categories, preferably into new products that were purchased by the same customers that Wilson already serviced. Our recommendations were adopted.

At the beginning of this example, I identified Wilson as a company that did a good job of strategic planning. As you can tell by reading this, this pat on the back for Wilson is probably a little exaggerated. In reality, the circumstances, that is, their need for a rubber stamp and their willingness to have their conclusions challenged, prevented them from pursuing the wrong course of action. However, I do give them credit for being willing to investigate all options before investing.

I should note that I doubt if they would have been able to talk a Japanese company into investing in the United States market, even if they had tried. My experience with Japanese companies is that they never fail to investigate before they invest. Wilson would have ended up wasting a lot of energy.

7

Avoiding Bad Apples
(ACQUISITION SCREENING AND ANALYSIS)

When I'm getting ready to reason with a man, I spend one-third of my time thinking about myself and what I am going to say—and two-thirds thinking about him and what he is going to say. — ABRAHAM LINCOLN

Apples, as we all know, may be sour or they may be sweet. When they're on the market, a smart seller will polish them to whet your appetite. Inside, even the shiniest, most delicious-looking apple can be sour, rotten to the core, or even filled with worms. Unfortunately, the same is true of acquisition candidates.

The purpose of this chapter is to show you how to avoid disenchantment with your acquisitions. I feel that somehow I should be emphasizing the positive (acquiring good companies) rather than the negative (avoiding bad apples), but, in reality, most acquiring companies also take an apparently negative view. That is, most companies are not as interested in finding a gem of a company, as they are in avoiding a lemon. Corporate executives will usually take great care to avoid being known as the one who championed a bad acquisition.

There are really two portions of an acquisition analysis—internal and external. Internal acquisition analysis includes analysis of financial records, equipment, and buildings. This type of analysis is, of course, the function of financial experts, accountants, and appraisers. External acquisition analysis includes close scrutiny of the candidate's markets, its image in the marketplace, its growth relative to its competitors, its technological position, and its product innovation; it also reveals how a company has done and how well it is likely to do in the future. It is, in my view, more important than the readily accessible, yet less future-oriented, internal analysis.

ACQUISITION SCREENING

Before we begin external acquisition analysis, I'd like to discuss briefly acquisition screening. Acquisition screening is the process of narrowing down the universe of possible acquisition candidates to a manageable number. A thorough acquisition screening process involves two distinct steps. The first step is to analyze and compare industries to identify the one or two that appear to be the most desirable. The degree to which this step is relevant to a particular company depends on its acquisition philosophy. Some companies make it a policy to acquire companies only in businesses that are related to their own. Obviously, industry screening and ranking would have no relevance to a company with this policy. Other companies will acquire any company in any business as long as it promises profit, is legitimate, and won't tarnish their reputation.

A story I heard from the head of acquisitions for a major conglomerate illustrates this last point. It seems a business broker introduced him to a publisher that was for sale. On paper the publisher looked like a very promising acquisition candidate. At a preliminary get-acquainted meeting, one of the conglomerate's representatives asked this routine question, "Have you people ever been involved in any messy legal actions?" The publisher's lawyer looked at the publisher and said, "Well, Harry, I guess we'd better tell them now. They'll find out sooner or later. We were tried and acquitted on a magazine publishing pornography charge." That was the end of the merger discussion. It wasn't the legal action that did it, but the taint of pornography. The conglomerate could not risk a blemish on its reputation. The mere thought of a headline in the *Wall Street Journal* reading "Major Conglomerate Acquires Accused Pornographer" settled the question.

The second step in the acquisition screening process is the screening and ranking of individual companies within an industry. The purpose of this step is to identify the one or two companies within an industry that are both desirable and acquirable.

Of course there are some companies that have no organized approach to acquisition screening. I was once involved in a shotgun acquisition analysis of a candidate that was turned up in the cocktail lounge of a New York City hotel. It seems that a large chemical company's chief executive (who was also the leading stockholder and son of the founder) ran into an old college classmate in the Hilton lounge. The classmate soon let it be known that his small food ingredient company was for sale. An option to buy was signed the next day. The first thing the following Monday we got a call from the chemical company's panicked corporate development vice president. He asked us to find out by Friday all we could learn about this food ingredient company. The deal was being closed the following week. Acquisition screening has no meaning to a company that operates like this!

The first step of the screening process, industry analysis, requires that enough information be collected so that relevant characteristics of various industries can be compared and ranked. Basic information on each industry should include industry size (at manufacturer's price level); historic real growth; an estimate of future growth, profitability, and return on investment; an indication of industry concentration; identification of the major customer group; awareness of manufacturing processes and equipment; and an understanding of distribution and selling techniques.

Much of this type of information is available from trade associations, brokerage house reports, trade magazines, and government statistics. In addition, some market research companies do a good job of putting together low-cost industry reports. A decent overview of a given industry can be purchased from a company like Predicast, for example, for several hundred dollars. In some instances, it may also be necessary to make a few phone calls, or even pay a few personal visits, to major customers or to distributors to put all the information together.

Once an attractive industry has been identified, the company analysis can begin. The basic purpose of this information-gathering effort is to become knowledgeable enough to identify and know something about the leaders in an industry. Information needs include an indication of market share, form of ownership, company profitability, the segments of the market that each company operates in, and the innovativeness of each leading company. Again, this type of information is available from published sources, or it can easily be gathered through phone calls or personal visits with appropriate industry representatives.

Sometimes finding just one attractive candidate in an industry becomes a problem. This is especially true if the industry is highly fragmented. Often the best approach here is to order Dun and Bradstreet reports on companies listed in purchasing directories or even in the Yellow Pages. At one point in an acquisition screening study I was involved in, we even resorted to telephoning the companies themselves to find out more about them and to "hint" that someone might be interested in "some form of business partnership." It worked surprisingly well.

Acquisition screening is done in-house by many of the larger diversified corporations. Business brokers, who always try to be helpful to potential clients, are often quite useful in providing a lot of the necessary information for the screening process.

ACQUISITION ANALYSIS

Acquisition analysis usually refers to the analysis of a single acquisition candidate, no matter how that candidate is identified. The analysis itself follows the four-step approach to business problem solving used in most consulting assignments.

The first step is to define the problem and to determine the objectives of the analysis. This is very straightforward and requires that two major questions be answered.

1. Is the acquisition candidate's industry as attractive as we think it is?
2. Will the candidate make a good acquisition (that is, can we be sure it isn't a bad apple)?

These two questions are usually expanded into a detailed list of specific questions that must be answered during the course of the study. The best way to explain the nature of these questions is with an example.

Several years ago, I did an acquisition analysis study of a kitchen cabinet producer for a large, diversified client. Incidentally, the kitchen cabinet industry is a very popular acquisition analysis area. Growth and profitability figures are very favorable among kitchen cabinet producers, and so many big companies have taken a look at this industry at one time or another.

After the client company accepted our kitchen cabinet acquisition proposal, we met with several of their executives to develop a detailed list of questions to be answered during the study effort.

- What is the current size of the residential kitchen cabinet industry?
- How fast has it grown in the last five years in real dollars? What growth rate is projected for the next five years? Why?
- What are the market shares of the industry leaders? What share does the acquisition candidate control? Is it increasing or decreasing?
- How is the market segmented by end-use market? New construction? Repair and remodeling? Mobile home?
- How is the market segmented by construction and facing material? Plastics? Particle board? Structural foam? High-pressure laminate? Which product type is growing fastest?
- What is the acquisition candidate's position in the major market segments? Are they serving fast-growing end markets with fast-growing product types?
- What is the acquisition candidate's image with customers, noncustomers, dealers, mass merchandisers, and competitors?
- How does the acquisition candidate rank in product innovation, merchandising, sales aggressiveness, product reputation and management depth?
- What is the sales outlook for the acquisition candidate for the next five years? Are they expected to do better or worse than the kitchen cabinet industry as a whole?
- What impact will a slide in housing starts, or a drop in disposable personal income, have on their prospects?

It was apparent that the only way to develop reliable answers to these questions was to do a good deal of personal information gathering (step 2). A total of about eighty interviews were conducted in this study. Customers and noncustomers (including builders, do-it-yourself chain store buyers, and mass merchandisers), kitchen cabinet dealers (both the candidate's dealers and competitors' dealers), trade associations, suppliers of components to kitchen cabinet builders, and all major competitors were interviewed.

Management consultants have a possible important advantage in this type of study. They can go out to the marketplace and ask a lot of people a lot of probing questions without anybody finding out why the questions are being asked or who's really doing the asking. In this case we camouflaged the study as a general market study for a client with an interest in the business. If we were asked who that client was, we said we were sorry but we had been instructed not to disclose the client's name. ("They want to remain anonymous so they are sure to get impartial responses.") If an acquiring company wants to remain anonymous, it almost has no choice but to use consultants to do the acquisition analysis fieldwork, unless it is willing to set up a "dummy" market survey division with a name like Market Investigation, Inc., or something like that, so that the name of the parent company need not be used.

After all the information is gathered, the analysis phase begins (step 3 in the management consulting approach). You will recall that analysis means doing whatever is necessary to solve the problem. Well, in acquisition studies, if the information-gathering work is done well, the analysis is fairly routine. It usually just involves sorting out all the information and putting it in a meaningful order. Once this is done, it is rather easy to draw implications and reach conclusions. Actually only one basic conclusion must be reached: Will the company make a good acquisition or won't it? Quite often this conclusion becomes apparent while the information-gathering fieldwork is still in progress.

This was the case in the kitchen cabinet acquisition analysis. We found out nothing but good things about the candidate. They were one of the top three producers in the market, their products were well regarded, they were positioned in the fastest-growing segments of the market, they were recognized as product and merchandising leaders, and their management got very high ratings. We also found that the overall outlook for the factory-built kitchen cabinet industry was favorable.

Last comes the final step in the management consulting approach to business problem solving—recommendations and implementation. In most acquisition studies this means a final presentation to the client with a recommendation to buy or not to buy. Actual purchase arrangements are not usually handled by the consulting firm.

A DIFFICULT EXTERNAL
ACQUISITION ANALYSIS

The kitchen cabinet acquisition study which was just discussed was clean and neat. Unfortunately, not all of them are like that. In this section, I'm going to tell you about an acquisition analysis that was extremely difficult. It's a great example for illustrating some of the problems that can develop.

In March 1976 one of our regular clients, Diversified Corporation,* asked us to do an acquisition analysis of Techtronics,* a leading producer of home entertainment products. This was not an unusual request for Diversified. We do three or four acquisition studies for them each year. But since they are a regular client, they have come to expect a regular price, that is, about the same price for every study. (This "regular price" was to create one of the problems on the study, but back to that later.)

Diversified, a $3 billion plus operation, needed the study done in ten weeks because of the timing of their option to buy Techtronics. We said we could live with that schedule. Techtronics is a $100 million company that has a fantastic compound growth rate of almost 20 percent a year. It produces a broad line of home high-fidelity sound products such as receivers, speakers, tape recorders, turntables, and radios. These products are sold individually and also packaged as complete sound systems (generally for the lower-priced markets).

From the very beginning of the effort, confidentiality was a major concern. Both companies were listed on the New York Stock Exchange. Any leak could ruin the deal and cause a lot of problems with stock prices.

The study began with a meeting at Chicago's O'Hare Airport. The chairman of our firm, a second consultant, and I were there. Diversified's representatives included their acquisitions manager and their group vice president of home products. He was a former television manufacturing executive who loved to impress everybody with his knowledge of the television industry. It was apparent right away that he was anxious to make the Techtronics deal so he could get back into his beloved home electronics business.

That evening two members of our firm flew down to Houston to spend a day with the founder and major stockholder of Techtronics. He briefed us on his operations, his product line, his approach to marketing, and his understanding of competitors. We learned that some of the larger competitors were only extensions of Japanese parent companies, and that he had little concrete information on those companies.

We were now ready to begin the fieldwork phase of our study. At this point the first major problem was beginning to surface. Our preliminary exposure to the home stereo industry suggested that it was extremely fragmented, both by number of manufacturers and by type and price level of

*An assumed name.

products. For example, we quickly learned that there were well over 100 companies that produced and sold high-fidelity speakers, and to make matters worse, there was no small group of dominant manufacturers. We also found out that most manufacturers specialized in one or two product categories. Some made only electronics, some only turntables, and some only speakers, and only a few offered a full line of products. This situation created a coverage problem for us. We just didn't have the time or the money to interview a significant percentage of the competitive manufacturers. Even if we could have done so, it was questionable whether the information gained from many of them would be relevant to the overall market, since each was such a small part of the whole. We had serious doubts as to whether we could quantify this complex market accurately.

There was also a problem of multiple distribution channels. Stereo and electronic products are sold in all types of retail outlets including department stores, stereo shops and chains, mass merchandisers, catalogue showrooms, discount stores, drugstores, and even by mail order. This meant that we had to interview a meaningful sample of each type of outlet for both Techtronics and competitive products. We shrugged our shoulders and decided to just forge ahead and do the best we could. Oh, to be back working on a simple market like kitchen cabinets! Our fear about the competitors' lack of understanding of the size and segmentation of the market was soon confirmed. Two other problems developed in competitive interviews. First, since consumer electronics was a very competitive, almost cutthroat business, the manufacturers were less willing to share information than we had hoped. Second, some of the major competitors were too busy to see us because of an upcoming consumer electronics show in Chicago. We informed Diversified of the conflict, and they agreed to a delay in completion of the study until a week after the June show.

An informal status and review meeting was set with Diversified for the end of May. In preparation, the three of us from the firm who were working on the study had a Saturday afternoon session at my home. The purpose of the meeting was to try to agree on a preliminary conclusion concerning the desirability of the acquisition. We couldn't agree. The vote was stalemated: one "no," one "yes," and one "undecided." The "undecided" vote was the chairman of our firm. I was the "no"—not for any concrete reason but just because I didn't like the roller-coaster nature of the business. Big names of just a few years ago like Scott, Fisher, and Acoustic Research had gone into tailspins because of errors in judging this fickle market. The "yes" voter justified it because of Techtronics' strong position in the market. They were the recognized number two company in the business; they were far short of number one, but head and shoulders above the rest of the pack. We also knew that although Techtronics frequently seemed to use a heavy-handed approach with its customers, they were generally well regarded. We ended the meeting by deciding that we would tell Diversified, if asked, that it was too early to reach a conclusion.

At the interim meeting at Diversified, another problem developed. Both the acquisitions manager and the group vice president had become emotionally involved in the acquisition of Techtronics. There was no doubt that both of them had developed an illogical fondness for making the deal. This was the first time I had observed this phenomenon in all my years in the consulting business. I could understand it with the group vice president. He was just licking his chops to get back into consumer electronics. But for the life of me I couldn't understand the head of acquisitions for a Fortune 100 company losing his impartial point of view.

At this meeting we briefed them on both our positive and our negative findings. But they just didn't want to hear the negative information, and, if you can believe it, they cautioned us against being "too negative" when we presented our final report to the chairman of Diversified! Here we were in the middle of our acquisition analysis in a complex and volatile market, with too little time and money, and with our prime contact at the client company suggesting that we "doctor" our findings.

The whole thing was really beginning to bother me. Diversified had begun to remind me of another giant conglomerate that, for anonymity's sake, I'll call Conglomeration Corp. Conglomeration has a bad habit of making acquisitions without proper analysis—either by their own staff or by a consulting firm. They came to us when they bit into their shining new apple and found a worm in their mouth. Instead of proper investigation before purchase, they were forced into emergency corrective action after acquisition. I felt that if Diversified continued to get emotionally involved before making its acquisition studies, it wouldn't be much better off than Conglomeration.

The Diversified study was completed the week after the June consumer products show, and the final presentation was scheduled for the next week. As we had suspected, we were unable to quantify and segment the home consumers electronics market with confidence. We also concluded that Techtronics was a market leader but had several vulnerabilities: (1) Its recent entry into the low-priced market was floundering; (2) its management ranks were unproved below the founder (who was approaching retirement age); (3) its heavy-handed distribution practices were resented by the trade. Finally, we concluded that Techtronics' growth might continue in the 15 to 20 percent range for the next five years.

We handled the "doctoring" issue by deciding to hit hard on those negative aspects of Techtronics that we could support with solid evidence and deemphasize those negatives that were more subjective. After much debate we concluded that we would recommend the acquisition—with reservations! The reservations included concerns about only modest growth in consumer disposable income, movement of the war babies out of the stereo purchasing age bracket, fear of increased Japanese competition, and the possible repercussions if retailers retaliated against Techtronics by refusing to buy their products.

Several weeks later we heard from Diversified that they (I personally think it was the chairman of the board) had decided not to acquire Techtronics. The stated reasons were a policy of only buying the leader in an industry and a feeling that Techtronics, because of their rapid expansion, would be too much of a drain on Diversified's capital. These reasons didn't sound plausible to me, but whatever the reason, I was glad to hear that the deal was off. I felt that Diversified was just too conservative and too solid a company to make a major acquisition in such a volatile industry. If Techtronics went sour, for whatever reason, they could easily generate losses of $10 million annually!

IN-HOUSE ACQUISITION ANALYSIS

The approach to doing an acquisition analysis without the use of outside consultants is much the same as the approach used by consultants. The objectives of the study are the same—to judge the candidate and its industry. The information needs are the same, but there are some subtle differences in the way information is collected. The analysis is usually straightforward, as it is when outside consultants do it, and the recommendation and implementation is either a "yes" or a "no."

I should mention that I can write with some authority about an insider's approach to acquisition information gathering because I've gone out and interviewed internal consultants to find out how they do it!

The first thing to decide in information gathering is how you will identify yourself. There are basically two approaches. I referred to one approach earlier—that of creating a nonidentifiable division name which will serve to protect the true identity of your company. This is done frequently in consumer market research surveys, and it can also be used in acquisition information-gathering work. It's not unethical or illegal, just a little devious. The second approach is to be up-front and direct. That is, you just identify yourself as being who you are and with the company you are with.

Of course, a lot of preliminary information can be gathered before you ever have to identify yourself. You can start by gathering all the public information that is available (for example Dun and Bradstreet reports, annual reports, 10Ks, brokerage house studies). You can also use friends of the company, like lawyers and bankers, to make inquiries. Business brokers can also be extremely helpful. They can, for example, approach a possible acquisition candidate and solicit a good deal of meaningful information from the candidate without disclosing who they are getting it for. Good brokers realize that they must be willing to do this kind of thing to justify their commissions. Worthwhile brokers also screen possible acquisition candidates so they will maintain a reputation of presenting basically good candidates to acquiring companies.

If the preliminary information gathered on a candidate looks promising, the up-front internal consultant will then contact the acquisition candidate personally. Once some mutual interest is established, the candidate will often supply a significant amount of data on the company's operation and markets.

Of course, it's still essential to get out into the marketplace and ask the right people the right questions. The up-front internal consultant is direct and aboveboard in these efforts. Customers of the candidate are contacted either personally or by phone and told that your company has a potential interest in the particular business in question. The customers who are interviewed have no need to know *why* you are interested. The interest, for all they know, could be through acquiring a current supplier, through acquiring a license of a foreign company, or because of a new product that your R&D group has developed. And since purchasing agents are usually interested in more competition, they are quite willing to answer most questions. Internal consultants tell me that this type of interview is used mostly to fill in information gaps and to find out about the candidate's image. One word of caution. Since the interviewers know what company is asking the questions, it's important to screen out any bias in the responses that may reflect that knowledge.

Competitors to the acquisition candidate are also contacted and interviewed with a straightforward, honest approach. Your offer to exchange market information, coupled with their sense of curiosity, are usually enough to entice them into a discussion. Again, in these situations, it's important to sort out bias from fact. This can usually be done by corroborating all important information with a second independent source.

That's it. There appears to be no reason why an internal problem solver can't collect just as reliable information as an outside consultant, and, therefore, be able to do just as good an acquisition analysis.

8

Predicting the Success
of Newness

(NEW PRODUCT AND NEW VENTURE ANALYSIS)

*A new idea is delicate. It can be killed by a sneer or a
yawn; it can be stabbed to death by a quip and
worried to death by a frown on the right man's brow.*
— CHARLES BROWER

In the last chapter we looked at acquisition analysis, which is one avenue to
growth. The other avenue, of course, is internal development, and that is
the subject of this chapter.

Internal development, to my way of thinking, includes both new venture
and new product development. I say this because the approach used to
judge the success of new ventures and new products is the same: to get out
into the market and see what it has to say to you. Originally, I had planned
to have one chapter on new ventures and a second on new products, but I
combined them when I realized that I couldn't decide which chapter some
of my examples belonged in. When is a new product so risky, when does it
require so much in the way of new facilities, and when is it so different that
it is really a new venture? Since the management consulting approach to
evaluating both is the same, they can be treated simultaneously.

New products and new ventures are the lifeblood of a successful organization. Successful new products or services are required to stay ahead of, or
at least abreast of, competition. But as we all know, new product and service failures are much more common than new product and new service
successes. The purpose of this chapter is to demonstrate the management
consultant's approach to determining, as early as possible in the product
development cycle, those new products and services that have a high prob-
ability of success.

THE BASICS

I'd like to start this section by using a management consulting case to illustrate what new product and new venture analysis is *not*. A large grocery chain came to our firm for help in deciding whether to "venture" into the business of manufacturing their own line of snack foods (potato chips, corn chips, etc.). They were currently purchasing these products from outside suppliers, but they felt that their total profit margin could be improved if they manufactured them internally. Since the market was already established, (the products had established track records), there was no need for a sales forecast. The study concentrated on a return on investment and manufacturing cost analysis, and at the conclusion of the work, the quantitative analysis confirmed the wisdom of the "new venture." But to my way of thinking this snack-food study was *not* new venture analysis. It was rather, I suggest, a simple make versus buy analysis.

To me, a new product or new venture analysis implies newness in the marketplace. And it is customers' acceptance or rejection of this newness that results in success or failure. So the crux of a true new venture or new product analysis is estimating market acceptance, or penetration, or sales volume. Once this is done, it is possible to make all the ancillary estimates (start-up costs, manufacturing costs, packaging costs, pro forma income statements) that are integral parts of any new venture, but not the heart of it.

Market acceptance is the heart of new product and new venture analysis, not only because it is the most critical area, but because it is an area in which most companies don't have expertise. Numerous specialists are available to make ancillary estimates, but few companies have internal experts who can reliably estimate potential sales volume for a new product.

As with most consulting assignments, new venture and new product analysis studies begin with the problem definition step. Defining the problem in this type of assignment quickly boils down to defining what information is needed to make an accurate appraisal of market acceptance.

The second step, as with most consulting assignments, involves getting the needed information. Because new ventures and new products are foreign to the experience of the company, and because the major sources of information on market acceptance are outside the client company, almost all information gathering is done in the marketplace rather than within the company. The only exception to this is the briefing session for the consulting team at the beginning of the program. The backbone of the information-gathering process are personal interviews, although where appropriate, lower-cost telephone interviews can be substituted. Focus groups are also sometimes used.

The third step (analysis) is personalized to suit the circumstances. Sometimes it requires nothing more than sorting out basically uncomplicated information. At other times, it can include complex analysis of market segmentation, competitive strategies, product features, and price trade-offs.

If the results of the step 3 analysis are positive, the final step is to develop a marketing plan. This plan includes sales estimates, the steps required to bring the product or service to the market, a target list of customers, budgets, and a timetable.

The best way to show how to fit the basic approach to specific situations is by presenting some actual consulting assignments. The consulting assignments presented in this chapter are mostly industrial market situations because the management consulting approach to new venture and new product analysis is more appropriate in such cases. Consumer product companies use specialized consumer market research techniques such as controlled test markets, test panels, etc., rather than relying on consultants' interviewing techniques for new product analysis.

As you read these consulting cases, you will note that most resulted in a recommendation to terminate the new product or new venture. This isn't because I *like* to use that kind of example, but because that's the way most such assignments turn out. I'd say that 60 to 80 percent of new product and new venture studies done by consulting firms end in a negative conclusion, not because that was the safe recommendation for the consultant to make but because the new product or new venture in question was not commercially viable.

SHOULD YOU GO AFTER
NUMBER ONE?

This is the story of an industrial potato processor that wanted to penetrate the retail frozen french fried potato business. This meant going head on against the number one retail frozen french fry producer—Ore-Ida. At the time of this study, Ore-Ida had a healthy 30 to 50 percent share of most major metropolitan markets, and in some markets their share was up to 60 or 70 percent. Further, there really wasn't any notable second-place national brand. Our client (call them Idaho Specialties) wanted to become that strong second-place brand.

There are, however, two major factors in the retail frozen french fried potato market that we had to consider. The first is grocery chain private label brands, which account for 20 to 40 percent of a typical metropolitan market. These products are packed for the chains by Ore-Ida, Idaho Specialties, and a host of other processors. The other factor in the retail market are the typically lower-grade brands which sold at the time for as much as 40 percent below Ore-Ida's price. (Private label brands were usually priced at 10 to 15 percent below Ore-Ida.) These brands accounted for 10 to 20 percent of the market, and weak regional competitors to Ore-Ida made up the remaining small portion of the market.

The primary objective of our study was to determine if Ore-Ida had any market vulnerability. And if they did, we were to recommend a strategy for taking some of Ore-Ida's business away from them. It was assumed, and rightly so, that the Ore-Ida share of the market was the only possible penetration area. This was true because the private label share was very preciously guarded by the grocery stores themselves, and the low-priced portion was only a "seconds" market. It was hoped that Ore-Ida might be a "fat cat," vulnerable to well-planned competition. Possible vulnerabilities we were to look for included an overconfident attitude, inflated prices, lethargic promotional practices, or maybe even declining product quality.

Basically we wanted to answer the following questions: How was Ore-Ida doing in the market? What could an aggressive competitor do better? How good was their advertising support? How solid was their relationship with food chain buyers? Were their promotional price discount practices competitive? What could a "new guy on the block" bring to the market that would give that company an advantage, be it an improved product, better consumer advertising, or whatever?

It was decided that the best place to get answers to these questions was from food chain frozen-food buyers. It was planned to interview four to five buyers in each of eight major metropolitan markets. Emphasis was to be placed on leading chains in each market, such as Jewel in Chicago and Certified in Los Angeles. In addition, while visiting each city, the consultant was scheduled to visit three or four food stores for the purpose of observing promotional activity, shelf space allocations, etc. Often, the frozen-food department manager was asked his or her personal opinion about Ore-Ida's strengths and possible weaknesses.

The interviews with frozen-food buyers went extremely well. I'd say that we got as close as you can to total cooperation. Almost all the buyers, who are a very cunning group of people, guessed that we represented a client that was interested in going after Ore-Ida. And they were all for it—quite obviously, there's nothing a purchaser likes more than increased competition.

It's only too bad that the cooperation we got from the buyers didn't produce some encouraging results—but it didn't work out that way. Instead, we found that Ore-Ida was a fortress. They were as solid as any stockholder could hope for. Their product was considered excellent, as was their packaging. Their prices were judged competitive, and despite their number one position, they hadn't eased off on price promotions or cooperative advertising. It was almost as though they were preparing for an attack. Maybe they were!

So we couldn't recommend that Idaho Specialties attack. Instead, we told them that in our judgment the only way to successfully penetrate Ore-Ida's market was with a significant product improvement—an instant frozen potato, or a french fry that tasted like McDonald's, or some other spectacular innovation. We told them that if they didn't have such an ace in the hole they'd best forget their project. We also told them that if they did decide to take a run at Ore-Ida, it would take a massive and continuing commitment in advertising. This would be necessary to get and maintain freezer case space in stores by creating customer demand.

I'd like to make two points about this case before going on. First, although Idaho Specialties paid my firm over $20,000 to do this study, there is no reason they couldn't have done it themselves. Buyers would have given them the same information that they gave us. And they could have saved $5000 to $10,000. They would have saved four round-trip Chicago to Boise airline tickets, four days of consultants' time for meetings at an average of about $450.00 each, and the money paid to us for preparing a formal report (which they wouldn't have needed to bother with themselves—especially for a totally negative finding).

The second point I want to make is that if the findings of this study had been reversed, that is, if we had found that Ore-Ida was vulnerable, then a focus group would have been a beautiful tool to use in helping develop a viable market penetration strategy. I can just hear a group of frozen-food buyers and merchandisers sitting around a tape recorder and reeling off their great insights into the best ways of marketing frozen french fries. I'm sure their contributions could be helpful in developing a strategy.

EVALUATING A REVOLUTIONARY PRODUCT CONCEPT

In the previous illustration, a company was hoping to launch a new venture whose success would be based on exploiting a hoped-for weakness in the market leader. The next case is about a company that was looking for success by introducing a revolutionary product into the market. It all began in the early 1970s when a Japanese firm known as Yako Engineering was formed to develop and market a portable shot-blasting machine. Yes, I know. I said the same thing when I first heard it: "What *is* a shot-blasting machine anyway?" I found out quickly that a shot-blasting machine is a mechanical device that systematically propels metal shot at metal surfaces, such as ship hulls or outdoor storage tanks, for the purpose of removing rust and paint.

This new machine was expected to produce significant cost savings for the user, reduce the time required to do the rust- and paint-removal job, and improve the environment for the workers performing the job. Its goal was to displace manual sandblasting systems currently in use. About four years after work began on the Yako project, development had been completed, and it was rumored that approximately sixty machines had been sold throughout the world. Yako had a licensing agreement with an American company (call them Jefferson Corp.) to market the unit in the United States.

Subsequent to the development program by Yako, another Japanese company began development of a second-generation portable shot-blasting machine. Its major claims to fame were that it was smaller and lighter than the Yako unit and that it could work on curved surfaces (which the Yako unit couldn't do).

Our involvement in this situation began when a smallish American sandblasting company came to us on the recommendation of a mutual friend. This company, Price Corporation, had the opportunity to acquire the United States marketing rights for the second-generation Japanese machine. Al Price, the owner of the corporation, was a novice at new venture analysis, and he readily admitted it to us. His basic question to us was, "What should I do? This could be a great opportunity for me, but I need to know more about it before I decide." Mr. Price went on to say that he didn't have a whole lot of extra money to spend on this project. We agreed that we would do a "best efforts" analysis for a total of $8000, including all professional effort and out-of-pocket expenses. Typically a study of this type, if done for a large, prosperous client would cost $15,000 to $20,000.

A brief letter of understanding was drawn up to outline the study approach. The objectives of the study, as outlined in this letter were:

■ To determine the strengths and weaknesses of the Yako portable shot-blasting machine as viewed by existing customers in the United States

■ To define the present structure of the United States portable shot-blasting machine market and forecast its growth through 1978

■ To identify the opportunities and limitations which this market may offer

■ To recommend, if the opportunity warranted it, the most appropriate marketing approach

These objectives were then expanded into a list of specific questions:

1. *Current Practices*
   a. What procedures do United States shipyards now follow regarding the painting and resurfacing of ships? What equipment is used? How often are these procedures performed?
   b. Are there any problems in accomplishing these maintenance functions, for example, air pollution, worker environment, cost,

time to complete, etc.? Are there any technical problems with the equipment which require solutions?

c. In Japan, the cost of cleaning up a ship is estimated at $7 to $10 per meter. How does this compare with existing costs in the United States market? (Consider both costs without the Yako unit and costs for those using Yako.)

2. *Portable Shot-blasting Machines*

a. What type of portable shot-blasting machines are now used in the United States? For what applications are these units used: ships, tanks, bridges, etc.? What is the present size of the United States portable shot-blasting machine market—in dollars and units? How is the market structured? By type of portable equipment within each end-use application? What is the cost of this equipment? What is the cost of the shot (pellets)?

b. What manufacturers produce equipment for the portable shot-blasting equipment market? What share do they control? Is there a tendency for these manufacturers to concentrate on a specific application or do they cover most applications?

c. What is the image of each manufacturer in regard to technology development, advantages and disadvantages of equipment, type of sales effort, and service after sale? Do these manufacturers produce the shot also? Do they supply shot-blasting services or do they limit themselves to equipment manufacture only?

d. What has been the growth pattern of each major end-use application for portable shot-blasting equipment? What is expected in the future? Are any new applications developing which could offer opportunity?

3. *Yako*

a. What is the attitude of users of Yako's equipment? What do they like the most? What do they dislike the most? Are there maintenance problems with this equipment? Is the required use of a crane with Yako's unit a problem? Has the Yako unit been able to reach the 1000 square meter performance per day expected? If not, why?

b. A recent purchase by the Navy in Texas of Yako's portable shot-blasting equipment is also of interest. Specifically, the questions to be answered are:

  ▪ What is the present status of this equipment? How has it performed?
  ▪ What pollution problems, if any, were experienced?
  ▪ What has been the reaction of the end users, labor

unions, etc., toward the reduction in labor required through the use of such equipment?

- Why did the Navy purchase Japanese-made equipment over United States suppliers? Who sold the equipment to the Navy? Distributors? Direct from the manufacturer?

4. *New Product*

   a. Another company is developing a portable unit able to work on curved surfaces; Yako's unit can only be used on flat surfaces. Is there a need for such a product? If so, in what applications and what is the potential over the next three to five years?

   b. The proposed unit is lighter in weight and thinner, permitting access to the ship's surface in restricted quarters. Is this an important advantage?

   c. What is the attitude of United States end users toward a foreign supplier? Consider quality, image, sales effort, service, spare parts, etc.

   d. Are there United States government import regulations which would limit the potential for an imported machine?

   e. What opportunity exists for the proposed equipment? How should the market be approached? Distribution? End-use application concentration? Leasing program versus outright sales versus establishing a shot-blasting service company? How many units could Price expect to sell over what period of time?

Because of the bare-bones program budget limitation, only a small number of interviews were possible First, about four telephone interviews were done with marine trade associations and publications. These were designed to collect published background information and statistics. These interviews gave us a good understanding of the shipyard population and concentration. (Incidentally, it was assumed at this point that large oceangoing ships, especially large tankers, were the major potential market for portable shot-blasting equipment.) We found that of the 440 shipyards in the United States, only about 40 had dry-dock facilities large enough to accommodate oceangoing ships over 200 feet long. Further, there were only two major multishipyard companies in the United States: Todd Shipyard (8 yards) and Bethlehem Steel (7 yards). So over one-third of the large yards were controlled by two major corporations (and, more significantly, two purchasing entities). In addition, the Navy operated eight ship repair yards.

It was decided to personally interview six of the largest shipyards and to interview another four on the telephone. While traveling to accomplish this personal shipyard work, we also interviewed the four significant shot-blasting manufacturers and Jefferson Corporation (the Yako licensee). Because travel costs that would be necessary if we visited the East Coast, the Gulf Coast, and the West Coast would go over our projected budget, further fieldwork was not possible. Fortunately more was not required to make a judgment.

Our major findings included the following: In the United States, portable, manual sandblasting is the dominant technique for blast cleaning oceangoing ships and large oil storage tanks. A large distinction existed between naval and commercial applications. The Navy fleet of about 500 ships is sandblasted down to white metal every three to five years. But to minimize maintenance expenses, commercial ships are generally not sandblasted to white metal on a regular basis. Coast Guard regulations call for dry-docking for inspection every two years. But typically only a light sweep blast cleaning is done to remove marine growth, loose paint, and scale. Blasting to bare metal is done only to repair locally corroded areas. This was not good news because both the Yako unit and the proposed Price unit were designed only to do bare metal blasting.

Investigation of the secondary potential application, oil storage tanks, also resulted in less than encouraging findings. In-place storage tanks were not even sandblasted at regular intervals. Only locally corroded areas were sandblasted to bare metal on an as-needed basis in preparation for repainting.

Sandblasting on both ships and tanks was being done using scaffolding and a hand-held nozzle connected by a long hose to the blasting machine on the ground. Ship hull sandblasting was almost always done by the shipyard, not a subcontractor. Oil storage tank blasting was usually done by painting contractors.

We determined in discussions with shipyards that there were four companies actively involved in the development and/or marketing of portable shot-blasting machines. The first was Jefferson Corp., which *had* been the sole Yako distributor. That's right. Jefferson had given up on the Yako machine. In two years Jefferson had not sold a single Yako unit, even though they had invested almost $500,000 in seven Yako machines, licensing fees, and development marketing expenses. All the Yako sales success was in Europe and Japan where large supertankers are dry-docked. Jefferson told us that a major problem was that large tankers which could best utilize the flat surface blasting capability of Yako units didn't call on United States shipyards because of the small obsolete Unites States dry-dock facilities. Jefferson also said that since light brush-off blasting predominated in the United States, there was little need for Yako's white metal blasting capability—except in naval yards. Then Jefferson said that the Navy had never purchased or tested a Yako unit (this was later confirmed by the Navy).

The other three shot-blasting companies had all dabbled in portable equipment, but each predicted and justified a small market potential. Two of these companies had built expensive (almost $1 million each) prototype units for the Navy. These units were larger than the Yako units, could be operated faster, and required only one operator.

The Navy also said in an interview with us that they are bound by law to purchase equipment from United States companies "unless comparable equipment is not available from United States companies." And then the Navy representative told me, off the record: "We'll be damn sure to encourage [through development contracts] United States companies to make comparable equipment." That ended any potential for use of Japanese equipment in the Navy.

Our brief presentation to Al Price concluded that he'd best pass up the chance to market the second-generation Japanese unit. This conclusion was based on two independent factors. The first was the failure of the Yako machine to penetrate the United States market. The second was our well-documented prediction that the second-generation machine was also doomed to failure.

This example emphasizes an important point in new venture analysis work: A new venture can be reliably evaluated without analyzing a past track record. I feel that even if there had been no Yako experience, our analysis of the marketplace would have caused us to reach a negative conclusion on the Price Corporation opportunity. Analysis in the marketplace can tell you if a new concept has merit if you are just willing to listen and absorb what the marketplace has to say.

AN ATTRACTIVE NEW PRODUCT CONCEPT

I'm going to close this chapter with a consulting assignment that illustrates that consultants sometimes do actually recommend that a company proceed with a new product concept. This little study also illustrates a situation where the do-it-yourself approach to business problem solving would have been appropriate.

Collins Corporation is about a $70 million manufacturer of air-moving equipment such as fans and blowers. Their products are used in heating, ventilation, and air-conditioning equipment, and to a very minor extent in the rapidly growing electronics equipment market. At the time of the study, Collins's previous attempts to penetrate the electronics equipment area had been rebuffed by strong competition. Its arch rival, Caltron, in addition to dominating the sales to electronics equipment manufacturers directly, had a stranglehold on the distributor market. (This distributor channel caters to small customers, but represents a significant total volume.)

But Collins sensed a vulnerability in Caltron's distributor relationships. Because of heavy demand by the large direct accounts, rumor had it that Caltron was being forced into a severe back-order problem on most distributor accounts. Collins felt that by offering distributors prompt delivery, they might be able to get a foothold in the distributor market (and therefore in the electronics end market).

We did only seven interviews for Collins on this study, for which they paid us over $4000. The interviews were all done personally with large electronics distributors. Our purpose was to determine how severe the Caltron back-order situation was, what Caltron's distributor policies were, and if an opportunity existed for Collins.

We found that Caltron's delivery to distributors was an unbelievably long forty to sixty weeks. Average delivery was just over one year. Although Caltron was well liked by distributors (well-designed and highly reliable product, good company reputation, excellent people), most of the distributors told us that they needed better delivery and if Caltron couldn't deliver more promptly, they would consider buying from someone else.

We recommended that Collins proceed as quickly as possible to exploit the distributors' demand for the product. We suggested they offer a product line characterized by high reliability and interchangeability with Caltron's popular items (Collins's few current offerings in this market were not interchangeable). And finally, we emphasized the need to not only offer, but demonstrate, prompt delivery.

I can think of no reason why Collins had to pay us $4000 to analyze this opportunity. They could have done it themselves for three days worth of employee effort plus travel expenses of about $1000. And, if they had done it themselves, they would have already been on their way to establishing rapport with the distributors. In fact, several of the distributors we interviewed guessed we were doing the study for Collins anyway!

9

Achieving Marketing Success

(MARKETING STRATEGY)

> *Goodwill is the only asset that competition cannot
> undersell nor destroy.* — MARSHALL FIELD

> *The man who will use his skill and constructive
> imagination to see how much he can give for a dollar,
> instead of how little he can give for a dollar, is bound
> to succeed.* — HENRY FORD

Franklin Corporation is an old-line company that grew large producing automotive and industrial batteries. About five years before Franklin became a client of ours, they started on a diversification program that included the purchase of a chain of retail car repair centers. Also during this period Franklin acquired a very small company that specialized in designing and producing some of the sophisticated components used in light aircraft braking systems. Franklin named this little operation its Metal Products Division.

The Metal Products Division puttered along in oblivion, contributing a small profit each year to the corporate annual report. But then, in the early 1970s, the federal government decided to get involved in heavy truck safety standards. One of the government's first actions was to require that, by 1977, all heavy trucks (particularly semitrailers) be able to stop in a shorter distance without jackknifing.

The Metal Products Division saw this new braking standard as an opportunity to make a name for itself in the Franklin Corporation. So it assigned a three-man engineering team, headed by its most creative senior designer, the task of developing a heavy truck braking system that could meet the 1977 regulations. Since none of the braking systems then on the market met the regulations, the Metal Products Division was sure that all the other established heavy truck brake suppliers would also have to initiate product design and development programs.

Eventually, the Metal Products team did develop what they thought was an extremely attractive braking system. They tested it with very satisfactory results in both the laboratory and on highway test vehicles. A decision was made by the division to begin marketing the system to truck and trailer manufacturers. In total, there are about twelve significant heavy truck manufacturers and about fifteen to twenty sizable trailer manufacturers. All the vehicle builders have traditionally bought new vehicle braking systems from a small established group of about five suppliers. Now a newcomer (Franklin Metal Products Division) was going after a piece of the action.

To everybody's surprise (maybe even their own), they did get a piece of the action. In fact, for the 1977 model year (the year the federal standards became effective) it looked like the Metal Products Division would have braking systems on about 15 percent of all heavy trucks and trailers. Not a bad start for a battery company! In retrospect, the Metal Products Division's success up to this point was attributable to the fresh-start design approach it took. They started with a clean slate and with no preconceived ideas, while the established brake suppliers were shackled with tradition and a factory full of tools and equipment that "couldn't" be scrapped.

It was at about this time that the Metal Products Division (at the behest of the corporate planning manager) called us in. The 1977 model vehicles were about six months away from hitting the road, and the Metal Products Division's early success with truck and trailer manufacturers had created the need to make a strategic marketing decision regarding brake replacement parts.

You see, heavy truck brake replacement parts (which are manufactured by brake suppliers—not by the truck and trailer manufacturers) reach the truck owners through several different distribution channels. The first channel is through the truck and trailer manufacturers' dealer outlets. This is, of course, where new vehicles are sold, and where truck and trailer manufacturers want customers to buy all the replacement parts they'll need during the life of the vehicle. But, as is true in auto parts, there is also another source for many truck and trailer replacement parts—the independent parts distributor. In the jargon of the heavy truck industry, these independent distributors are called *fleet specialists,* because they specialize in selling replacement parts (and repair and service work) to heavy trucking fleets. In the brake replacement parts category, the fleet specialists purchase almost all their parts directly from the brake system manufacturers. Thus the fleet specialist is in direct competition with the truck and trailer manufacturers' dealers for all truck and trailer replacement parts and service business. And some brake system manufacturers are in the peculiar situation of selling replacement parts to the vehicle manufacturers (to supply their dealer network) and at the same time selling replacement parts to fleet specialists (who compete with vehicle dealers).

This situation is a constant source of frustration to truck and trailer manufacturers, who feel that they have the inherent right to their own parts and service business. And besides, it is the most profitable part of the whole operation. The gross profit margin on service labor is as high as 60 percent and as high as 30 percent on replacement parts. In contrast, gross margins on new truck and trailer sales are only about 10 to 15 percent. So vehicle manufacturers cherish their parts and service business, and resent the fact that some of their brake suppliers sell parts to independent fleet specialists.

At the time of the study, truck and trailer manufacturers had lost a large segment of the parts and service business to fleet specialists. In fact, Franklin felt that about two-thirds of the brake replacement parts business had been lost to the independent channel. With the introduction of the new 1977 federally mandated braking systems, most truck and trailer manufacturers decided to take a stand. Some overtly hinted that they would only buy brake systems for their new trucks or trailers from brake manufacturers who refused to supply independent fleet specialists with replacement parts.

Which brings us to the problem that Franklin's Metal Products Division faced. In their successful brake marketing effort they had told truck and trailer manufacturers that they indeed intended to provide replacement parts and technical service support *only* to the vehicle manufacturers' distribution channels—that is, they would not sell parts to fleet specialists. This made the vehicle manufacturers happy, and no doubt influenced some of the truck and trailer manufacturers to choose Franklin brake systems. At the time, it seemed like an easy decision to make since Franklin had no established relationships with fleet specialists and no knowledge of how to deal with them.

But the management of Franklin Metal Products Division was beginning to have second thoughts. They knew through the grapevine that some of their competitors had plans to sell replacement parts for the new braking systems to independent fleet specialists. Franklin also found out by visiting some large trucking fleets that many large fleets preferred to purchase brake replacement parts from fleet specialists because fleet specialists offer parts at lower prices than do truck and trailer dealers and because fleet specialists are expert in brake repair. Franklin also heard that truck and trailer dealers are notorious for carrying inadequate stocks of brake replacement parts.

To make matters worse, it became clear to Franklin that many large truck and trailer users could dictate to vehicle manufacturers (because of their purchasing power) which manufacturers' brakes would go on the trucks and trailers they purchased. Which meant that if large users couldn't get parts for Franklin brakes easily and cheaply (which to them meant the fleet specialist), they might not specify Franklin on new vehicle orders.

There was one last factor in Franklin's dilemma. They had a feeling, call it a hunch, that some brake system manufacturers sold replacement parts to fleet specialists (even though it was frowned on by new vehicle manufacturers) because it was very profitable business—perhaps more so than the replacement parts business with the vehicle manufacturers. So their promise to vehicle manufacturers might be hurting their bottom-line profit figures.

The first contact we had with Franklin's Metal Products Division was in the form of a long letter entitled "Request For Proposal." It said that Franklin was seeking a consulting firm to conduct a study with this objective:

> We believe that the primary objective of this study should be to resolve the fundamental question of whether or not our distribution strategy and long range plan should make provision for additional replacement parts distribution capabilities independent of the vehicle manufacturers and, if so, how could this best be achieved.

Franklin requested that we submit a proposal and indicated that the study must be completed eight weeks after the kickoff meeting. This was a tight schedule, but they hoped it was achievable.

We and one other consulting firm (which was headed by an expert in truck marketing and distribution) submitted proposals. A week later we were notified that we had been chosen "because we could approach the problem without any preconceived opinions." I guess this means that having little or no experience in an area is an advantage at times.

The kickoff meeting was held almost immediately at the Metal Products Division headquarters office near Philadelphia, and then we charged ahead. The first week we completed a quick literature search and prepared interview guides. Then for the next four weeks two consultants and I ran all over the country, feverishly doing interviews. Between us we completed 130 personal interviews with trucking fleets (67 in total), fleet specialists (18), truck or trailer dealers (18), truck manufacturers (11), trailer manufacturers (5), and brake system manufacturers (11). All this work was done anonymously. At Franklin's request, Franklin's identity as sponsor of the program was not revealed. The next two and a half weeks were spent feverishly analyzing findings, calling back people to fill in holes, and writing the report.

We concluded in our presentation that Franklin had no choice but to reverse its position, and institute a strategy that would include replacement parts distribution through both vehicle manufacturers' dealers and through independent fleet specialists. Here's how we supported this conclusion:

1. We found that almost 90 percent of brake parts purchased by large fleets were bought from fleet specialists, but that small users bought over half of their parts from truck or trailer dealers. So it was apparent that both channels were necessary to serve the entire user population.

2. Four of the six major brake component suppliers had told us during interviews that they planned to sell replacement parts for the new braking system to fleet specialists.

3. It was obvious that large fleets would continue to specify the brake manufacturer for all their new truck and trailer purchases. So the desire of the large fleets to purchase parts from fleet specialists couldn't be overlooked.

4. We found strong indications that profits to brake manufacturers were higher through the independent channel than the vehicle manufacturers' channel.

5. Brake manufacturers who were committed to both distribution channels had been using Franklin's promise to supply only vehicle manufacturers' dealers as a sales tool in dealing with large fleet accounts. Some even tried to talk users out of specifying Franklin brakes because "you'll have trouble finding parts."

6. Our discussions with truck and trailer dealers confirmed that they do an inadequate job of keeping brake parts on hand. There was no reason to assume that this situation would improve in the future.

7. Finally, we determined in our anonymous discussions with truck and trailer manufacturers that they would probably reluctantly accept Franklin's change of policy. This was true because brake parts are not "major dollar" items like transmissions and drive axle parts.

Franklin management "bought" our conclusion, which was not surprising since the substantiation presented was similar to the rumors and intuitive feeling they had presented to us at the kickoff meeting.

At the presentation we also developed our recommended approach for implementing the new distribution strategy. Franklin really had four choices:

1. Utilize the auto repair chain that Franklin Corporation owned to distribute replacement parts

2. Acquire an existing distribution system

3. Form a joint venture with a company that has an established distribution network

4. Develop a distribution network of fleet specialists from the ground up

This situation illustrates an important point. One message I want to get across in marketing strategy studies is the importance of considering *all* available options. Comparison of alternatives is the key to making proper strategy decisions. We did this in the Franklin case. Each of the above four

EXHIBIT 10   Ranking of Alternative Distribution Plans

	Cost		Impact on:							
Alternative	Initial capital	Implementation program	Ability to market new products	Image	Operating flexibility	Control & operation	Customer buying practices & service	Market & product knowledge	Rank
Repair stores	Low	Moderate	Poor	Poor	Poor	Poor	Poor	Fair	Poor
Acquisition	High	High	Good	Fair	Fair	Fair	Good	Fair	Fair
Joint venture	Low	Low	Poor	Fair	Poor	Poor	Fair	Poor	Fair-Poor
New distribution system	Moderate	Moderate	Good	Good	Good	Good	Good	Good	Good

alternative approaches were compared for relative strengths and weaknesses. A summary of this analysis is presented in Exhibit 10.

Basing our recommendations on this comparison, we advised Franklin Metal Products Division to choose the fourth alternative—developing a new distribution network. The implementation section of our report discussed the type of fleet specialist Franklin should solicit, what to include in its distributor agreement, the necessary number of fleet specialists for their network, and geographically desirable locations, and, finally, it discussed a recommended approach for notifying and appeasing the truck and trailer manufacturers. This approach suggested offering parts to the vehicle manufacturers at a price which allowed their dealers to compete effectively with Franklin fleet specialists. And in order to implement all these considerations, we recommended that Franklin hire an experienced heavy truck parts marketing executive, preferably someone who had extensive knowledge of fleet specialist operations. (By the way, we didn't sell them an executive search study.)

THE BASICS OF MARKETING STRATEGY PROBLEM SOLVING

The last illustration is typical of many marketing strategy problems. Most of them are rather involved, extremely complex, and far from straightforward. To make matters worse, even though the four basic steps of business problem solving apply, there are still a great number of discretionary judgments involved. What is required in each step is highly dependent upon the particular set of circumstances, more so than in corporate growth planning or acquisition analysis, for example.

As is the case in almost all problem situations, after defining the problem and the objectives to be achieved, the next step in a marketing strategy analysis is to gather the needed information. Which raises the obvious question: "How many and what kind of interviews are necessary?" Let me address this question in the context of the Franklin example. You may recall that we did 130 interviews on that study. I feel that was overkill. In retrospect, I think we could have done just as good a job with about half as many interviews. Thirty truck fleets would have been plenty (instead of sixty-seven). Half of the total of thirty-six truck and trailer dealers, and about 10 fleet specialists (instead of 18) would have done nicely. I wouldn't have cut back on the number of interviews of truck manufacturers, trailer manufacturers, or brake system manufacturers, however. These were all critical. In most studies, the farther up you get in the distribution channel, the more meaty the information becomes. So it's not wise to cut corners on manufacturer interviews. After all, a manufacturer interview doesn't cost any more than a customer interview, but is usually worth a lot more in information value.

One justification for the overkill on the Franklin study was the short time frame in which the interviews were conducted. When 130 interviews are done in four weeks, some are useless, some are done with a stand-in for the right person, and, most important, there is little time for cross-fertilization of ideas between the consultants who are doing the field work. When cross-fertilization is lacking, it almost becomes necessary for each consultant to do enough interviews to solve the problem single-handedly.

In a marketing strategy study, while the fieldwork is being done (or even before, if possible), it's critically important to begin formulating alternative strategies and approaches to implementing these strategies. If this is done, you can be collecting the facts needed to judge all these strategies and possible implementation approaches as the interviews are being done.

While developing alternative strategies and implementation approaches, it's often useful to use the "plausible scenario" technique. For example, in the Franklin Metal Products Division case, it might be wise to consider these plausible scenarios:

1. What if the federal government postpones the effective date of the braking regulation?

2. What if the federal government modifies the regulation to make it less stringent (so that competitors' past production designs could meet it)?

3. What if the regulation is cancelled?

Any of these developments could have a major impact on the desirability of Franklin's initiating an independent distribution strategy, and, what is possibly more important, on the proper timing for such a move. The usual way to develop this contingency approach to strategy planning is first to assign probabilities to each scenario. Then strategies to meet each contingency are developed, or strategies currently in effect are reevaluated under the assumption that each scenario actually will become reality. For example, if the federal government postpones the regulation, how would the strategy chosen by Franklin be effected? Obviously, it should make Franklin at least reconsider notifying vehicle manufacturers of its decision too quickly, since this would give them time to possibly phase Franklin right out of their production schedules.

Could the Metal Products Division have done this study without the use of a consulting firm? Based on their market position and their frame of mind, I would have to say "no." I say this (1) because they put great emphasis on protecting their anonymity, probably because they sensed a vulnerability in their newly developed market position, and (2) because they appeared to have a need for an independent confirmation of a strategy change that they seemed to feel all along was inevitable. This is common for a company that is entering a new, unfamiliar market.

Fortunately, the Franklin case is not typical in this respect. There are many marketing strategy situations that can very easily be handled without outside consultants. An example of this is presented in the next section of this chapter.

In summary, here are the basics of sound marketing strategy decisions:

1. Determine all plausible alternatives.
2. Lay out all possible implementation approaches.
3. Get out into the field to gather the facts necessary to make a proper judgment.

The last of the three guidelines is the most important. You can't solve a marketing strategy problem sitting behind a desk.

THE CLIENT THAT GAVE US A
SECOND TRY

This is the story of a client company that had a chronic marketing problem. We did a study to solve the problem, presented our results, and left. Two years later, things hadn't improved (in fact, they were worse), so they called us back in to try it again.

This case is a fascinating illustration of a situation where the client would have been far better off without outside consultants had the right steps been taken internally.

The client, a large diversified manufacturer, decided to invest in the machine-tool business. (This was a basic mistake in the first place, but that's another story.) After purchasing three totally unrelated machine-tool companies, the client merged them into a unified group. At this time machine-tool sales were on the wrong side of their highly cyclical sale curve. And it was also the time we came in to do the first study, with these objectives:

• To evaluate the market dynamics associated with the three product lines.

• To develop alternative marketing strategies for each product line, and to recommend that strategy which would be most likely to increase each product line's sales and profits over the next five years.

In our vain attempt to achieve these objectives we conducted a total of 109 personal interviews with end users (68), competitive machine tool manufacturers (23), the client's sales representatives (11), and the client's division staff (7).

Our complete strategy recommendation for one of their product lines (lathes) boiled down to this:

1. Strive to improve your manufacturing efficiency in order to be more price-competitive.

2. Continue to develop capability to manufacture and supply automatic parts handling equipment which will enable you to compete better with transfer machines (another type of machine tool).

3. Introduce a twin-spindle lathe, and determine the attractiveness of introducing products in other segments of the lathe market.

I'm embarrassed to expose the lousy job we did. I recall spending most of our analysis time during this study concentrating on market size and segmentation numbers, on whether the market would grow at 3 or 4 percent a year, and on other relatively minor details. We did this because we couldn't come to grips with the strategy. Not that we didn't sincerely try. We tried our damnedest, but we just didn't get the facts we needed in the interviews. The multitude of specifics and variables in machine tools and metalworking techniques overwhelmed us, even though we were all graduate engineers.

For example, we were unable to generate meaningful competitive price data because each machine tool is a semicustom product. No two are exactly alike. Two seemingly identical lathes may sell for a 20 to 50 percent difference in price because of special features and requirements. So when an interviewee told us that they paid $120,000 for a specific machine, we had no way of knowing what exactly they got for $120,000. We tried asking them, of course, but the responses were usually incomplete and almost useless.

In the ensuing two years, our client went on to develop and market the twin-spindle lathe we recommended (but that we neglected to describe for them). Unfortunately, they developed a lathe that was *too* expensive and *too* heavy for all but a few applications. In the first year, they managed to sell a grand total of *one* machine!

Then they made another mistake. They summoned us back to do more work. Specifically, they wanted a study to determine the requirements for the successful introduction of a new twin-spindle lathe. This time we did sixty interviews. We had the same problems; we couldn't communicate on a sophisticated enough level with the interviewees to define a successful new product or the strategy to introduce it.

Here are the sum and substance of our second set of recommendations (which I'm even more embarrassed to disclose).

1. Initiate a preliminary design effort to define the machine's characteristics (size, swing, and horsepower range; maintenance requirements; etc.).

2. Develop a specific list of potential customers.

3. Complete a product concept and market potential survey using the preliminary design data and the list of potential customers.

We finally told them to do what they should have done before we ever darkened their door. We told them to "take a preliminary design and get out and ask your potential customers what they think of it." In their highly specialized and customized business, we finally realized that this was the only way to get meaningful feedback. Unfortunately, sometimes the most obvious approach is the hardest to recognize, and sometimes companies feel more important if they hire a consulting firm to do legwork.

Back to the message of this section. You can do marketing strategy studies internally, and, at times, you *must* do them internally. Successful internal market strategy development only depends on a company's ability to generate the necessary market information. If there is no strong reason why you can't get out into the marketplace and generate this information, then there is no reason why you can't solve marketing strategy problems internally. Strong reasons for not generating this information yourself include premature disclosure of company strategy and an absolute necessity to remain anonymous. These were not present in the example that was just presented, and they're not present in many other situations.

10
Using the Crystal Ball
(SALES FORECASTING)

Nothing is so easy as to deceive one's self, for what we wish, that we readily believe. — DEMOSTHENES

Sales forecasting is as much an art as it is a science. Seat-of-the-pants decisions, human judgment, and plain old common sense are a surprisingly important part of forecasting in this age of sophisticated computers and complex mathematical models. In fact, it sometimes seems that the more sophisticated and complex a forecasting technique becomes, the less faith everybody (except the creator of the technique) has in its accuracy. This lack of faith in technology is too bad in a way, but many of us have been burned once too often by a "great new forecasting technique."

There is no way to avoid making forecasts, or judging the merits of someone else's forecast, because forecasting is an integral part of business decision making and problem solving. It permeates all levels of business, including market strategy, capital equipment expenditures, production scheduling, budgeting, and new ventures.

There are hundreds of sales forecasting methods. I remember a business associate of mine once saying sarcastically, "You know, sometimes it seems that there are more forecasting techniques in this world than there are accurate forecasts!"

The purpose of this chapter is not to survey or criticize forecasting methods. Instead, the intent is to present a straightforward approach to sales forecasting that is used quite frequently by management consultants for a wide variety of purposes.

THE BASICS

Although there are a multitude of forecasting techniques, all of them fall into one of three basic categories. Since the approach I'm presenting in this chapter "borrows" a little bit from each basic category of forecasting, it's probably worthwhile to describe these basic categories.

Qualitative Methods

Professional, full-time industrial forecasters (who have a tendency to look down on qualitative methods as guesswork) would say that the usefulness of qualitative techniques is limited to situations where data are scarce (in a new product situation, for example) or where reliable data are nonexistent. This attitude suggests that if good data are available, they should be relied upon almost exclusively in making a forecast. I disagree. Any forecast worthy of being called a forecast should consider qualitative (or judgmental) input.

The most popular and probably the most well known of qualitative forecasting methods is the Delphi method. The objective of the Delphi method is to gain the consensus of a group of experts. This is usually accomplished by questioning them individually. During each questioning session, anonymous feedback information from other members in the group is provided. This process continues until there is a convergence of estimates, or opinions, of the entire group of experts. The purpose of the individual questioning is to eliminate prejudices, stubbornness, public embarrassment caused by a change in position, and other psychological factors.

Times-Series Analysis

Time-series analysis is just what its name implies: an analysis of historic sales data. The assumption of time-series analysis is that past sales-trend patterns will continue into the future. Obviously, this assumption is more likely to be accurate over the short term than over the long term. Therefore, time-series techniques are usually limited to use in a three-month to three-year time frame (that is, unless some extraordinary long-term pattern is determined and faith that it will continue into the more distant future is strong). The *moving average* and *exponential smoothing* techniques are the most widely known time-series analysis and projection methods.

Causal Models

This forecasting technique basically takes time-series analysis one step farther. It takes the pattern of the item (that is, its time series) to be forecasted and tries to determine explicit relationships between it and other historical data patterns such as related businesses, economic trends, and socioeconomic factors. Causal models are the most sophisticated forms of forecasting. Regression models, econometric models, and input-output models are all causal model techniques.

Of course, the key to accurate causal model forecasting is to find a solid relationship between the item you want to forecast (dependent variable), and predictable external elements (independent variables). If external elements are not predictable, they will be of little use in forecasting. Causal models are very helpful tools in contingency planning, even if the independent variables are not so completely predictable. This is true because you can play the "What if?" game. For example, you can ask, "What would happen to widget sales if personal disposable income went down 3 percent next year?" Then the computer can tell you that the sales of widgets would go down 7.4 percent.

An Example

This discussion about various sophisticated forecasting techniques reminds me of a study we did in 1971. It was a multiclient technological forecasting study done for a group of eight manufacturers of passenger car components. All these companies made their living by selling components (wheels, ignition systems, steel, radiators, etc.) to General Motors, Ford Motor Company, Chrysler Corporation, and American Motors. The overall purpose of the study was to predict what the passenger cars made in America would be like in 1975 and 1980. What size would they be? What type of engine and drive train would be used? What materials would be used in major body components? The list of questions to be answered went on and on.

The first major step in the study was to forecast the overall domestic passenger car market for 1975 and 1980. How many units would be sold? What share would imports account for? How would domestic production be divided among compacts (there were no subcompacts back in 1971), intermediates, specialty cars, standard cars, and luxury cars? And what share of each class of car would be powered by Wankel (or rotary) engines? (You remember the Wankel. General Motors reportedly spent over $200 million on its development in the early 1970s, and Mazdas were humming all over America.)

Our approach to developing this forecast was simple. We went straight to the experts—the four major auto makers. We told each of them that if they would give us their forecasts, we would combine the four forecasts and give each maker the results. It seemed like a great idea. We would combine the expertise of four of the most sophisticated forecasting companies in America. (I could just imagine their computers grinding it out!)

As it turned out, the forecast was only partially accurate. The auto makers hit the import figures right on the nose, and they weren't too far off on the overall market sizes. But the engine forecast was dead wrong (20 percent Wankel engines in 1980), and the segmentation of sales by car class was way off. (Who'd have thought there was going to be an oil crisis or the need for energy conservation?)

What this means is that all sales forecasters (no matter how sophisticated) make mistakes. Hopefully, however, a conscientious and careful approach will minimize errors, or at least minimize the repercussions of error.

A COMBINATION APPROACH

Sales forecasting is an integral part of many management consulting engagements. For example, it is necessary to develop forecasts in acquisition analysis, marketing strategy studies, product potential analysis, and facilities planning studies. Often, the same forecasting technique is used in all these different types of studies. It's a combination of several different forecasting techniques, and it is sometimes called the *modified Delphi method.* Its primary appeal lies in the fact that it is very versatile and reasonably simple to use. The modified Delphi approach is basically a pragmatic and logical procedure, and it offers good reliability.

The modified Delphi method is not new or revolutionary; it's been around and in use for decades. Further, it is not a secret weapon of the management consulting industry. It can be, and is, used by many industrial organizations. I'm emphasizing it in this book because my experience has shown me that it works surprisingly well in a wide range of situations.

The first step of the modified Delphi method is to gather all the historical data that are available, including sales records for past years (in dollars and units) and statistics concerning market size and historic growth. If possible, an understanding of reasons for changes in sales or market growth trends should also be developed. (For example, "The drop in product sales two years ago was caused by a price cut by our major competitor." "This increase was caused by prebuying in anticipation of a Teamsters' strike.") Once all data are collected, yearly product and market growth rates and a compound annual average growth should be calculated. Always be sure to use real (i.e., deflated) dollars; better yet, use units (for example, barrels, pounds, tons, cases). These growth numbers and the understanding you have gathered as to why growth trends have taken place will be helpful in the next step.

By the way, if you are attempting to forecast the sale of a new product, obviously you can't collect any historical data. However, if data on a similar product or service are available, collect and calculate growth rates on that product. If nothing is available, so be it. The modified Delphi method is still applicable.

The second step in this forecasting method is to discuss the past and the future with anybody and everybody who can relate to the product or service you're interested in forecasting. These "discussions" are in reality, specialized field interviews.

The best place to start the interviewing step is with buyers of the product or service (assuming it's an industrial situation). Question them about their past and future requirements. Do they expect to be buying more or less? Why? If it's a new product or service, would they buy it and how much would they buy? Distributors, brokers, and manufacturers representatives are also very worthwhile sources of input in this step. Many of them have a unique perspective on their markets and its trends. They also may be aware of competitors' future plans, similar products that "bombed nine years ago" (and why), and anticipated changes in customers' purchasing practices and policies.

A third (and invaluable) group to interview are fellow industry members, or, as consultants would call them, the client's competitors. Past and future market and product sales trends should be discussed in detail, as should specific growth rates and projections. Finally, a major purpose of these competitive interviews is to find out what sales forecasting techniques each interviewee has tried in the past, and which ones each is currently using.

The fourth and final group to interview are any people who could be classified as experts. This group could include economists, government specialists, university professors, trade association experts, or anybody else who may have a meaningful insight.

Speaking of "anybody else" reminds me of a guy I interviewed during the kitchen cabinet acquisition analysis I described in Chapter 7. Early in the fieldwork phase of this study, three or four people mentioned a knowledgeable, experienced man who was with the Kitchen Cabinet Association in Louisville. Each person referred to the man as a "must" interview. There was only one problem. I had already interviewed the Kitchen Cabinet Association and this fellow wasn't there. I telephoned the Association's director to inquire and he said, "Oh yes, old Walter. He retired three months ago, but I'm sure he'd welcome a call from you. Here's his phone number." So I called Walter at his farm. He was just great. I learned more about kitchen cabinet sales trends and forecasting approaches from him than from all the others I talked to.

During all the discussions or interviews in the modified Delphi method it's essential to be aggressive. The interviewer must politely challenge assumptions and conclusions, probe for underlying meanings, and "bounce off" other people's opinions to stimulate fresh reactions. In a real sense, the interviewer is serving as the moderator in the Delphi method.

After all the interviews are completed, it's time to put it all together:
- Customer's attitudes and opinions
- Distributor's and wholesaler's inputs
- Competitor's approaches to forecasting
- Experts' opinions

This material is not put together through use of any predetermined equation or specialized formula, but is analyzed entirely on the basis of what makes sense to the interviewer. The information gatherer in effect becomes the expert in the process of questioning all the right people. And, again, the relative importance of the input for these people is not judged by a weighted average or some other formula, but on what makes sense to the interviewer. In the kitchen cabinet situation, for example, the man on his retirement farm in Kentucky made a lot of sense to me. So in that study, I relied more on his approach and less on what other people said.

Let me show you how all this works by presenting several illustrations. The examples in this chapter are pure forecasting studies, but I want to emphasize that the modified Delphi approach is applicable to any type of business problem-solving situation where a sales forecast is required.

ELECTRIC HEAT IN CANADA

It was late Spring in 1974. The long lines at gas stations that were precipitated by the "oil crisis" were still fresh in everybody's mind. And up in Toronto, Canada, the electric heating products subsidiary of a large multinational company had just presented to its group vice president a market plan it felt could capitalize on the fear of future high prices for oil and natural gas in Canada. This marketing plan called for a major and rapid expansion of the division's production facilities (with an associated multimillion dollar expenditure of capital). The basis for this request was a sales forecast that predicted an increase in product sales (in real dollars) from $6 million in 1973 to a whopping $80 million in 1980. This increase represented a phenomenal 45 percent average annual growth rate in division sales. It was also projected that in the same period the overall market would grow at the rate of 34 percent a year.

Obviously, these numbers sound too good to be true. The question was, *were* they? The group vice president had no reliable way to make a judgment. So he called us in to develop an independent forecast. We presented a proposed program to him that was designed to answer the following questions:

1. Will electrical generating capacity expand rapidly enough to support a 34 percent a year electric heating market growth?

2. What population and housing trends are expected to take place that will have an effect on the use of electric heat in both existing and new construction?

3. What is the size of the market for electric heating products in Canada? How is the market divided among baseboard heaters, wall heaters, floor heaters, electric furnaces, etc.? How is the market divided among residential, commercial, and industrial segments?

4. How fast has the electric heating products market been growing in Canada in the last five years? Why and how has this growth been achieved? How fast is the market expected to grow in the next seven years? What factors will influence this growth?

The program began with a meeting at division headquarters in Toronto. We were briefed on the division's products, markets, and sales efforts. They also explained their forecast to us, and gave us all the historical sales data available on their products. (These data suggested a modest 6 percent growth rate. However, the division said these data were irrelevant because they were gathered "pre-oil crisis.") Surprisingly, these division people seemed like conservative, rational businessmen. We wondered how they could come up with such an optimistic forecast. At dinner that evening the group vice president reiterated the same feelings. He said, "In the past these guys have always been realistic and accurate in their forecast. That's why I'm half tempted to believe them this time."

The division forecast that was in question was based on the premise that electric heat would quickly become so inexpensive compared to fossil fuels that it would be the "only way to go." The division predicted that by 1980, 63 percent of new residential completions would utilize electric heat (despite the fact that only 1 percent of in-place housing in Canada in 1969 was heated electrically), and that 25 percent (or about 1 million units) of the homes in Canada that were more than fourteen years old would convert to electric heat in the next seven years.

We approached our task with the attitude that the market would "tell us" what the realistic growth rate was going to be. This was basically the modified Delphi method. During the course of our fieldwork we interviewed the following groups:

Customers (architects/contractors)		14
Distributors		21
Competitors		7
Experts		30
Government agencies	(11)	
Trade associations	(6)	
Public utilities	(13)	
	Total	72

This may seem like an extravagant number of interviews for just a sales forecast, but we found out very quickly that Canada is quite a diversified country. What's true in Ontario may or may not be true in British Columbia or Quebec. Because of this situation we decided to do a province-by-province forecast and then build these up to arrive at a national forecast. Also, when measured alongside the proposed multimillion dollar capital expenditure, a forecasting effort of this size (which cost the client about $30,000) is a relatively modest investment.

Through our process of questioning people, probing for explanations, challenging their reasoning, and bouncing their opinions off other peoples' opinions, we arrived at a very reasonable consensus.

We concluded that indeed there would be sufficient electrical supply to support a 35 percent per year growth rate. (This was an easy conclusion because we found that much less than 1 percent of electrical demand was currently used for electric heat.) We concluded that population and housing trends and the projected higher cost of fossil fuels would indeed promote an increased use of electric heat, but not at the rate predicted by the division's forecast (which was 45 percent). To substantiate our forecast in our final presentation, we broke it down into two separate categories. The first prediction was based on a summation of provincial forecasts (which were derived from interviews); this predicted a compound annual growth rate of 11 percent. A separate forecast, based on the division's competitors' forecasting methods applied to the next seven-year period, is summarized below:

	Average Annual Growth
Competitor A	9%
Competitor B	12%
Competitor C	10%

Each of the forecasts by these competitors (who between them controlled 60 to 75 percent of the total Canadian market) confirmed our provincial forecast. The division people initially fought our results, but in the end the weight of our findings brought them around. We recommended an expansion to meet an anticipated 10 to 12 percent real growth. Our analysis of the division's position suggested that they would experience little, if any, change in market share.

TELEVISION SET SALES

One of the leading television set manufacturers was having trouble developing a reliable method of forecasting television set sales. The current statistical approach, which was basically an exponential smoothing time-series analysis and projection system, had proved unreliable. Production scheduling was tied to the forecast for each individual model, and so, often, finished-goods inventory was either excessive or totally nonexistent. This situation was resulting in excessive production and inventory costs and was making some of the client's television set distributors unhappy.

The situation here basically involved short-term forecasting—from three months to one year. In a series of preliminary meetings with the client's forecasting people, the current approach was discussed and five years of past sales records (for each major model) were assembled. However, rather than going right into the interview step, it was decided to test some statistical techniques first. This decision was made for one basic reason. It was felt (and it turned out to be almost correct) that the number of "meaningful" interviews we could carry out would be rather small. The entire universe included only distributors, retailers, competitive manufacturers, and possibly some forecasting experts. In this universe, probably only the competitive manufacturers would have any valuable experience or insight into statistical short-term forecasting vis-à-vis television sets. (Obviously, in a consumer product situation, interviews with end users, that is, customers, would be meaningless.)

Because we thought the sources were so limited, we decided to prime ourselves thoroughly before beginning our interviews. We did this by testing various techniques using historical data. For example, 1970 through 1975 data were used to see which known method would best project 1976 quarterly sales (which were, of course, available historic figures). Various regression models were tested in this way for numerous screen sizes and models. Our results were mixed. Some approaches worked well at times, but collapsed in other situations. Finally, however, we felt ready to talk knowledgeably with competitive manufacturers.

Unfortunately, luck was not on our side. Almost all the manufacturers agreed to a "visit"—if we exchanged information with them, which we did. Unfortunately, all we found out was that most of them knew less than we did about short-term statistical forecasting in the area in question. One exception was a leading company that had just converted to a new forecasting system that they wanted to keep to themselves. They spent most of the interview being evasive, and I really don't blame them for their secretiveness. I think I'd do the same thing if I were in their place.

It looked as though we had come to the end of the line. We applied what little we learned in the competitive interviews, but we didn't come up with anything to get excited about. We did some telephone interviews with large retailers and appliance distributors which confirmed our earlier suspicion that these sources would be of little assistance. But then something dawned on us. Other types of appliance manufacturers face similar forecasting problems. A refrigerator or a dishwasher or a hi-fi system isn't that much different from a television set. Why not interview Maytag and Hotpoint and other big-name appliance manufacturers? If they had a good system, they'd probably be willing to discuss it with a consulting firm representing a *noncompetitive* manufacturer.

We decided to implement our delayed revelation. And to our pleasant surprise, appliance producers cheerfully suggested several refinements to our tentative techniques that greatly improved their reliability. The modified Delphi method had proved its merits once again.

11

Drawing Lines and Boxes

(ORGANIZATIONAL PLANNING)

> In a balanced organization, working towards a
> common objective, there is success.
>
> — T. L. Scrutton
>
> You can employ men and hire hands to work for you,
> but you must win their hearts to have them work
> with you. — Tiorio

There are basically three types of organizational studies, whether done internally or by a consulting firm. The first type involves development of new organizations, for example, creating an organization plan for a new division to be built around a new product concept.

The second type of organizational work involves what is sometimes politely referred to as drastic organizational planning. This type of work often results in the termination of whole departments, and, because of the sorry shape some companies find themselves in, it often requires urgent, overnight analysis and implementation.

The third type of organizational study falls somewhere between the other two. It involves conscientiously improving a basically healthy, ongoing organization. All organizations need monitoring and periodic improvement, because change is an inevitable part of corporate existence. Markets change. Products change. The economy changes. Technology changes. People change. And organizations must change also. This raises the critical question, "Will organizational changes be made at random in reaction to environmental changes or will organizational changes be conscientiously planned and executed?"

The purpose of this chapter is to show you how to institute a comprehensive, ongoing approach to planning the structure of your organization. This approach is applicable to any existing organization, whether it is in trouble or just in need of modernizing and fine tuning. Effective organizational planning begins with a thorough description of the organization as it is. This description, which focuses on establishing a comprehensive organizational data base, leads to the analysis and improvement steps. The process described in this chapter can be used to improve the organization of a department, a division, or an entire company. To simplify the descriptions in this chapter, the organizational unit in question is assumed to be the entire company.

STAFFING AN ORGANIZATIONAL STUDY

I'd like to briefly suggest several approaches to staffing an organizational study. This is extremely important because most full-blown organizational studies are labor intensive and time consuming. Of course, many consulting firms are able and willing to staff the entire study—at about $300 to $400 per staffer per day. On the other hand, if a company has one or two people with organizational expertise (or even a willingness to learn it), an internal task force can be built around a coordinator who provides guidance, direction, and advice. A compromise approach is to engage an outside organizational consultant to serve as this coordinator, thus utilizing outside expertise while still saving most of the cost of complete outside services. This compromise is an excellent idea for companies whose personnel lack expertise in organizational planning techniques. It might be a good idea to assign a bright young employee to be chief assistant to the consultant/coordinator. Once into things, this person will probably be able to spearhead the company's ongoing organizational planning.

DEFINING THE PRESENT ORGANIZATION

As is true with most situations, you've got to know what you've got before you can begin to improve it. So it is with organizational planning. Most employees know who reports to whom, and everybody can pull out an organization chart from the files explaining how the company is organized, but formal reporting relationships and organization charts are a far cry from a meaningful description of a company's true organization.

To define an organization thoroughly and meaningfully (and to uncover its shortcomings), a series of steps should be taken. Even a large and complex organization can be defined in a meaningful fashion if these steps are followed one by one.

Step 1. The Overview This initial step involves establishing an overview of the company's basic organizational pattern. The major organizational changes that have taken place in the last five to ten years are of primary concern. Past and present corporate objectives, and the corporation's formula for achieving these objectives, should be defined.

This information and the other input necessary for the overview can usually be obtained from a small number of senior officers. Some of it will be readily available; other specifics probably will have to be assembled. This overview step also orients the consulting team or task force, so that subsequent steps can be undertaken smoothly and efficiently. (It's not unlike the program kickoff meeting that initiates most consulting assignments.)

A list of all the functions performed at each level and a brief description of each function should be compiled. Then a preliminary evaluation by the senior executives of how effectively each function is being performed should be solicited (often it will be volunteered, sometimes almost as an apology for neglect). Next an estimate of the total cost of the current organization is needed. This should include salaries and wages (including bonuses and fringe benefits), office space, communications costs (primarily telephone), and out-of-office costs such as travel. The consulting team or task force should also learn the functions and purposes of all major committees.

A personnel summary including income categories, age distribution, educational level, seniority, experience in various functional positions, and income history for the past five years should be obtained. In conjunction with this, it is also desirable to develop an understanding of the corporate compensation system.

Finally, it's important to understand the contribution that each organizational unit has made to company successes and failures. This judgment should be based on analysis of corporate financial records, senior officers' input, and on a close look at the competitive environment each unit operates in.

Step 2. Formal Communications   Fortunately, step 2 is easier than step 1. Its purpose is to complete the overview information—to collect all formal communications documents such as manuals, policy documents, memos, etc. This will also allow the task force or consulting team to develop an understanding of the company's reporting and information system. Understanding this system will be very useful in identifying organizational strengths and weaknesses as step 3 gets under way.

Step 3. Organizational Interviewing   This step is the heart of a good organizational planning study. Not only is it the primary basis for determining the structure of the current organization, but it is the heart of the analysis and improvement process. Therefore, it's fitting that organizational interviewing is the most work-intensive portion of the entire effort. It's also where the task force's least experienced members play an important role.

The major purposes of organizational interviews are to:

- Define how the organization *really* functions
- Build a basis for comprehending even a large, multifaceted organization
- Detect weaknesses, problems, shortcomings, and friction points in the organization
- Create an interchange of ideas that will lead to improvement

Procedurally, organizational interviews are done this way. A task force member or outside consultant sits down and talks to key people in the organization. These interviews are always conducted privately, and the interviewee is guaranteed beforehand that all facts and opinions will be treated confidentially. These key employees are encouraged to talk about their work, their authority, and their relationships with others in the company. Often, interviewees show some initial hesitation, but, in most cases, if the interviewer is patient and friendly, these inhibitions will vanish and meaningful facts and opinions can be obtained.

As these interviews unfold, it is possible to construct an accurate description of the total organization. When the task force or consulting team completes the organizational interviews, each key employee's perspective of the organization should be clear. Reasons for what is right in the organization, as well as reasons for what is not right, are usually apparent at this point.

Most consulting firms have specialized interview forms for use in organizational studies. Some even have the important page headings printed on the bottom of each page, with each page slightly longer than the one before it, so that the interviewer can quickly turn to the proper page while taking notes. (Note taking on some type of form is essential. The interviewees will accept it as part of the process, and it will not inhibit a free exchange of information.) A typical seven-page interview form is summarized in Exhibit 11.

ANALYSIS OF THE PRESENT ORGANIZATION

The next step is to analyze the information obtained from the interviews along with the findings of steps 1 and 2. This process begins with an exacting evaluation of the overall health of the present organization. Are the objectives of the organization as a whole adequate? Do the specific one-year and five-year plans match the objectives? Is the company living up to expectations? Is the level of success consistently good (or poor) throughout the organization? What accounts for the successes and failures? Are the

EXHIBIT 11   Organizational Interview Form

Page number	Page title	Specific questions
1	Organization chart	■ Name of interviewee, title, department, date ■ Sketch of organization
2	Duties, functions, and responsibilities	■ Major responsibilities ■ Detailed duties and functions ■ Accountability and reporting procedure
3	Departmental operations	■ Present operations ■ Future outlook
4	Duties and functions of subordinates	■ Listed for each subordinate
5	Authority and relationships	■ Authority and limits ■ Standards of performance ■ Relationships with nonsubordinates
6	Problems and suggestions	■ Ideas, suggestions, and recommendations for change and improvement
7	Personal	■ General background (education, age, marital status) ■ Experience prior to company ■ Experience in the company ■ What interviewee can do and wants to do

reasons organizational, or nonorganizational? (All problems not directly associated with organizational difficulties should be put aside at this point.) It should be kept in mind at this juncture that the sole purpose of the organization is to fulfill the goals and objectives of the corporation. If the organization is not living up to its objectives, preliminary opinions about its shortcomings should now be developing.

Next, the basic structure of the organization should be analyzed. This includes the levels of management, the functions of each level, the degree of centralization, the compensation system, the management information system, the reporting and authority relations, and even office locations and layouts. Basic structural analysis focuses on a company's *necessary* functions, noting whether they are performed well, poorly, or only partially. The interactions of various groups and departments must also be scrutinized.

After the basic structure has been reviewed to determine if it is consistent with corporate objectives, all the other elements of structure which complete the system can be analyzed. These include the information system, the reporting and control systems, and all the formal and informal communication practices. It should be determined if these elements are compatible and consistent with the basic structure, and discrepancies should be noted for corrective action.

Obviously, people are the difference between an organization *plan* and an organization in action. So the next step in analyzing the organization is to assess the organization's personnel. Preliminary information on personnel is gathered in step 1, and much more detailed information is gathered in the organization interviews. This information can now be combined to assess the organization's personnel potential. The task force or consulting team must also be prepared at this point to defend its evaluations of personnel, since some will surely be challenged by senior executives.

The next step in the analysis is the most nebulous. It focuses on determining whether the essence, or spirit, of the organization is in harmony with the corporate objectives. Variations in attitude from division to division, or even from person to person, must be determined. This step is difficult to describe, but when you are involved in organizational planning, especially in the organizational interviews, telltale signs of positive or negative attitudes and morale are easily detectable.

The last step in reviewing the organization is to develop a summary of findings and conclusions. Problems should be identified, reasons for their existence should be put forth, and the effect of these problems on profitability should be judged (at least subjectively).

DESIGNING AN IMPROVED ORGANIZATION

As was the case in defining the present organization, designing an improved organization requires several steps or phases.

Phase 1. Establishing Business Objectives The term "business objectives" in the context of organizational planning refers to the results that a corporation desires year after year in order to consider itself successful. You may recall that the initial step in the corporate growth planning process was to establish growth objectives, which was typically accomplished by a meeting of senior executives or by having a member of the consulting team or task force meet with each senior official and listen to their views about present and future objectives of the enterprise. The objectives, and the process for arriving at a consensus, are the same in organizational planning.

Objectives should be set for at least a five-year time frame. Planning organizational improvement with shorter-term objectives is not advisable. It's also important to make the objectives consistent with the portion of the organization under examination. For example, if the organizational entity is the engineering department, then the objectives should be tailored to it.

Business objectives established in this process should be as specific as possible. Profit improvement and sales increase goals should be quantified as yearly percentage increases, or dollar increases. Beyond profitability and growth, other objectives that might be considered include cash flow, vertical integration, international expansion, and diversification.

Phase 2. Reviewing Success Factors   In the first phase, establishing business objectives showed the direction in which a company should be heading. The next phase involves a review of the conditions and circumstances that led to past success and that will be necessary for attaining future objectives. Obviously, some of these success factors are external to the company. But the internal success factors should be clearly defined, recognized, and controlled by the company.

The most pragmatic way to review success factors is to isolate each business objective. The success factor that contributes to attaining each goal is then listed. For example, attainment of a 10 percent real growth rate for a materiel-handling equipment company may require introduction of a new line of front-end loaders, which in turn will require expanded engineering and development, increased production capacity, added financial resources, and even an additional marketing channel. Once success factors for a given business objective have been isolated, the next step is to relate these factors to the company division that has ultimate responsibility for their accomplishment. If appropriate, success factors are ranked in order of relative importance. These rankings may help to suggest the necessary compromise for designing an organizational structure that can best accomplish its stated business objectives.

Phase 3. Developing the Basic Structure   The preliminary phases of organizational design are now accomplished. It's time to move on to the heart of the process—developing the basic structural design for an improved organization, one which retains the advantages of the present organization and corrects its shortcomings. This phase begins with a search for the *ideal*. An ideal organization is one which is designed without regard to the constraints that the existing organization may impose in forms of personalities, established relationships, and tradition. In other words, in the beginning we do not worry about any of the obstacles that will interfere with the transition from the present organization to an ideal organization. As the design process nears its conclusion, there will be time to compromise—to translate the ideal organization into a *workable* organization.

We begin by considering all the functions that must be performed. For example, at the general management level, the primary functions are definition of corporate philosophy, setting corporate objectives, and planning, coordination, and leadership. Finance and accounting functions include cash management, credit management, accounts receivable management, accounts payable management, control of assets, dividend and stockholder interest management, capital expenditure evaluation, and information system management, among others.

Once all functions are identified, a value judgment must be made as to the relative emphasis that should be placed on each function in order to achieve the basic objectives of the organization. For example, if diversification through acquisition is an objective, it will be important to give this function significant emphasis in the improved organization. This may call for a special position within the corporate planning division, or even a vice presidential position reporting to the chief executive officer.

The next step is to design a number of alternative organizational structures. Variations may include changing the number of levels in the organization, the positioning of functional groups, and the degree of centralization. The purpose of developing these alternatives is so that each can be evaluated against the others, and against the present organizational structure.

There are at least six basic ways to organize a department, division, or entire corporation. These basic methods are usually referred to as organizational groupings; they include:

- Function
- Product
- Geography
- Process
- Customer or end market
- Product management

The basic characteristics of these methods are briefly presented below. A more thorough discussion of each can be found in many business texts. You will notice that some are applicable to an entire organization, while others are suited to division or department organization only.

One of the oldest organizational groupings is grouping by *function*, that is, by the nature of the work activity being performed. Traditional functional groupings include finance, engineering, manufacturing, marketing, and personnel. Most small organizations utilize functional groupings. The advantages of functional organization are that the personnel within divisions organized that way become experienced specialists and, because all work effort is directed at accomplishing specific goals, the objectives are usually fulfilled. A major disadvantage is that functional groups typically fail to keep the interests of the total company in mind. This divergence of goals leads to the second major disadvantage of functional groupings: Conflict between functional groups occurs frequently. For example, marketing says that manufacturing is so slow that it has caused a back-order problem, while manufacturing accuses marketing of promising unrealistic delivery dates to customers in order to meet sales objectives.

The second type of organizational grouping is by *product*. Activities directly associated with a single major product, or group of related products, are grouped together. For example, Du Pont has numerous product groups, including textile fibers, organic chemicals, explosives, and elastomer chemicals. Product grouping is most common in large companies that produce a variety of unrelated products. The primary advantage of this type of structure is that it encourages profitable emphasis on a given group of products, since each group manager has total responsibility for one group of products. A possible disadvantage is that duplication of many administrative functions within each product group may detract from overall corporate profitability.

The third major type of organizational grouping is *geographical*. Here activities carried out in a given locale are grouped together. This type of approach is common in service industries, sales organizations, and, sometimes, worldwide organizations such as major oil companies. Geographical grouping permits a functional organization to give personalized attention to the needs of a given city, state, or group of states. It allows personnel to concentrate all their efforts on a single territory. A possible danger is an overemphasis on one territory at the expense of the organization as a whole.

Another major type of grouping is by *process*. Activities are grouped by the steps through which the work moves. Some oil companies have process grouping which includes the exploration group, the transportation group, the refining group, and the marketing group. Process groupings are also found in clerical operations and engineering departments (for example, product design, drafting, product development, and production engineering).

Customer or end-market grouping is also common. Here the intent is to give emphasis to a specialized group of customers. This grouping is employed quite often where the same product is sold to several widely divergent customer groups. For example, some oil companies have two entirely distinct sales organizations—one to sell gasoline and oil products through retail service stations, and another to market these products to commercial accounts. Commercial account sales may be further segmented into agriculture, metalworking, home heating oil, and so on. A personnel department may likewise be grouped to serve managerial, salaried, and hourly accounts. The obvious advantage to this approach is that customers receive specialized and knowledgeable attention. Disadvantages include inefficient sale routes and the fact that personnel are often exposed to only a small segment of an organization's total efforts.

The last major grouping approach is sometimes referred to as *matrix grouping* or *product management grouping*. It is designed to benefit from the advantages of product grouping (such as good coordination and profit consciousness) without incurring the excessive costs usually associated with such arrangements. It is, in effect, a compromise between functional grouping and product grouping. Engineering, production, and marketing remain as they would be in a functional grouping; however, product managers are assigned to coordinate functional group decisions with their given product lines. Product management groups are also used in some marketing organizations to direct emphasis for the field sales force. The primary disadvantage of this arrangement is that there is a crossing of the lines of authority and responsibility, which can result in a good deal of friction, infighting, and finger-pointing.

With each of these groupings and the list of functions to be included in the organization in mind, it should now be possible to design several alternative organizational structures. They need not be completely detailed at this point, but they should have enough substance so that meaningful judgments can be made about each. While formulating these alternatives, keep in mind the problems that were uncovered while analyzing the current organization. Your primary purpose in developing alternative organizational approaches is to eliminate these weaknesses.

Begin the comparison and selection process by listing the advantages and disadvantages of each alternative on a series of comparison charts. Review these alternatives in light of corporate objectives. Trade-offs, compromises, and modifications are an integral part of the evaluation process at this point.

It is important for the senior consultants, or task force leaders, to work closely with the senior management group. There are so many possible combinations of structure, grouping, and placement of personnel, that it is impossible to select an *optimum* design, substantiated with hard evidence. Top management must be made to realize this and to understand that the final selection must be based on their best judgment. They should be involved in the evaluation of the various alternatives, in the review of the strengths and weaknesses of each, and in the final selection.

Criteria for judging various structural alternatives are available. Important criteria include:

1. *Control:* How does each alternative facilitate management control?

2. *Coordination:* In which option is cooperation between functional groups likely to be at its best?

3. *Management attention:* Does the proposed organization allow for adequate attention in each critical area?

4. *Management development:* Which structure is most likely to develop managers with varied and meaningful experiences?

5. *Cost:* Which alternative will be the most cost effective?

Cost comparisons of alternatives can usually be made by looking at the present organization. Present organization costs (which include salaries, fringe benefits, information systems, communications, travel, office space, secretaries, and stationery and supplies) were calculated earlier in the process, and costs of alternative structures can be estimated by an incremental process.

Once a particular alternative structure has been selected, it can be developed in great detail. Detailed charts can be drawn, titles selected, primary functions and performance standards determined for each job title, and a preliminary compensation structure determined.

Development of the basic structure of the improved organization is now complete. It's time to evaluate the company's current personnel against the requirements of the new organization.

Phase 4. Staffing the Improved Organization   This phase begins with the development of detailed tables which indicate the number of people required in each organizational unit. These numbers are determined by the amount of emphasis desired, the specific work to be performed, and, of course, an organizational cost parameter. The next step is to prepare qualification specifications for each person in each organizational unit. The specifications should be brief. They are intended to capture the essence of the qualifications necessary to achieve each position's part of the corporate objectives. Qualifications include necessary education, specific type of past experience desired (including range of years), desired personality (such as "outgoing," or "precise"), and a rough indication of the age range desired.

Once these qualifications are set down, a matching process begins. The present employees are matched with positions in the new organization wherever possible. Retraining should always be considered as an alternative to seeking a new employee. If one of the primary objectives of the organizational planning process was to trim organizational costs (which is often the case), a sizable number of current employees may unfortunately be designated as surplus at this point. Close liaison with top management is again recommended at this juncture. Their concurrence on match-ups, surpluses, and the possible need for seeking personnel from outside the present organization is essential.

When agreement is reached, the last step in this phase is to write down all the necessary position descriptions. Good position descriptions are precise. They delineate the exact functions to be performed by the person assigned to the position as follows:

- A brief statement of the basic job function
- The position's reporting procedure
- The position's authorities
- Indirect (or lateral) relationships
- Methods of measuring the position's performance
- Details of the basic job function
- The qualification specifications

Position descriptions serve as a guide for recruiting personnel and as a foundation for executive compensation plans, and can provide assistance in the process of appraising the executive structure. For senior and middle levels, individual descriptions are required for each position, but at lower management levels, it is often possible to use one description to cover many similar positions.

Phase 5. Design Completion   The purpose of this phase is to recheck and fine tune all previous work and to make any necessary final adjustments. A judgment should now be made concerning the spirit that the improved organization will project. Is it the essence of that which is desired? The designers of the new organization should also make transition plans at this time. These should provide for minimum disruption and frustration of the employees. As a part of the transition planning work, it may be decided that one, or even two, interim organizational structures are desirable before the final plan can be implemented. When major changes are involved, interim steps are often desirable to minimize shock and encourage a smooth transition.

If the implementation plan calls for interim organization structures, it is necessary to design interim charts, interim qualification descriptions, and interim position descriptions. Of course, care should be taken to prevent interim materials from getting out of hand. In one organizational planning study I know of, the final report was loaded with large graphic foldouts depicting all sorts of interim organizational details. They were extremely detailed and complex, and the president of the client firm finally politely inquired about the cost of all that interim graphics. The consulting firm balked at revealing the cost figure, but finally disclosed, to the president's dismay, that all the graphics in the consultants' report cost the company almost $3000!

Final cost estimates comparing the new organization with the present organization are also prepared at this time. These estimates should include projected impact of the new organization on profit and loss, organization costs, and the cost of new versus old information systems. Finally, the blessing of top management is sought for the entire package.

IMPLEMENTING THE
ORGANIZATION PLAN

Whether an improved organizational plan is designed by outside consultants or by an internal task force, its implementation will probably be difficult and hazardous. The key to successful implementation is the uncompromising support of the top person (or persons) involved in the change. If it's a divisional reorganization, then the division president or general manager must believe in it. If the entire company is being changed, the board of directors, the chief executive officer, and the senior executives must be convinced that all the effort and frustrations related to the transition will be worth the end results.

Unfortunately, uncompromising support can disappear just when it is most needed. Often this happens at the first sign of uprising or discontent, precisely when the top executive must stand firm. He or she may even have to get a little angry and say something like "God damn it, this is a good plan and we're going through with it! And that's final!" If the top executive is to develop the necessary confidence and conviction in the merit of the plans for improvement, it is important that he or she be involved during their inception and design. If the key person is familiar with the alternatives that were discarded, with the compromises that were made, and with all the other tough decisions necessary to make the proposed organizational design work, then that person will very likely recognize that the proposed plan is indeed the most workable plan and that it truly merits support.

Of course, supporting any major organizational change requires the conviction to do what must be done in the way of personnel changes. If several new vice presidents are needed to improve things, then the old ones will probably have to go. If a high-level corporate staff position is being decentralized into the various divisions, it is unlikely that the person presently in that position will accept a demotion to a comparable position in one of the divisions—so that person must also go.

This brings us to the process of notifying the organization of an impending change. Most people in the organization will probably know that a change is coming before any formal notification, if for no other reason than the fact that an interview process such as that described above is an almost sure sign of change. About a week before formal announcement of the new organization, it is essential to inform all key people, all people who will be directly affected, and especially all people who will be hurt. This is not only good business, it is also the decent thing to do. These sessions should be conducted personally and privately.

Formal notification to management-level personnel is probably best handled through a series of group meetings. At these sessions, it should be announced that the consultants, or the organizational planning task force, have developed a plan for an improved organization, and that this plan has been approved and has the wholehearted support of management. A new organization manual, including tentative position descriptions, should be distributed. Suggestions and advice on implementation of the plan should be actively solicited. Personnel should also be asked to review their new position descriptions and suggest changes. The schedule for implementing the improved organization should also be presented and discussed.

The implementation schedule will vary greatly depending on the situation. If drastic action is necessary, a company of medium size *can* be reorganized in several weeks, but this approach should be avoided if at all possible. Ideally, an orderly transition should be scheduled over a three- to six-month period. There is little to be gained by going beyond six months, however. Employees can become disturbed by a long period of change, uncertainty, and doubt.

During the implementation of the plan, it's critical to schedule regular review meetings to monitor progress and correct difficulties. Don't be dismayed when problems do occur. Problems are a part of all new ventures—and organizational improvements are no exception. The key is to recognize them and to deal with them promptly and deliberately.

Tolerance for inefficiencies during the transitional period is also a must. There will be a time during the implementation of a plan for improved organization when the new organization will actually function worse than the previous organization. This is to be expected. People are learning new jobs, and many employees will be new to the organization. New reporting procedures and information systems are being instituted, and limits of authority are being tested. The greatest boon to modern business, the telephone system, is probably being uprooted and revised. The key words here are patience and perseverance. Eventually, everything will settle into place and begin functioning properly.

CONSULTANTS OR INSIDERS

The process of defining, analyzing, designing, and implementing an improved organizational structure is complex and very labor intensive, and some measure of expertise is desirable, especially in the design phase. Unfortunately, organizational planning requires a permanence of function that is lacking in many companies. Often organizational planning is done to cure serious ills, rather than in anticipation of future opportunities, and an organization may change (since change is inevitable) in a haphazard and sometimes unfortunate way. A new marketing manager will decide she no longer needs a market research manager when the position becomes vacant. Then, perhaps, a market opportunity will emerge that cannot be exploited "because there isn't anybody available to do the job."

In a large company this type of situation needs the attention of an executive who has an overview of the objectives of the entire corporation. To fulfill this function, some large companies have created a position entitled vice president of organizational planning. This vice president's responsibility is to oversee and manage organizational change. The person in this position should be able to anticipate the impact of proposed changes on information flow, personnel requirements, compensation systems, morale, and the future growth and profitability of the organization.

If there is no existing in-house mechanism for planning and carrying out organizational changes, a qualified consulting firm may be hired to do a major organizational study. In this situation the client can take advantage of the consulting firm's expertise, but will have to pay a great deal for the service. Conversely, if a company chooses to do the entire study internally, it can save a good deal of money, but it may lack the expertise to design an effective new organization. These two extreme approaches suggest an attractive compromise. Why not hire a consultant to direct and advise an internally staffed task force for organizational planning? The consultant will be most useful in helping to interpret interview results, in directing the preparation of alternative structures, and in suggesting an appropriate format for position descriptions. At the same time, the bulk of the work can be done by the task force. I understand that some smaller consulting firms (that can't staff large organizational studies properly) actually welcome this type of arrangement. Of course, if a company feels it has the necessary organizational expertise, there is no reason why the entire effort cannot be done internally. If the effort is very large, the interviewing work can be divided among two or even three interviewing teams in order to shorten the definition and analysis phases. All interviewers should be carefully selected and thoroughly briefed before they talk with each key person, since they are trying to determine how the interviewee perceives his or her job, how he or he or she performs it, and how he or she feels the job could be done better.

I'd like to share with you a fascinating variation on the use of management consultants in an organizational planning study. Several years ago one of the major oil companies came to us with an unusual request. They wanted us to find out the commercial marketing organizational structures in use by their major competitors. They were in the midst of organizational restructuring, and they felt that it would help them if they knew how and why competitors were organized the way they were. (They also wanted to know what previous organizational structures had been tried and discarded by competitors.)

At first this seemed like a job for the Central Intelligence Agency, not for a consulting firm! We tried to talk them into letting us get involved in their basic organizational planning effort, but they wanted no part of that suggestion. We told them that we had serious doubts about our ability to obtain the information they requested using ethical practices, but they pleaded with us to try at least a few companies. We agreed, but only if they let us go about it our way. We said we would contact the oil company's competitors and tell them we were participating in some organizational planning work for a major oil company. Then we'd go on to say that we were interested in visiting with them to discuss the development and current structure of their commercial marketing organization. And, finally, we would promise them that in exchange for their cooperation we would verbally share with them all the information on the structures of the other oil companies that we obtained, including the company requesting the study, without disclosing the names of the companies. The client agreed to our plan. I guess the competitive oil companies' curiosity got the best of them. Nine out of ten major oil companies that we contacted agreed to a visit, and eight out of ten answered just about every question that we asked. Personally, I was amazed at what good solid information we were able to develop, and our client, to say the least, was very pleased. The information gave them an insight and a perspective that they didn't have before. Now don't misunderstand me. I'm not advising you to copy a competitor's organization plan. But knowing *how* and *why* everybody else in your industry is organized has got to be valuable in a company's planning process. If it is possible to get this insight in an open and ethical manner, more power to you.

You might be saying, "Sure your client got what they needed, but everybody else also got the same scoop, so the client lost his competitive edge." That's not exactly true, because when we visited each company we spent almost all the time talking about *their* organization. We invited them to visit us after the fieldwork was completed to ask us about everybody else's organization, since we had only partially completed our interviewing at the time of the visits. This approach seemed fair because we were talking "on our dime," and therefore wanted our questions answered first. Competitors must have gotten involved in other things, because none of their people ever visited us or even gave us a call. Because of this lack of follow-up, or lack of interest, our client got what they wanted, in exchange for very little. I should make it clear that had the oil company's representatives come to talk (or even called us), we would have felt obligated to tell them as much about everybody else's organization as they had told us about their own.

A closing note. I facetiously titled this chapter "Drawing Lines and Boxes" because I knew that this was going to be one of the longest and most complicated chapters in the book. If nothing else will do it, *just* the length of this chapter alone should make even a novice realize that good organizational planning involves much much *more* than drawing lines and boxes.

12

Finding Good People

(EXECUTIVE SEARCH)

> The best executive is the one who has sense enough
> to pick good men to do what he wants done, and
> self-restraint enough to keep from meddling with
> them while they do it.   — THEODORE ROOSEVELT

To the uninitiated, executive search may not appear to be related to business problem solving. I know the first time I heard executive recruiting and problem solving used in the same sentence, I was confused. A veteran headhunter had said, "My job is solving problems for clients. You see, if sales are lagging because of a personnel deficiency, I find *the* person who will revitalize the sales function. I solve the problem." It's hard to argue with that logic. Many business problems are people related, and in such cases executive recruiting is truly one approach to problem solving.

Executive recruiting is one of the most lucrative of all consulting specialties. This is true because search firms use a value pricing system, rather than a per day pricing system. Typically, executive search firms charge 30 percent of the recruited person's first-year salary (payable by the client, of course), plus out-of-pocket expenses. So if in a given year a headhunter completes twelve searches with a total salary value of $600,000, he or she collects $180,000. Not bad for finding twelve people! A management consultant providing other types of services and using the traditional pricing system would not be able to come anywhere near $180,000 in yearly billings. (If you multiply 230 work days per year by a daily billing rate of, say, $400, you reach a total professional revenue of $92,000.)

By doing executive recruiting internally, a company can save proportionately more money than by doing other types of consulting assignments internally. And, fortunately, executive search is a process that can be done internally in most instances. One large, diversified company I know of hired a consulting firm with a great deal of headhunter experience to analyze their recruiting function and then to prepare a report detailing an effective plan for recruiting both at the corporate and divisional level. This report was, in effect, a concise manual of executive search. [Although this consulting firm had earlier instituted a policy of declining executive search assignments (because of potential conflict-of-interest difficulties), and so preparing the report was not really giving away inside information, I'm sure that some search firms would frown on the preparation of such a manual.]

THE BASICS OF EXECUTIVE SEARCH

The executive search task is usually divided into the following distinct phases:
- Assessing the problem
- Writing the specifications
- Planning and scheduling the search
- Preliminary searching
- Advertising
- Sourcing (locating outside candidates through personal recommendation)
- Screening resumes
- Contacting likely candidates
- Interviewing
- Checking references
- Presenting candidates
- Making a choice
- Making the offer

As you can see from a look at Exhibit 12, the thirteen phases of executive search are really just a convenient way to subdivide the universal four-step approach to business problem solving. Now let's examine each phase of the recruiting process in some detail.

Assessing the Problem

I'm going to put the first phase (and the twelve that follow) in this context: Assume your company has decided to recruit management personnel internally, and that you, a well-thought-of manager in the personnel department, have been assigned the responsibility of directing the searches. Your client in any particular search will be defined as the direct supervisor of the position you are engaged to fill.

Your first step in assessing the problem is to interview in detail the manager (your client) for whom the new recruit will work. You should strive to answer the following questions in your meeting:
- Why is the position open? What are the requirements of the job?

EXHIBIT 12   Business Problem Solving and Executive Search

Universal approach to business problem solving	Thirteen phases of executive search
1. Defining the problem	1. Assessing the problem
	2. Writing the specifications
	3. Planning and scheduling
2. Gathering necessary information	4. Preliminary search
	5. Advertising
	6. Sourcing
3. Analysis and conclusions	7. Screening resumes
	8. Contacting likely candidates
	9. Interviewing
	10. Checking references
	11. Presenting candidates
4. Recommendations and implementations	12. Making a selection
	13. Making the offer

- Is there anyone within the manager's operation who might be a candidate?
- What performance pressures does the client seem to be under? Is the client only defining a short-term position to meet a current crisis?
- Are there any personality peculiarities and internal politics which would influence the choice of the candidate?

It's important to visit the plant or office where the new employee will work. Develop profiles of the client and the principal associates the new person would be working with. Evaluate their background (in and outside the company), interests, work habits, and personality. Also ask the client and the client's associates for names of people who may be candidates and for the names of acquaintances who can be used to suggest additional candidates. Finally, ask the client to identify the types of companies from which appropriate candidates are most likely to be recruited. Press hard for information—do not leave the client without a thorough understanding of the situation. When you do leave, promise to keep the manager informed with periodic progress reports.

The purpose of assessing the problem is to tailor the search process. This will help you uncover the best candidates. This assessment ensures that the client's problem is realistically perceived and that a search is the best solution to the problem. It also provides a clear picture of the environment in which the new employee will function and acquaints you with the client's operation so you can (1) write precise specifications for the position, (2) evaluate candidates effectively, and (3) speak knowledgeably with candidates about the position.

Writing the Specifications

Executive search specifications are the criteria against which candidates are measured. They are therefore "ideal" in nature. Specifications are intended to delineate clearly the kind of person who can fill the position in question. Typically, specifications are divided into three elements: (1) the company, division, and position, (2) the ideal person, and (3) the ideal experience.

The company and position section briefly describes where the position is, its title, to whom the position reports, who reports to the position, how many people are under its direction, the position's duties and responsibilities (be specific and list figures, amounts, etc.), and any unusual requirements (such as extensive travel).

The ideal person section includes age range, education, physical requirements, human characteristics (such as personality traits, ways of working, appearance, and manner), and special requirements (such as, for example, public speaking.)

The ideal experience section should include the type and minimum amount of experience the candidate should have, how long the ideal person should have been functioning in various capacities, and what industries or even companies the person should have worked for. Essential and nonessential experience should be identified.

A draft of the specifications should be reviewed and approved by the client. Once specifications are finished, they become the standard for measuring and judging. A typical specification is as follows.

SAMPLE SPECIFICATION
FOR SALES MANAGER

The company is a producer of specialty paper products involving printing, die-cutting, and pressure-sensitive paper. These products include electrocardiogram and x-ray mounts which are already being marketed, principally to the manufacturers of original medical and dental equipment.

The Position

Direct, train, and recruit salespersons. Develop marketing, sales, and promotion plans in conjunction with the vice president. Gradually, sales manager will assume complete responsibility for all sales activities

- Position reports to the vice president and general manager
- As planner, he or she would analyze markets and establish sales strategies and objectives
- As manager of salespersons, he or she would guide them in their daily activities. The sales manager would have little or no account responsibility

The Ideal Person

- A college graduate, preferably an M.B.A.
- Thirty to forty years old, a mature, sober person of judgment and balance, but with a desire to take normal business risks when possible gains are apparent
- An articulate, persuasive individual with well-developed human relations skills
- A general manager type committed to building an oragnization; oriented toward profit and results; capable of developing personnel
- Interested in solving problem
- An innovator, but one who can work with detail
- A person who is achievement oriented and destined to climb in business

The Ideal Experience

- Sold products or services to industrial customers. Familiar with buying situations where buyers plus others in the company must be favorably influenced simultaneously
- Managed sales or assisted a general manager for a minimum of two years. Preferably has had successful experience in the hiring, training, and directing of salepersons
- Worked in a profitable, fast-paced operation where modern management and marketing techniques were well developed
- Developed sales and marketing plans to meet defined objectives
- Direct experience in the printing and graphic arts industries not mandatory. However, the sales and management experience should have been in a situation where various manufacturing capabilities were applied to solving problems at different levels in many industries

Planning and Scheduling of Search

The purpose of this step is to determine the resources and steps needed to set the strategy of the search and determine when each step should be completed. A schedule should be used as a daily and weekly guide and as a means to check progress. This schedule should include the following items:

- Finalization of specifications
- Completion of search plan
- Presenting plan to client
- Preliminary search
- Advertising
- Sourcing
- Screening, interviewing, and checking references
- Presenting top candidates to client

A typical search will take from ten weeks to three months The schedule should call for timely completion of each step at an appropriate point within this overall time interval. The longest period of time should be allocated to sourcing, screening, interviewing, and checking references. Some searches, because of unusual circumstances, scheduling problems, or whatever, will take as long as four or five months. However, extended efforts and delays are not usually necessary if the search is aggressively undertaken.

Preliminary Search

The preliminary search involves looking in the more obvious places. Begin by checking the company personnel files to generate sources to contact in later steps. An effective search file system should be cross-referenced by functional, industrial, and company area. Some executive search firms organize their primary file by company. Each company entry contains the names of all personnel known to be working for a company, as well as previous employees. This company-type filing system will also help internal executive search operations. It can be initiated by asking all management personnel in the company about anyone they know who is or has been associated with major competitors or related businesses.

After looking in the files, the next step is to check directories. These include trade journal directories, professional association directories, and so on. Pay special attention to the promotion sections. Next, prepare a letter to send to contacts, friends, and acquaintances, describing your need and the type of person you're looking for. Ask in the letter if they know of anybody who might be appropriate. In the sourcing portion of the search, you may also contact some of these same people by telephone.

The preliminary search is then completed by contacting "suspects." Suspects is a label used by searchers to refer to readily identifiable candidates. This list may include names suggested by the client or the client's associates, as well as names found in the unsolicited resume file. These people generally can be contacted immediately and evaluated quickly.

Advertising

Sometimes advertising can be useful, although its value has always been questionable. At best, you may find one good candidate through space ads. The reason for this is quite simple. Searches are undertaken to find people who are not looking for a job—people who are successful and basically happy in their present jobs, people who generally don't answer space ads.

The purpose of the advertisement is to attract as many high-quality responses as possible. It should not be written to try to screen *out* candidates, which is a separate task. The most useful advertisement will be worded to bring forth the largest number of exceptional people who are *not* looking. It should tell a little about the company, summarize the major responsibilities of the position, indicate the experience required, and refer to the opportunities. Much of the content of the advertisement can be taken from the already completed list of specifications.

The key is to keep in mind the goal of the ad—to appeal to the ambitions and self-interests of outstanding people, people who may see more opportunity in your advertisement than in their present position. Study advertisements in the *Wall Street Journal* and other major publications as a guide. Try to avoid superficial and trite language. I'd suggest the use of blind (box return) advertisements in order to avoid having to acknowledge all replies.

Although you should not expect too much from advertising, it is usually wise to advertise, nonetheless. A good search must be comprehensive and thorough.

Sourcing

Sourcing is obviously an insider's term, but it is so descriptive of the action involved that it is appropriate to use it. Sourcing refers to the process of locating outstanding candidates through the use of personal recommendations. Impartial third-party referrals are almost always more reliable and informative than the resumes submitted by candidates actively seeking a job. As I said before, the ideal person is not looking for a job. He or she is successful and valued where he or she is, and is likely not to answer (or even look at) an advertisement.

Begin by sourcing people in the company who could be useful. Every new employee should be sourced immediately. Other likely people to source include the deans of the industry, veterans in the field who "know everybody," association executives, and trade magazine editors. Many experienced corporate headhunters suggest that it's best to review an already prepared list of candidates with a source. Perhaps the source will know one or two and be able to provide a quick evaluation. Regardless, the source will be stimulated to suggest others, which is what you want. When a name is offered, you should probe for the following basic information:

- Age
- Position
- Company
- Previous experience
- Outstanding characteristics
- How to get in touch with the person

When specific industry experience is not a prerequisite, sourcing can be undirected. In the sales manager example presented earlier in this chapter, the recruiter checked several different industries, and, in fact, the person finally hired was from the automotive industry.

Sourcing can also be very highly directed. One executive search consulting firm uses the words "target search" to describe its approach to directed sourcing. Directed sourcing implies a concentrated effort to locate two or three strong candidates from a limited group of companies in one industry. Say, for example, that the recruiter is looking for candidates currently working as marketing managers in machine-tool companies. While doing the telephone sourcing work, the searcher will push to get the names of as many such people as possible. If this doesn't work, more direct efforts are required, even to the point of camping out at a restaurant located near a target company and placing calls. The first call may locate a sales supervisor, who is convinced to come over to the restaurant for a cup of coffee and the chance to hear about an attractive opportunity. The recruiter may get the sales supervisor to sketch an organization chart of the entire marketing group and supply the name of the marketing manager. As soon as the sales supervisor leaves the restaurant, the recruiter hustles over to the phone and calls the marketing manager, "for a cup of coffee and some interesting conversation." Nine out of ten times, if the marketing manager is in the office that day, he or she will make up some excuse to leave the office and will be in the restaurant in fifteen minutes. This example illustrates the single most important aspect of successful sourcing—being aggressive. A good executive recruiter will scratch, dig, and push to locate a strong group of candidates.

Screening Resumes

The purpose of this step is to decide which, if any, of the resumes sent in response to advertisements are worth pursuing. Usually the best approach is to sort all resumes into three groups, keeping the specifications in mind:
- Excellent possibilities
- Marginal possibilities
- Rejects (not qualified)

An advantage of blind advertisements is that this sorting can be done at your own pace. Add a summary sheet to each resume you have an interest in. Enter the applicant's name, the date you received the resume, and the date you reviewed it. Then write two or three key strengths and reservations you have about the applicant, being sure to measure him or her against the specifications. Concisely note your impressions of such things as the candidate's diction, decisiveness, demeanor, etc. Finally, this sheet will be used to record each contact or attempted contact with the applicant.

Promising but nonappropriate resumes should be filed for future needs. Be careful not to overburden your files with resumes of underqualified candidates. Only keep resumes from well-qualified, high-potential people, and people who are in, or have been in, good companies.

Contacting Likely Candidates

At this point in the search you should have a group of likely candidates gathered from advertising and sourcing efforts. People in this group should be contacted as soon as you decide that they have promise. Always use the telephone, not the mail. It's usually best to keep the initial conversation brief. Ask about his or her experience. Find out what the candidate's compensation is. If there are any inconsistencies or unclear areas, get them clarified now.

It's essential to make a judgment about your next step while you are talking. If he or she continues to be attractive, arrange to meet soon in the most convenient way. If the candidate appears to be marginal, put him or her in a hold position that you can pick up or drop later. This can be done simply by saying something like, "Well, I enjoyed chatting with you. After we've completed some of our preliminary analysis, I'll be back in touch with you if it would appear to be mutually beneficial." Finally, if you conclude that the candidate is not suited for the position, indicate it, and terminate the conversation. If you choose, you can leave the door open for future positions that may open up.

All initial contacts should be made by the person coordinating the search assignment, not by the requisitioning manager. It's important always to control the initial contacts and to take the initiative in the conversation.

Interviewing

The purpose of interviewing is to continue the evaluation process begun in the telephone contact. The first interview should, if possible, be handled by the recruiter. The recruiter must decide if the candidate warrants further interviewing. The initial interview with each candidate should take place in the field—at an airport conference room, in a regional company office, or even in a restaurant. Ideally, these first interviews should be grouped or coordinated along a prescribed route that will minimize your time and travel. Since you may have to promote your company, be prepared with brochures and other materials. Describe the division and locale where the candidate would work. Be reassuring about career opportunities, the company's plans for the future, graduate school opportunities, living conditions, and recreational opportunities.

If additional interviews are warranted, the candidate's travel schedule should be learned. A list of references should be obtained. While references are being checked, one or two other people in the company (from personnel or from the division seeking the new person) should interview the candidate. Each successive interviewer should have the benefit of input from previous interviews. At times, it may be best to bring the candidate into your offices for these interviews.

Reference Checking

The purpose of this step is to uncover areas for further questioning, to learn everything practical about the candidate (particularly things the candidate does not or cannot tell), and to lend support to findings and conclusions concerning the candidate.

Reference checking is the most revealing measure you can take short of working with the candidate for years. It may even be superior to shared work experience because it permits you to see the candidate as several people have over a span of time in both business and social situations. Reference checking is far more revealing than reviewing a resume; it is also more revealing than most interviewing.

The person making the check should identify himself or herself, the candidate, and the position for which the candidate is being considered. Checks can be made by people other than the recruiter, but they will suffer from lack of knowledge of the situation and persons involved. Ask the people providing the reference if they have a few minutes available to help place a person they know in a positon that offers fine opportunities.

Among the key questions to ask are the following:

- How well do you know this person? How do you happen to know him or her? Professionally? Socially? How long?
- What is your general impression of him or her? As a business person? As a friend?
- Have you ever worked with the candidate? In what capacity? How did he or she perform? (Refer to the resume as appropriate.)
- How is he or she regarded by others?
- How does he or she work with superiors? With workers under him or her? How does the candidate delegate responsibility? Does he or she keep close control?
- What are his or her strengths? (Ask for examples.) What are his or her limitations? (Probe. In what capacities would it be difficult for him or her to function?)
- Do you think that the candidate could handle the position we have described? How well?
- Would you employ the candidate? In what capacity?
- Is this person a loner? A team player?
- What do you know of family background?
- What can you tell me about personal habits? How is the candidate's conduct off the job? Interests? Activities?
- Is there anything else that I should know that I haven't touched on? For example, is there anything that would embarrass him or her?

Always be sure to write the answers to all questions in quotation marks. You may need to edit them for clarity and brevity, but be careful not to distort the respondent's answers in your rephrasing. A finalized version of a typical reference check is shown below.

REFERENCE REPORT

William G. Smith

Mr. John R. Casey
Retired Executive and Consultant

Mr. Casey was contacted by telephone and made comments essentially as follows about Mr. Smith:

"I know Bill pretty well, for ten years as a matter of fact. I met him playing softball on the same team in Park Forest. I was the founder and a former president of the Park Forest Athletic Club.

"My general impression of Bill is very good. If I had an opening, I would hire him. He's a great guy—conscientious, intelligent, thinking marketing all the time. He has a great sense of responsibility to his family and his job.

"I knew him when he was in marketing at Goodyear. I was director of sales for a local printing firm and Goodyear was one of my accounts. He was doing fairly well, but wanted to do more. He has to be envied for having the courage to open his own business. So many of us do nothing more than talk about it.

"He's a very competitive guy—lots of leadership qualities, among men especially. He must have been a great athlete in college. He seems to do everything well.

"He has no personality problems. He gets along with everybody. He seems to communicate well at all levels. He easily wins your respect. His speaking voice is impressive. When he talks, you find yourself listening.

"I would say that Bill should be a prime candidate for the position you have described. As a skilled marketing man, I think he would do well given the responsibility to get the job done in an organization where policy lines are clearly defined.

"As I mentioned earlier, I worked in a similar position with a printing firm a few years ago. It's not a glamour industry. Return on investment is typically low. To be profitable, a firm has to specialize in the printing industry today. Why, there are more printing firms in Chicago than drugstores!

"Stepping into a position such as the one you describe, a man isn't likely to achieve overnight results. The firm's management will have to show some patience regardless of whom they select. Given the authority, I'm sure Bill could handle the job. He's a marketing man in the broadest sense and he can definitely motivate salespersons.

"In terms of his adaptability to the printing business, I think he could pick up what he would need to know rather quickly. The production equipment wouldn't scare him. I think he has achieved a basic familiarity with some of the machinery over the past year as a consultant. Bill has done some graphic arts work developing catalogues and promotional materials for a number of his clients, providing him with far better than a layman's understanding of the business.

"Bill has a fine family and a lovely wife. We get together occasionally on a social basis, and I would describe him as a moderate drinker. He's very much involved in Park Forest's young boys' athletic program. He's the best football coach these kids have ever had in the Peewee Football League. He's the first one to ever teach them real fundamentals. I also think he's active in the school and the Presbyterian Church—a Deacon, I believe.

"As a friend and business acquaintance, I highly recommend Bill to you. If there is any other way in which I may be of assistance, please feel free to contact me."

Presenting Candidates

The purpose of this step is to present the candidate finalists accurately and in the best light. By doing this, you will provide the client with much needed help in his or her interviewing of the candidates. Usually, two or three final candidates are presented.

Prior to introducing the candidates to the client, the recruiter should have done three things:

1. Interviewed the candidates personally, and had them interviewed by others from the personnel department or client's department

2. Checked all references and written reference reports

3. Prepared a summary appraisal of each candidate measured against the specifications

The summary appraisal for each candidate should be written in identical formats for ease of comparison. The information included in a typical summary appraisal is presented in Exhibit 13.

It is often desirable for final candidates to have met several people in the company before getting to this step, more to give the candidates a feel of the group he or she might be working with than to let the company people appraise the candidates. Creating the very best impression possible of your company at this stage is as important as evaluating the candidates, since,

EXHIBIT 13   Information to Include in Summary Appraisal

General data	Educational background	Summary of experience
■ Residence	■ Degrees	■ Dates, companies, and positions listed on one page
■ Telephone numbers 　Home 　Business	■ Schools ■ Years	
■ Age and place of birth		
■ Marital and family status		

Professional and civic activities	Details of experience	
■ List each	■ Extensive description of responsibilities, accomplishments, etc., in each major position	

EXHIBIT 14 Sample Candidate Qualifications and Ratings (Sales Manager)

		Base Rating/Weighted Rating*			
	Weight*	'A'	'B'	'C'	'D'
		BSBA	CPA Equiv.	BSBA	BS Ch.
WHAT HE SHOULD BE:					
A college graduate, preferably an M.B.A.	5	8/40	9/45	8/40	7/35
Between 30 to 40 years old, a mature, sober man of judgment and balance, but with a desire to take normal business risks that are sound compared to possible gains.	4	8/32	7/28	6/24	6/24
An articulate, persuasive individual with well-developed human relations skills.	4	7/28	9/36	7/28	7/28
A general manager type, profit- and results-oriented.					
Skilled in working with others. Dedicated to selecting, training and developing salesmen to the end that he creates a highly effective organization.	5	9/45	9/45	5/45	5/45
Interested in solving problems.	4	8/32	8/32	8/32	8/32
An innovator with a well-developed sense of new products' commercial possibilities. Capable of working with detail.	4	8/32	8/32	7/28	9/36
A person who is achievement-oriented and destined to climb in business.	5	8/40	8/40	7/35	7/35
Point rating (of possible 70/310)		56/249	58/258	48/232	49/235
WHAT HE SHOULD HAVE DONE:					
Sold products or services to industrial customers. Be familiar with buying situations where buyers plus others in the company must be favorably influenced simultaneously.	4	8/32	7/28	6/24	8/32
Managed sales or assisted a general manager for a minimum of two years. Preferably he will have had successful experience in the hiring, training, and directing of salesmen.	5	9/45	10/50	2/10	2/10

Specification	Weight				
Worked in a profitable, fast-paced operation where modern management and marketing techniques are well developed.	3	8/24	6/18	9/27	9/27
Developed sales and marketing plans to meet defined objectives.	3	7/21	8/24	7/21	7/21
Specific experience in the printing and graphic arts industries is not mandatory. However, his sales and management experience should have been in situations where various manufacturing capabilities are applied to solving problems at different levels in many industries.	5	8/40	5/25	6/30	8/40
Point rating (of a possible 50/200)		39/157	36/145	30/112	34/130
Subtotal		95/406	94/403	78/344	83/365

PERSONAL TRAITS:

Specification	Weight				
Basic intelligence	5	8/40	10/50	8/40	8/40
Adaptability; quickness to learn	5	9/45	10/50	8/40	9/45
Apparent emotional stability and temperament	5	9/45	6/30	7/35	7/35
Personality; magnetism	3	10/30	9/27	7/21	7/21
Physical appearance and stature	3	10/30	8/24	7/21	7/21
Point rating (of a possible 50/210)		46/190	43/181	37/157	38/162
TOTAL POINT RATING (of a possible 170/720)		141/596	137/584	115/501	121/527

* Weights have been assigned to each specification reflecting its relative importance. The scale of 1 to 5 should be interpreted such that the higher the assigned number, the greater the importance of that particular specification. Base Rating is on a ten-point scale: very weak (0) to very good (10). / Weighted Rating is a product of the base rate and specification weight.

after all, interviewing and reference checks have already told you a great deal about the finalists.

Making a Selection

It is important for the recruiter to assume considerable responsibility in making the final selection. This responsibility includes making a recommendation based on an objective comparison of the finalists. The basis for this comparison should be the specifications. A comparison chart can be built, using the specifications as follows:

- Enter each item of the specifications in the leftmost column.
- Assign a value to each item based on its relative importance to the total qualification.
- Enter the name of each candidate at the head of columns to the right of the itemized specifications.
- Grade each candidate from 1 to 10 on each item and multiply the figure by the value of the specification.
- Finally, total the results for each candidate. These totals will provide a basis for comparison.

A sample candidate comparison chart is presented in Exhibit 14.

Making the Offer

The purpose of this final step is to reach an agreement whereby the candidate will come to work for your company at a fair price, at a mutually convenient time, and in a positive frame of mind. Prior to acceptance, the selected candidate will probably want to visit the home office, the division office, and the plant and community where he or she will work. Usually the candidate's spouse will also want a chance to evaluate the new location. It is probably best to make a tentative offer prior to such visits, since this may avoid duplicate trips (one by the candidate alone and another by the candidate and spouse). The final terms can usually be worked out during the early part of the visit, so that the couple can begin house hunting.

Making the offer should be planned well in advance, taking into account the person's values and expectations. Discussions should be low-key and have the sole purpose or having your company and the candidate come to terms during the visit.

Two things that can be done to help the couple are (1) provide them with a good map of the area and introduce them to a knowledgeable real estate agent; and (2) provide them with an evaluation of schools and introduce them to a couple who have successfully moved into the area recently.

SOME HELPFUL GUIDELINES

In most organizations the need to locate and attract capable, bright managers is an ever-present challenge, and recruiting must be a high priority for all managers. Each manager must recognize that organization building through strengthening team members is vital. Each should be alert to identifying outstanding people wherever and whenever possible. The peoples' names and observations about them should be contributed to a common pool, without regard to whether they are available or not. Managers may have worked with good people at one time, or met them in travels, at association meetings, or at trade shows. Managers should have a sense that sourcing is an ongoing process.

Even though personnel may officially be responsible for recruiting and for doing most of the search work in specific assignments, the manager who directs an unfilled position is ultimately responsible for properly filling the job when the need arises. It is not enough to requisition a person from personnel and then sit back and wait. Managers must take responsibility for deciding who works for them. It is important to remember that there are subtle but real differences between acquiring management talent and filling routine lower-level positions. In lower-level positions it is possible to requisition employees from the personnel department, but real managerial involvement is required for hiring at higher levels.

A productive company-run recruiting function must be designed to reach out aggressively for highly capable, desirable people. Your company must take the initiative. You must search for and find the people needed. Executive search and recruiting mean exactly what they say. Do not simply take the best person who is readily available. The proper attitude and approach to working are essential to management organization building through recruiting. Every step must be geared to an aggressive thrust, including advertising, sourcing, interviewing, traveling to see people, reference checking, and presenting attractive employment packages.

In a large company, the management recruiting function should be organized to maximize its resources. Recruiters are best positioned in a central corporate personnel department. Corporate personnel should take the lead in developing, sustaining, and coordinating the "people building" effort. Only corporate personnel is in a position to have overall knowledge of the company's talents and needs, to deal directly with each division or plant, and to develop meaningful outside contacts. In summary, there are seven key guidelines that will help your company find and hire winning executives time after time.

1. *Pinpoint* search responsibility. In a small company, the manager who has a need should assume responsibility. In a large company, either the client or recruiter should assume or be assigned primary responsibility.

2. *Develop* an exact specification of the manager you want. Aim this specification at the ideal person. Don't compromise at this stage in your work. The specification should be detailed enough to thoroughly address specifics of the position, the ideal person, and the ideal experience.

3. *Search* as widely as possible. Seek out the largest possible number of potential candidates. Remember that the person you want is almost certainly employed and probably not answering help-wanted advertising.

4. *Conduct* thorough interviews and ask tough questions. It's impossible to cover the experiences, background, and attitudes of a seasoned executive in a short interview. An hour or more should be spent with strong candidates, and meaty questions must be asked. A good candidate will have good answers.

5. *Always* ask for and check secondary references. Talk to the references the candidate supplies, but also be sure to talk to people supplied by the primary references. Don't neglect to talk to all previous bosses, whether they surface as references or not.

6. *Insist* on a choice. The search effort should result in presenting at least two outstanding candidates. If only one candidate is presented, there really is no choice at all.

7. *Turn* to an excecutive search firm when appropriate. Senior positions (e.g., chairman of the board, president, general manager), members of the board of directors, and any other key position that has remained open beyond a reasonable time period should be turned over to a competent search firm.

13

Keeping Good People
(EXECUTIVE COMPENSATION)

*The law of work does seem utterly unfair—but there
it is, and nothing can change it; the higher the pay
in enjoyment the worker gets out of it, the higher
shall be his pay in money also.* — MARK TWAIN

The purse may be full and the heart empty.
— ROBERT LOUIS STEVENSON

The title of this chapter infers that executive compensation is somewhat
narrower than it actually is. In addition to keeping good people, an executive compensation system should attract new people to the staff and, perhaps most important, motivate employee effort toward fulfilling the objectives of the organization.

People who should be considered executives for the purposes of executive compensation planning are, of course, all corporate officers and high-
level managers. In addition, all companies have certain employees who are
important enough to the operation of the company to compensate with the
purpose of retaining. Maybe a company has a researcher with a list of
patents that could choke a horse, or a field service troubleshooter who
always seems to get things straightened out or a critically important sales
force. These personnel, though technically "nonexecutive," should be part
of any executive compensation system.

The purpose of this chapter is to illustrate an approach to solving a broad
range of executive compensation problems with two case histories. The first
is a sales compensation study that was done by a consulting firm for a large
food company. This study was done in conjunction with a reorganization of
the client's field sales force. The second is an executive compensation study
that I did for a consulting firm while a member of its staff, which again
illustrates the basic message of this book—in many cases an organization
can solve consulting-type business problems using an internal approach.

IMPROVING A SALES
COMPENSATION SYSTEM

The primary business of the client in this illustration, American Foods, was selling national brand name consumer food (and some nonfood) products through supermarkets. Six or seven of their brand names were household words. American also sold its food products to the food service market (restaurants, fast-food chains, etc). This food service operation accounted for only about 10 to 15 percent of American's total revenue, and was not considered to be a meaningful market. In fact, some company executives referred to the food service market as a "low-margin dumping ground."

But things began to change in the late 1960s. Retail food sales growth began to weaken because of a national obsession with fast-food chains and other away-from-home eating establishments. Consumers were spending less of their food budgets in supermarkets and more in establishments such as McDonald's. This trend was acknowledged by most retail food companies, and many, including American, began to consider the food service market as an alternative growth market. American initially replaced their food service brokers with direct field salesmen in some high-volume markets, and soon after instituted a national accounts program for big food service customers.

In 1976, American introduced sweeping organizational change. In recognition of the growing importance of food service, a food service division having equal stature with the long-standing retail division was formed. American was also involved in a process of strengthening and reorganizing its food service field sales team at this time. A sales compensation study, done by our firm, was to be an integral part of the overall reorganization plan. Our specific objective was to assist American Foods in the design and implementation of a revised sales compensation program for the food service direct sales force, which would emphasize motivational incentives, both short-term and long-term.

The kickoff meeting was attended by two members of our firm and the newly appointed divisional management, including the food service division president, marketing manager, and national sales manager. At this meeting the requirements for the revised compensation system were agreed on, as follows:

▪ The system must be responsive to changes, such as the addition and deletion of products and changes in the definition of national accounts. (It was unanimously agreed that the system would fail if it could not keep pace with the rapidly changing market environment.)

▪ The program must lend itself to easy administration. Details that should be conveniently and easily administered include handling transfers, terminations, new hirings, how sales credits are to be allocated (where split responsibility exists), and how quotas will be established.

▪ The system must provide for automatic review. It was recognized that while most plans would work the day they were implemented, the real need was to revise the present system so that it would continue to function effectively over a period of years.

The methodology for developing and instituting the revised system consisted of five steps.

Step 1. Defining Objectives   Divisional management did not feel that the current field sales compensation system provided the proper motivational emphasis. Salespersons did not appear to be pushing the right products, for example. To begin to correct this situation, we met with the food service management team long enough to absorb their understanding of the current plan and to develop a ranked list of objectives for the new plan. For example, it was suggested to us that the revised plan should emphasize the development of new accounts, and should favor newer products.

Step 2. Analysis of Present System   This step focused on developing an understanding of the shortcomings of the present system. It began with a review of the duties and responsibilities of each individual included in the compensation program. Some of this was done through review of manuals and position descriptions. But, as is the case in most problem-solving situations, interviewing was the prime methodology. Personal interviews were conducted with twenty-six field sales personnel in all five sales regions. These interviews were designed to solicit ideas for improving the present system and to involve field people in the development of the planning process. The five regional managers were included in the interviewing effort.

Step 3. Developing the Revised Plan   This step began by designing various alternative plans that might be appropriate for American. A comparative ranking system was developed which included factors such as:

▪ The company's capability to administer each plan

▪ The necessity for detailed accounting and financial data for each alternative

▪ The relative emphasis on base pay versus incentive pay in each alternative

We also conducted field interviews with other leading food service companies. This effort was made to determine the kinds of programs that had been tried and discarded by these competitors, and to determine the compensation system that most direct competitors were using at the time. At the conclusion of this step, a revised compensation program was presented to the food service management team.

Step 4. Testing the Plan   Following the presentation of the improved compensation system, the program was tested by utilizing prior data to estimate its effectiveness in meeting objectives. This was, of course, not totally realistic, since the prior data reflected prior motivational patterns. This exercise was prompted by the client, and I don't recommend it as a valid measure. A more practical, but more time-consuming, approach is to test the system in one sales territory before full-scale implementation. The disadvantages of this approach include bias caused by the fact that salespersons will know they are involved in a test and the possibility of claims of special treatment for the portion of the sales team involved in the test.

Step 5. Implementation   Successful implementation of any compensation system depends on management's understanding and support. This support was encouraged by having all appropriate executive personnel involved in the entire analysis and development process. A meeting was held at division headquarters to brief the operating sales management group, including the regional and assistant managers. At this meeting, two-way communication was encouraged to offer a final opportunity for sales management to expose potential problems and to suggest revisions in administration provisions.

The revised compensation package was then presented to the field salespeople through a series of five regional meetings. This type of meeting is very important because people are naturally apprehensive concerning decisions that could affect their income. If a new system is not communicated properly and understood fully, resistance can develop which may compromise or delay the full effectiveness that the plan can and should achieve.

Let's take a look at what we, the consulting firm, actually contributed to developing and implementing the revised compensation system. Our major involvement included:

Step 1: Assisting in defining objectives

Step 2: Interviewing divisional field salespeople

Step 3: Developing and analyzing alternative systems, including conducting competitive interviews

Step 4: Designing measures to test the new plan

Step 5: Presenting the plan to field sales management

The client could have easily done all these things themselves, with the possible exception of the competitive interviews. Even the information developed in these competitive interviews could have been developed in other ways (such as cocktail conversations at association gatherings and meetings with similar, but noncompetitive, companies). In retrospect, I feel that our implementation efforts were marginal, because after we made the presentation of the plan to field sales management, the client did the rest of the implementation (the paperwork, forms, training, explanations, and ironing-out of problems). The one indisputable positive contribution we had to make was our experience in compensation work. Whether this was worth $25,000 in fees and out-of-pocket expenses is open to question. Our experience and guidance was apparently worth it to this company. To other companies, it might not be.

INTERNAL CONSULTING IN A CONSULTING FIRM

Unfortunately, consulting firms are among the most poorly managed businesses, not because talent and knowledge are lacking, but because consultants are either so busy solving others' business problems or so busy looking for clients that they don't have time for their own problems.

But neglected problems don't go away; indeed, they often get worse. So it was with a consulting firm I once worked for. This firm had three levels of professionals. At the lowest level were the senior consultants—these were the doers. At the second level were program managers—obviously they managed projects. And the highest-level positions, the sellers, were called principals. A green consultant advanced from the senior consultant level to the program manager level by developing competence in project work and in client relations (no sales competence was required). But at the program manager level emphasis switched from project performance to sales performance. The program manager's salary increases and year-end cash bonus depended pretty much on how well he or she was progressing as a seller of consulting services, and promotion to the principal level required a twelve-month sales level of $100,000 in professional fees. At the principal level, both base pay and year-end cash bonuses depended almost entirely on sales performance.

There were six principals in the firm at the time the problem started to develop. Four were founders of the firm, another had worked her way up through the ranks, and the sixth was "acquired" when our firm absorbed a two-person consulting firm. Neither of the nonfounding principals was truly producing enough sales volume to justify the rank. There were supposed to be seven program managers, but two of the most senior managers had recently resigned. Both had been struggling for almost three years to generate the required $100,000 sales volume needed for promotion to principal. (One of them had managed to reach $55,000 in a twelve-month period.) Both emphatically expressed their reason for quitting somewhat like this:

> It's impossible to make it under current circumstances. A program manager should get some sales help from the principals—shared sales credit or something. But instead, the principals greedily hog all their clients and *all* the sales credit. We're expected to develop new clients while they grow fat on repeat business.

Soon after these resignations, one of the nonfounding principals resigned to become vice president of marketing with a client company. This resignation was followed by a series of hastily called closed door meetings of the founding principals (this group was called the executive committee). It was obvious that they had become concerned by the sudden high turnover rate and employee discontent, especially at the program manager level. It soon became obvious what decisions had been made in the executive committee meetings.

An intermediate position, that of associate principal, was created between the program manager level and the principal level. It required $50,000 in sales credit for a program manager to merit promotion. A larger office, a free company car, and a larger base salary were the announced rewards for attaining the position of associate principal. Although most program managers seemed to be positively impressed by the change, none qualified for the new position.

Then the executive committee made a serious error in judgment. They began to treat two program managers better than the others. One, named Barbara, was given all the accounts of the recently departed principal. She soon garnered enough sales credit from these accounts to justify promotion to associate principal. The second program manager, Bill, was taken under the wing of the president (the most successful seller). Soon shared sales credit came his way, and then some existing accounts were turned over to him. Before long, Bill was also an associate principal.

During the six-month period it took all this to happen, three program managers were promoted from senior consultant. That brought the total staffing at the program manager level (after the promotion of Barbara and Bill to associate principals) to six. To say the least, none of the current group of program managers was happy about the favored treatment being accorded Barbara and Bill. Each, in turn, complained to members of the executive committee. Some protests were polite and others were downright vicious. The executive committee's reaction was unsympathetic: "Barbara and Bill reached the $50,000 goal so we promoted them. If and when you reach it, we'll promote you, too."

Discontent continued to grow until some project managers were almost refusing to manage projects. And all were openly threatening to quit.

The president of the company came to me one afternoon, closed the door to my office, and sat down in front of my desk. He said, "This morale problem at the program manager level is getting out of hand. You're a program manager. Why haven't you complained more vocally?" I replied, "Jim, to be honest, I haven't bothered because I don't think it would do much good. You know what your special treatment of Barbara and Bill has done. Yet you're unwilling to do anything about it." Jim replied, "What do you think we should do? Sure I've shared some of my sales credit with Bill, but other principals either won't or can't be as generous. And we had to give the account we gave to Barbara to somebody. She seemed the most appropriate."

I sat silent for several seconds and then said, "Jim, maybe we ought to do a study of the whole sales credit and promotion system. That's what we'd do if a client had our problems. Our current system is divisive. It creates ill will. And I suspect that this Barbara and Bill thing is just the tip of the iceberg. I know I've been hearing complaints about sales credit and its impact on bonuses and promotion ever since I've been here. But things don't seem to get any better."

The meeting ended with an understanding that I would prepare a brief outline of a proposed approach to evaluating and improving the sales credit and compensation system of the firm. It was agreed a week later that I would be a study committee of one and that I could solicit assistance from anybody else in the firm if and when I felt it was necessary.

The approach I planned was very straightforward. I would gather information from two basic sources: (1) fellow consultants (at all levels) on our staff, and (2) members of other consulting firms. I began my quest for internal facts, opinions, suggestions, etc., by calling a company staff meeting for 4:30 on the following Monday afternoon. At this meeting I announced that I was doing an internal study of the sales credit and compensation system with the support and blessing of the executive committee. A wide-open discussion was held concerning the key issues to be addressed and the questions to be answered. It was apparent that there was going to be a good deal of interest in the study. At the close of the meeting I told each person to expect a visit from me in the next several weeks—for the purpose of interviewing each of them. I was looking forward to trying my hand at interviewing a group of professional interviewers, and I think a lot of my associates were looking forward to being the interviewees for a change.

Each staff interview was conducted privately and in confidence. And let me tell you, I had some great interviews. People were candid and open, and gave their opinions on most everything. Suggestions for improving the system flowed on almost endlessly. And, as I had suspected, the "Barbara and Bill situation" was only one of a number of problems. My fellow employees seemed very relieved to be talking to a sympathetic staff member who hopefully represented a force for positive change in the system.

I recruited other staff members to help me gather information from outside consulting firms. What we wanted was an understanding of the systems of sales credit, compensation, and promotion that were being used by similar consulting firms. This information turned out to be easy to obtain. As is true in most industries, almost everybody in our firm knew somebody else at another firm. All that was required to develop the data we wanted was a series of lunches with previous acquaintances. We found people willing and able to discuss the type of noncompetitive information we were after.

After analyzing all the data and considering alternatives, I developed a series of recommendations, which were received enthusiastically by both the staff and the executive committee. This internal study not only resulted in an improved compensation system, but it opened up the company's communications channels and improved morale by clearing the air of pent-up hostility and frustration.

14
Bricks and Mortar
(FACILITIES PLANNING)

> *When we build, let us think that we build forever. Let it not be for present delight, nor for present use alone; let it be such work as our descendants will thank us for, and let us think, as we lay stone on stone, that a time is to come when those stones will be held sacred because our hands have touched them, and that men will say as they look upon the labor and wrought substance of them, "See! this our fathers did for us."*
> — JOHN RUSKIN

Facilities planning is one of the oldest consulting specialties. It encompasses many of the course areas in an undergraduate industrial engineering curriculum. And the word "facilities" embraces most corporate physical assets, including production equipment, factories, administrative offices, warehouses, depots, retail outlets, regional offices, and R&D facilities.

Some of the most common consulting assignments in facilities planning include:

- *Plant Location Studies:* A systematic approach to selecting an ideal plant location by balancing raw material and transportation costs; market locale; labor costs; power availability and cost; water availability and cost; variations in taxation; climate; and the assets of various local communities
- *Plant Layout Design:* Analysis of physical arrangement of factories, plants, laboratories, commercial areas, etc., with the objectives of improving operations, increasing output, reducing costs, serving customers better, and creating a pleasant work environment for company personnel
- *Equipment Analysis:* An organized approach to equipment evaluation and selection designed to improve efficiency, productivity, and profitability
- *Warehousing and Physical Distribution:* Analysis and planning of raw materials, finished goods, and distribution-related systems, equipment, and facilities

Rather than getting involved in a long, dry presentation of the basics of each of these areas, I'd like to present a wide-ranging facilities study that dealt with a total appraisal of a small company's equipment, plant, and warehousing facilities.

Incidentally, this case illustrates a point I made earlier: In many consulting assignments the junior people carry the bulk of responsibility in an engagement. I handled almost all of this particular assignment after only six months of consulting experience. I did have the right credentials—a master's degree in mechanical engineering and six years of industrial experience. But there is a big difference between classroom work and the real world, and to make matters worse, none of my real-world experience involved facilities planning! Fortunately, the consultant in charge of the study was a Ph.D. in industrial engineering with ten years of consulting experience. Although he wasn't very deeply involved in the study, he was on emergency call when I needed him. Because of his presence and an unbelievable turn of good luck (which I'll explain later), I feel we ended up doing a very good job for the client.

THE COMPANY

Creative Products Company was a producer and marketer of specialty consumer paper products—holiday and special-occasion (for example, birthday) paper tableware. Primary product lines included plates, napkins, tablecloths, and cups, which were shipped directly from the plant and office located in Detroit to specialty shops, bookstores, and greeting-card shops throughout the country.

Annual sales volume was about $10 million, and sales had doubled in the last 4½ years. The president, a bright young Harvard Business School graduate, had bought the company five years before with the help of several silent partners. The president and the four people reporting to him (comptroller, production manager, sales manager, and creative design chief) comprised the entire management team.

Although Creative Products had only four basic product lines, there was what seemed to be an almost endless variety within each line. There were five different-sized plates, including luncheon, dinner, snack, tray, and party varieties. There were eight napkin sizes, four tablecloth sizes, and about five types of cups (cups were purchased in bulk and then repackaged). Each size offered color and design variations for special occasions such as birthdays, weddings, graduations, Easter, the Fourth of July, Thanksgiving, Hanukkah, Christmas, and New Years. All told, the four basic product lines involved over 450 different products. This situation was the major difficulty we faced in our efforts to improve the client's facilities.

THE PROBLEM

The principal in charge of the engagement (the Ph.D., Frank Lazard) and I flew to Detroit to discuss a possible study of the Creative Products situation with its president, Bob Anderson. We had been recommended to him by a large client of ours in a Detroit suburb. Bob called us in because his entire facility was being strained by the rapid sales increase that had taken place under his direction. In fact, efficiency in the plant and warehousing system had become so disrupted that it was beginning to impede future sales growth. After a discussion with Bob and his plant manager, the following problems surfaced:

- Stock-outs, at times, had reached 16 percent of sales.
- In an attempt to reduce stock-outs and minimize finished goods inventory volume (storage space was limited) production runs were being shortened. This was resulting in excessive setup time on the production equipment.
- In some instances (to satisfy back orders) only that portion of production runs which was needed immediately was packaged. The remainder was held in the production area.
- Some of the production equipment was "old," slow by current standards, and suffered frequent breakdown.
- Order picking of finished goods was done using an oversized grocery cart. And there were no storage locations for permanent items in the warehouse, which complicated the picking process. And, finally, because the company was "smallish" and expanding rapidly, there was only limited capital available for modernization and expansion.

After lunch, the plant manager took Frank and me on a thorough inspection tour of the facilities. We noticed some additional problem areas. Excessive raw materials (napkin tissue and plate roll stock) were being "stored" all over the production area. And, because there was no more room in the finished goods warehouse, cartons of plates, napkins, tablecloths, and cups were also stacked all over the production area. All these excess materials in the production area resulted in duplicate material handling and production inefficiencies. All in all, Creative Products' facilities and operation were in quite a state of disarray!

After returning to our offices in Chicago, I submitted a proposal to Creative Products which suggested that we analyze and recommend improvement, where justified, for:

- All production and packaging equipment
- Raw material and finished goods space requirements
- The finished goods warehouse (storage procedures and order picking)
- Plant layout

INFORMATION GATHERING

Bob Anderson authorized our study effort the same day he received our proposal in the mail. I then returned to Creative Products to gather all the necessary information and data. This work began with a long meeting with the production manager. Then I interviewed department supervisors and the warehouse supervisor. The purpose of all these discussions was to gain a thorough understanding of the current practices and procedures. I also solicited opinions concerning problem areas and suggestions for improvement.

Another major purpose of my visit was to gather quantitative data. To this end I put together equipment lists with details on each item including age, production rate, setup time, operator involvement, and repair cost and time. In addition, I observed and recorded the flow of materials from receiving of raw materials, through production and packaging, to storage of finished goods. Next, I examined very carefully the current procedures for loading finished goods in the warehouse and for order picking. And, finally, I used building layout drawings and a long tape measure to determine things like aisle widths, storage space in various sections of the warehouse, and work-in-process movement distances.

All this was accomplished in a very busy three days. Then, contrary to consulting tradition, I flew back to our offices to begin the analysis work. Usually, a consultant or a group of consultants working on a facilities planning study will practically camp out at the client's facilities. They fly in every Sunday night and fly home every Friday night until a project is nearly complete. This method of operation is used to demonstrate to the client that *100 percent effort* is being devoted to the problem. The obvious drawback to this procedure is that it really runs up the out-of-pocket expenses (which the client pays, of course). A rental car, meals, and lodging can easily approach $100 per consultant per day. Because of Creative Products' small size and cash crunch, it was decided to hold down out-of-pocket expenses by doing as little work at their facility as possible.

ANALYSIS AND CONCLUSIONS

The analysis and conclusion effort on this project was divided into three separate sections. First, the manufacturing and packaging equipment was analyzed. Next, detailed analyses of operating procedures regarding raw materials and finished goods storage space were made And, finally, the overall plant layout was analyzed.

A planning horizon of five years was decided on before the analysis was begun. It was agreed (with Bob Anderson) to forecast a 15 percent per year compounded real sales growth for this period. This projection resulted in an anticipated doubling of output in the period. The sales forecast was based entirely on past company performance.

Manufacturing and Packaging Equipment Analysis

Creative Products owned and operated four basic types of equipment: (1) plate manufacturing, (2) napkin manufacturing, (3) tablecloth manufacturing, and (4) packaging. Our approach to analyzing each of these equipment categories was the same. We began by determining the capability of present equipment to meet production demand based on a 15 percent per year increase in output. If the present equipment would fall short of anticipated output, and in most instances this was the situation, alternatives were evaluated. But in several cases, some pieces of equipment could, indeed, double production output if used on a full two-shift operation. Even in these cases, alternatives were considered for two reasons. First, much of the equipment was old and unreliable. Second, it was felt that in some situations, new equipment might lower total costs by lowering operator labor, downtime, and repair costs.

In all cases, equipment was evaluated by personal discussions with the appropriate supervisor and the plant manager. Then, back at out offices, appropriate suppliers were contacted concerning the possible purchase of new equipment. (In some instances used machinery dealers were also contacted.) About a dozen equipment dealers visited our office to present their equipment offering. Quotations for equipment that could "fit" Creative Products' needs were requested by us. Once all these data were available, an analysis of alternatives was undertaken.

Creative Products operated about forty pieces of equipment. To illustrate our approach in equipment analysis, I'm going to use a group of six napkin machines. (A napkin machine takes rolled tissue stock and prints, cuts, and folds it into finished napkins.) Creative Products' napkin machine data is summarized in Exhibit 15.

The first step in analyzing this group of machines was to determine how efficiently they were being used. This was done by dividing actual average

EXHIBIT 15   Production Machine Data

Machine number	Age, years	Purchase price	Napkins produced	Machine capacity, pieces/hour
1	22	$15,200	10-inch	20,300
2	27	6,700	10-inch	18,200
3	24	16,100	13-inch (3-ply)	15,600
4	22	14,800	13-inch	15,800
5	8	40,300	13-inch	25,000
6	22	16,100	17-inch	9,200

EXHIBIT 16   Running Efficiency

Machine number	Machine capacity, pieces/hour	Actual average production, pieces/hour	Running efficiency
1	20,300	7,600	36%
2	18,200	6,900	38
3	15,600	11,900	64
4	15,800	6,300	40
5	25,000	6,500	26
6	9,200	3,900	42

production by each machine's capacity, which yielded a running efficiency percentage for each machine (see Exhibit 16).

The most striking conclusion we gained from these calculations (besides the fact that all the machines had low running efficiency) was the extremely low efficiency for machine 5, which was the fastest and the only new machine. It was producing at only 26 percent of capacity. Checking determined that this poor utilization was caused by the practice of scheduling all the short runs for 13-inch napkins on machine 5. This resulted in 74 percent of its time being devoted to changeover and setup. We suggested to the client that in the future every effort should be made to schedule the longer production runs on the higher-production-capacity machines.

Next, the forecasted production increases for the next five years were applied to each machine. This calculation was made assuming current actual production rates and a 230-day work year. Results are summarized in Exhibit 17. As can be seen, two of the machines (4 and 5) would be overloaded, even assuming a three-shift operation in five years, and machines 1 and 2 would also be pushed to their maximum capacity.

Finally, an economic analysis was done to compare the present napkin machines with alternative new machines. For example, production information was assembled for three alternative 10-inch napkin machines. This information is summarized in Exhibit 18, where actual production levels for these machines were based on an assumed 40 percent running efficiency.

EXHIBIT 17   Machine Daily Loadings

Machine number	Daily loading, hours	
	Now	Five years from now
1	11.5	23.0
2	11.5	23.0
3	4.5	9.0
4	13.5	27.0
5	13.5	27.0
6	4.8	9.6

EXHIBIT 18   Alternative 10-Inch Machine

Manufacturer	Model	Capacity, pieces/hour	Estimated actual average production	Quoted price
Paper Converting	Standard	36,000	14,400	$65,000
Paper Converting	High-speed	48,000	19,200	73,000
FMC	Standard	36,000	14,400	79,200

Several methods are available for comparing equipment alternatives. These include simple rate of return on investment, total average life, payback period, discounted cash flow, present worth method, and uniform annual cost. All these methods are discussed in detail in the literature. In the Creative Products' case, we chose to use the uniform annual cost method since it is straightforward and easily understood. In this method, annual equipment, labor, repair, and maintenance costs are calculated for each alternative, based on minimum rate of return criteria. The results of these calculations for the 10-inch napkin machines are summarized in Exhibit 19.

We determined from the result that it was difficult to justify the purchase of new 10-inch napkin machines on one economic comparison. This was because existing equipment was fully depreciated, and new equipment expense could not be fully compensated for through increased labor cost savings. In fact, with the initially assumed 15 percent rate of return and twenty-year life, the cost of new equipment would not even begin to be compensated for. That's why the analysis was also done for a 10 percent return and a thirty-year life. However, a subjective judgment was also necessary in this situation because the age and condition of existing equipment might result in unpredictable and excessive operating costs. Maintenance

EXHIBIT 19   Economic Comparison of 10-Inch Machines

Machine	Minimum rate of return	Assumed life, years	Estimated uniform annual cost			
			Equipment	Labor	Repairs & maintenance	Total
Present			$7700		$1,500	$ 9,200
Paper Converting						
Standard	15%	20	$10,300	3700	500	14,500
Standard	10	30	6,900	3700	500	11,100
High-speed	15	20	11,600	2650	500	14,750
High-speed	10	30	7,800	2650	500	10,950
FMC						
Standard	15	20	12,600	3700	500	16,800
Standard	10	30	8,400	3700	500	12,600

and repair costs were already high and future expenses could go even higher. Further, the loss of production due to excessive downtime is always costly.

Analysis of Raw Materials and Finished Goods Storage

As you may recall from the problem definition, storage space for raw materials and finished goods was a critical problem. The production floor was being used for storage of materials that overflowed the warehouse. The first thing we did in our storage analysis was to consider raw materials (cups, knocked-down cardboard cartons, inks, and rolled paper stock). The cups and the cartons were being stored in a steel shed, but all inks and rolled stock were scattered around the production floor. Ink, for example, was stacked in a designated area to a height of 4 or 5 feet. The ceiling height was 18 feet, and so only about 25 to 35 percent of the committed cubic footage was actually being used.

The proper way to approach a raw materials storage analysis is as follows. First, yearly demand is calculated (using sales forecasts) and then the optimum inventory level is calculated by balancing ordering cost against carrying cost. We went through this process for Creative Products to determine future inventory levels for the five-year period, and used the information to determine building needs. But the calculated results had to be adjusted to account for real-world circumstances. For example, cups had to be purchased in larger than optimum quantities, and paper roll stock purchases were at least partially dictated by suppliers' mill schedules. The result of this analysis was a forecasted raw materials storage space need (in cubic feet).

A similar analysis of finished goods storage space utilization indicated that the present finished goods warehouse was not designed properly. For example, in the newer portion of the warehouse, there were no shelves or racks, and so in many instances loads were only stacked to 6 or 7 feet in an area with a 12-foot ceiling. The other section of the warehouse had a mezzanine which required climbing up to load individual cartons. Overall, usable storage efficiency (usable space divided by total space) in the warehouse was about 63 percent. Aisles accounted for most of the unusable space. Because of a lack of shelving and the inaccessability of much of the "usable" space, only 28 percent of usable space was, on the average, occupied by finished goods.

A five-year projection of finished goods requirements indicated that additional (or much more efficient use of) space would be required in the future. This projection was based on a 15 percent per year increase in production, past seasonal demand pattern (September sales were almost double those in February), the economic production lot size, and a calculation of safety stock levels for major items. The procedure for carrying out an analysis of this type is available in any good production and inventory control text, and I won't bore you with the details here. The important point to note is that it doesn't take a consultant to make these calculations. Anyone who can read the procedure and who has mastered high school math can do it. I only wish the problem that confronted us in developing new systems for warehouse loading, storage, and picking had been as easy.

Analysis of Finished Goods Warehouse Systems

Two steps were currently being used to load the warehouse. Cartons (loaded with napkins, plates, or other products) were normally loaded on four-wheel platform trucks. Warehouse personnel pushed these loaded trucks to their available storage location in the warehouse. The cartons were then individually placed on the floor or up in the mezzanine. Then order picking was done manually, using picking carts. (The average order had something like thirty-five different items in it, and the average quantity of an item in an order was one.) Order pickers traversed the warehouse, at times using ladders or poles for hard-to-reach items. And sometimes cartons were even tossed down from the mezzanine by one picker to another!

It may seem that it would be easy to improve on such a system. *Improvement* was easy, but significant and meaningful improvement proved to be elusive. We developed a warehouse concept ranking system that included:
- Building and equipment costs
- Minimum manual handling
- Accurate order filling
- Safety and efficiency
- Ease of implementation
- Growth potential

But none of the possible alternative systems we compared with the old system looked that much better. We even tried to analyze the systems being used by Creative Products' major competitors, but obtained no useful results. These competitors were either too small or too big or too diversified to be relevant to our situation. Unfortunately, my project leader, with all his experience and education, was at his wit's end also.

Then we got lucky. Some unidentified mailcarrier saved the day by delivering a magazine to an associate of mine. One morning this associate walked into my office and said, "Aren't you doing something on warehouses, Ken?" I nodded, and he said, "I just got this magazine in my mail. It's got a cover story about some company's new warehouse. I thought you might be interested." I thanked him and went back to pondering Creative Products' problems. An hour later I decided to browse through the newly arrived magazine for a few minutes of diversion. On the cover was a man standing in the aisle of a brand-new warehouse. The caption identified him as Ronald Schultz, the warehouse manager and brainchild behind its design. As I began to read the article, I realized how close the magazine situation paralleled our client's. Although Mr. Schultz was in a different business, his problems were the same. He had hundreds of different items packed in cartons. His demand was seasonal, and a typical order required picking about thirty different cartons. The article briefly described the company's new system and expounded on how happy everybody was about how well it worked.

I needed to know more about Schultz's system so I telephoned him and said, "Hi, my name is Ken Albert and I'm with a consulting firm in Chicago. We do a lot of warehousing work for clients and I just happened to notice the article about you in the current issue of *Plant Engineering Magazine.* Your system sounds very interesting. Could you tell me a little more about it." A half hour later when I hung up the phone, I knew I had the answer to Creative Products' warehousing problems, or should I say that Schultz had the answer. His system (which included a pallet rack, one loading lift truck, and two operator-controlled picker trucks) was the answer to my prayers. And during our phone discussion he told me everything about it. He told me what it cost, what start-up problems he encountered, how he overcame them, how inventory records are kept, and on and on. My only concern was that our client might have seen the *same* magazine article. Fortunately they didn't—or at least they never let on that they were aware of it! This is obviously a situation where public knowledge contributed more to solving a client's problem than consulting expertise did.

Plant Layout Analysis and Design

Plant layout work, as I mentioned in the beginning of this chapter, has the primary objectives of improving operations, increasing output, reducing cost, serving customers better, and improving the working conditions for employees. The primary objectives in the Creative Products case was to improve efficiency and lower costs. We wanted to optimize the relationships among receiving, raw materials storage, manufacturing, packaging, finished goods storage, and shipping. Minimum transportation costs, effective space utilization, and flexibility for future growth were also major considerations.

The existing Creative Products' plant layout resulted in excessive material flow. About 70 percent of receiving was done in the finished goods warehouse. All this material was eventually transported to the other end of the plant where it worked its way back through production and finally back to the warehouse as finished goods. Four alternative plant layouts (including raw materials and finished goods warehousing) were considered in an effort to minimize movement of materials and improve efficiency. These were labeled alternatives W, X, Y, and Z. Total material movement (for paper roll stock, cartons and cups, and inks) for each alternative is summarized below:

Alternative	Total Material Movement, Feet
Existing	2005
W	1815
X	1410
Y	1655
Z	1570

After this calculation was completed, each alternative was rated on four subjective criteria:

1. Raw materials storage efficiency
2. Finished goods storage efficiency
3. Ease of adoption
4. Long-range expansion flexibility

Alternative X came out as most desirable. The only problem was that it required building an addition for finished goods storage at the opposite end of the plant from the present finished goods warehouse. Then the existing finished goods warehouse (where most raw material receiving is done anyway) would be converted to a raw materials storage area. These modifications would result in an extremely efficient and simple plant layout. Raw materials would go in one end of the plant and move through the production and packaging steps, and the finished product would be stored and finally shipped from the other end of the plant (just like the diagrams in textbooks!).

Recommendations and Implementation

The recommendations chapter of the report for Creative Products was fairly short. It took each major analysis area and recommended the most desirable alternative. Some new equipment purchases were recommended, but most recommendations in the equipment area focused on adjustments, modifications, and changes in operation that would enable Creative Products to meet a doubling in demand with current equipment on a two shift per day operating schedule. Of course, we recommended the finished goods warehousing system I had come across in the magazine article. And, finally, we recommended the plant layout system which I discussed earlier. We concluded our recommendations by offering a step-by-step approach for physically accomplishing the proposed layout.

We also presented a next-steps chapter, the heart of which was an implementation schedule that laid out all the actions to be taken (for example, modify the plate forming machines, select a contractor for the new warehouse addition, etc.), the responsible party (either the president or the plant manager), and the date each action should be completed. This table was, in effect, a simplified PERT chart. This chapter contained several "subtle" suggestions relating to the desirability of our firm assisting during the implementation. As it turned out, our implementation involvement was limited to a one-day visit to Creative Products by the principal in charge to answer some specific questions.

Lack of involvement in implementation is quite common in facilities planning studies. Clients think that they can easily, and at significant savings, do the implementation themselves, and in many cases they're right. In fact, in the Creative Products situation, there's no reason why the entire study couldn't have been done internally.

To do these kinds of "personal" analysis studies internally, it's important to assign the task to an impartial, autonomous individual. At Creative Products this project could have been assigned by the president to their industrial engineer, since I doubt if the plant manager would have been impartial enough to make objective judgments. After all, he had grown with and contributed to the existing situation over his ten years with the company. In fact, the president and the plant manager of Creative Products disagreed about the merits of some of our recommendations. Friction developed between them, possibly because the plant manager interpreted criticism directed at the facilities as personal criticism of him. Unfortunately, the plant manager resigned at about the time ground was broken for the new warehouse.

CONCLUSION

As illustrated by the Creative Products facilities planning study, there are four basic steps in doing such studies.

1. *Define the Problem:* This is usually fairly uncomplicated. Often observation and review of records, documents, schedules, back orders, etc., will pinpoint problem areas.

2. *Gather Information:* This step brings together all internal and external materials that can assist in solving the problem.

3. *Analyze Alternatives:* Four or five alternatives should be compared quantitatively and qualitatively. Ranking tables with weighted importance given to various factors is often helpful in identifying the best choice.

4. *Recommendations and Implementation:* Once a decision is reached, an implementation schedule (with actions and completion dates) should be prepared. This schedule should also assign responsibility for each action to the most appropriate individual.

part **3**

Solving Your Business Problems

15
Establishing Your Own Problem-Solving System

When you approach a problem, strip yourself of preconceived opinions and prejudice, assemble and learn the facts of the situation, make the decision which seems to you to be the most honest, and then stick to it. — CHESTER BOWLES

We've just completed a long series of chapters on how management consultants solve various types of business problems. Now we can move ahead to developing a system that you can use to solve your own business problems. This chapter will integrate all the previously discussed bits and pieces of do-it-yourself advice and expand them into a comprehensive approach to business problem solving.

TYPES OF INTERNAL PROBLEM-SOLVING SYSTEMS

There are four distinct types of internal problem-solving systems:
- Full-time internal management consultant
- Special assignment
- Task force
- Collaboration

One of them (or a combination of two or more) is appropriate for almost every size and kind of business. Each alternative is presented separately in the following sections.

The Full-time Internal Management Consultant

The internal management consultant has come of age. Industry sources estimate that 500 to 600 companies now have some in-house consulting capability, up from about 100 five years ago. Companies with internal troubleshooting staffs include prestige names like General Electric, Union Carbide, Travelers Insurance, Allstate, and Ford Motor Company.

These companies have always had the need for problem-solving expertise, but not until recently were permanent staffs assembled and recognized as consultants. Previously, tasks involving internal consultants were scattered among such groups as operations research, systems analysis, market research, market planning, and industrial engineering. And, primarily because of this fragmentation, these companies relied on outside management consulting firms to do most of their problem solving. I know one company that relied almost entirely on outside consultants until three years ago. During the last twelve months, however, their internal staff of six handled all but two assignments, which were given to outsiders, only because their internal people were too busy.

Internal management consultants recently formed the Association of Internal Management Consultants (AIMC). This group's objectives are to improve the individual professional effectiveness of members and to promote the internal management consulting profession. Its activities include educational seminars, national meetings, and publication of a newsletter. There is little doubt that AIMC has raised the status and position of internal management consultants in the companies which employ AIMC members.

Internal management consulting groups vary in size and scope from company to company. In some companies the "group" is a single individual, while in others it exceeds 200. A typical company troubleshooting team is made up of ten to twelve consulting specialists. These consultants represent a wide spectrum of functional disciplines including planning, management sciences, marketing, data processing, personnel, and industrial engineering.

As a rule the team goes into action only at the request of an operating unit or senior manager (the "client"). Once a study is authorized, however, the team is free to cross departmental and divisional lines to find a solution. Internal consultants are also actively involved in the implementation of their solutions to company problems, and internal management consultants consider themselves equals in every respect to outside management consultants.

The Special Assignment

Some companies use special assignments as a signal to the assignee to start looking around for a new job. One famous international corporation uses a so-called consulting group as a temporary decompression chamber for executives about to leave the company. This, obviously, is not what I mean by the special assignment alternative to business problem solving.

Rather, in companies that do not have permanent internal consultants, for whatever reason, a viable alternative is to assign problems to bright, energetic managers. Assignments can be given while the executive is carrying on his or her regular duties, or they can be full-time assignments scheduled between position changes.

Obviously, the key to establishing special assignments as a meaningful approach to business problem solving requires an understanding by employees that the assignment is an opportunity, not a step on the way out. This can probably best be accomplished by publicizing the policy and then demonstrating its worth through example.

The Special Assignment: An Example   Several years ago I did a study for a client that would have been ideal for the special assignment alternative. Our client, a leading chemical company, had established its position as a major supplier of base stocks used in synthethic lubricants. They sold these base stocks to oil companies who blended them with proprietary additive packages and then marketed them for use in jet aircraft engines. Although these synthetic lubricants were three and four times more expensive than petroleum-base lubricants, they were the only type that could withstand the high operating temperatures involved in jet engines. Of course, low-cost petroleum-base crankcase lubricants totally dominated the huge passenger car and truck market.

Then several things happened which made our client think that the day was rapidly approaching when their base stock would be able to invade the passenger car and truck engine market:

- The oil crisis occurred, leading the company to think crude oil might be in short supply and very expensive in the future.
- General Motors openly began pushing the Wankel engine, which might have been able to use a synthetic lubricant to good advantage.
- Two small oil companies announced new synthetic automobile and truck engine lubricants, the "pitch" being that use of the lubricant would extend oil change intervals, increase mileage, and reduce engine wear.

Our client asked us to evaluate the potential for using synthetic stock in automobile and truck engines—which we gladly did (for $10,000) by interviewing lubrication experts at the engine manufacturers and ten leading petroleum companies (including the two that introduced the synthetic motor oils).

I can't conceive of any reason why our client couldn't have assigned this study to the base stock sales manager or to a staff marketing specialist. The people we interviewed would have told our client the same things we were told. There were no confidentialities involved; there was no threat of competition from our client to any of the interviewees. In fact, our basic finding (that what the client suspected wouldn't happen in the near future, but they should by all means keep tabs on the situation) resulted in our recommending that the client assign someone to contact the engine manufacturers and petroleum companies periodically. We even supplied the names of the right person at each company, in effect turning the assignment over to our client. The main point is that they could have saved a good deal of the $10,000, and gained valuable first-hand knowledge, by conducting the study themselves in the first place.

The Task Force

Management task forces are used for numerous purposes, and they can be used effectively for solving problems that outside consultants would normally handle. Basically, a task force is an internal diagnostic team—a temporary group of managers brought together to analyze an unsatisfactory situation, pinpoint the problem or problems, develop a workable solution, and implement corrective actions.

A task force should be composed of representatives of departments in the organization most affected by the problem. Preferably, the people selected should be success-oriented middle managers who have excellent communication links throughout the organization, a grasp of the needs and requirements of their own departments, and the confidence of both senior management and subordinates.

The task force leader should be chosen from among the representatives. He or she should be the person most likely to assume responsibility for the group's recommendations. For example, the task force leader for a study of the system for procuring materials should be the purchasing department representative. The group leader must be willing and able to make a substantial investment of time and energy. Although it's possible to place the task force leader on special full-time assignment, most often task force assignments will be in addition to regular duties for all members. A person who is interested in a serious problem must be fully committed to the challenge of finding a solution.

To be effective, a task force should operate with a spirit of cooperation. And at each major decision point (for example, definition of the problem, analysis, stating recommendations) the task force should reach a consensus before proceeding. A spirit of constructive compromise must be instilled in each member by the task force leader. Then, when the task force has completed its work and its recommendations have been approved by the client, a core group of key people within the organization will have a thorough understanding of the current problem and will be dedicated to implementing an effective solution.

Collaboration

Collaboration is the last of the four approaches to establishing a business problem-solving system. In essence it is a partnership between an outside consulting firm and company problem solvers (be they internal management consultants, a manager on special assignment, or members of a management task force). Most often the partnership is temporary: It exists just for the time required to solve a specific problem.

Collaboration, especially between outside consultants and internal management consultants, is a fairly new trend. Three to five years ago many consulting firms refused to collaborate with internal problem solvers. At the time, many management consulting firms considered the internal problem solver as a potential adversary. Now, however, internal troubleshooters are permanently established in many companies, and almost all outside management consulting firms cooperate with them, maybe because they realize that a piece of the pie is better than none at all.

Speaking of "a piece of the pie," I'm reminded of an experience that was related to me by an internal management consultant with a large insurance company. About four years ago, he was assigned the task of speeding up and simplifying the flow of claims through the company's outdated processing systems. Analysis of the work required indicated that the task would be too big for the internal management consulting group to handle by itself, so they decided to collaborate with an outside firm. About six firms were called to discuss the problem—and a possible partnership arrangement. One of the largest and most prestigious firms refused to submit a proposal because the collaboration would prevent them from having full control of the outcome of the study, and one other firm submitted an unreasonable proposal. The others accepted the possibility of collaboration with enthusiasm. Total professional billing for the firm that eventually was selected reached almost $300,000—a large piece of pie for any consulting firm!

I should note that the insurance company's internal consultant recently told me that the prestigious consulting firm that refused to submit a proposal has since changed its mind concerning collaboration. The firm now actually solicits partnership assignments, and in fact got one with the insurance company which involved development of a training program for the company's newly hired internal management consultants! If that's not collaboration I don't know what is.

I was once involved in a collaboration effort that you may find interesting. It illustrates the changing attitude on the part of many companies toward relying entirely on outside consultants to solve business problems. About six years ago the consulting firm I worked for was hired to develop a strategic growth plan for a division of a billion dollar plus transportation company. This particular division's primary business (call them Ace Trailer Division) was the manufacture and marketing of on-highway truck trailers. At the time we did the study Ace was doing about $20 million annually and netting about 5 percent pretax. We developed a strategic plan which included seven basic recommendations:

1. Improve customer relations by streamlining communications, adding service personnel, and demonstrating more concern for customer problems.

2. Direct future new trailer marketing efforts at a more lucrative segment of end user.

3. Expand branch sales activities.

4. Establish a used trailer marketing network.

5. Improve quality control of existing products.

6. Broaden the product line to include drop-frame vans, flats, etc.

7. Add a second production facility after new marketing effort takes hold.

Our clients felt we had done a fine job and had presented them with a truly outstanding strategy for growth. They did grow, and at first they also made more money. But about four years after our work, the bottom fell out of the trailer market (a recession and government regulations disrupted truck fleet purchasing of new trailers). Eventually, the economy began to recover, but Ace Trailer Division did not recover along with it. Twelve months after the trailer market had begun to recover, Ace was losing money at the rate of $5 million per year on sales of about $45 million.

The parent corporation, a regular client of ours, called us back into the Ace Trailer situation. But their philosophy had changed over the six-year interval. They didn't want us to diagnose the current problem, but to collaborate with them in the effort. The corporate office had set up a management task force to address and solve the Ace Division problem. The task force leader, a corporate vice president, had formulated a plan for analysis and had assigned specific responsibilities to various task force members. For example, one member was to examine Ace's productivity and manufacturing cost situation, and another was responsible for a financial and credit review. My firm was assigned the task of assessing Ace's marketing effectiveness. Specifically, our objectives were to be:

- To evaluate the current market image of the Ace Trailer Division
- To ascertain the effectiveness, as perceived by the market, of the strategy our firm had recommended and the Ace Trailer Division had implemented as a result of our previous study
- To identify basic market factors that could assist in updating or revising the strategic plan

It was apparent that a collaborative approach was suggested by the client for two reasons. First, and most important, it would save them a good deal of money that otherwise would have gone for consulting fees. And, second, our client felt that our capability for carrying out *anonymous* field interviews with customers and competitors would be a vital part of the fact-gathering effort, a part they would not be able to perform as effectively themselves.

Incidentally, we did participate in the collaborative effort without any hesitancy, and the task force eventually concluded that Ace was losing money primarily because of production inefficiency and cutthroat pricing practices.

CHOOSING YOUR SYSTEM

Of the four types of internal problem-solving systems, only one requires a front-end commitment—the internal management consulting approach. With this system *at least* one individual is assigned a full-time position as internal management consultant, and the company must be sure that there is enough need for consulting services to justify keeping one or more consultants occupied full time. The staffing level should be set for average, not peak workload, which will minimize excessive slack time. In fact, staffing levels should be set so that there is always about a one- to two-month backlog of work. This backlog allows for a steady input of work and for built-in scheduling flexibility. For example, if a review meeting on one study is postponed because the client is suddenly called out of town, the consultant can switch his or her efforts to another program.

If you decide to use one or more of the other systems—special assignment, task force, or collaboration—it's best to let the circumstances of each particular problem dictate the most appropriate approach. For example, say one of your division managers arrives at what appears to be a breathtakingly attractive acquisition candidate, and a thorough analysis of the candidate's market and competitive position is called for. In this case, any of the four alternative systems is a distinct possibility. A collaborative effort between a manager on special assignment (or a task force) and an outside consulting firm may be most suitable, or the situation may simply require putting a person in the corporate planning department on special assignment for six weeks. That's the beauty of these three alternate approaches—they provide management discretion and flexibility.

EXPECTED BENEFITS

The most obvious benefit of using one of the systems discussed above is substantial cost savings—conservatively, I estimate a saving of 35 to 50 percent of the cost of an outside firm. Many of the reasons for cost savings are discussed in detail in Chapter 1, but there is one more which is significant. Outside consulting firms invariably hire only one caliber of consultant—people who will eventually be able to carry on all facets of client project work. This type of person (say, a bright college graduate with an M.B.A.) is expensive, and obviously commands a high daily billing rate ($300 to $400 per day). But portions of many consulting assignments do not require this level of talent, for example, quantitative data gathering associated with work simplification and frequent manual calculations associated with quantitative analysis. Companies which have developed internal consulting staff have saved a lot of money by having specially trained consulting assistants do most routine work of this nature.

Another benefit is associated with the inherent knowledge and familiarity of the company that insiders possess. Outside consultants invariably have to learn about each client company when an assignment is begun. This learning process takes time, and information is not always totally complete or accurate. But insiders know the company and where to get the necessary information. They know the company's operating procedures and practices so they can do a quicker and more comprehensive job.

Further, internal management consultants and people who have served on special assignment or management task forces almost universally maintain that insiders do a better job of implementing recommendations that have been generated internally. First, insiders, whether they be consultants, managers on special assignment, or task force representatives, have only one client—the company they work for. To maintain their reputation and to ensure repeat business they must implement effectively. They can't walk away from an assignment as outsiders can, and they will most likely still be on the payroll when results of their efforts—bad or good—come to the surface. The second reason insiders do a better job of implementation is because they are always around six months or a year later to modify or adjust the system they installed. Such fine tuning is essential because any new approach, no matter how conscientiously devised, can and will develop problems. Of course, most outside consultants will also sincerely try to provide modification and adjustment services. But if these require a round-trip ticket from, say, Chicago to Boston, and a day of their time, outsiders have little choice but to charge the client the going rate ($500 to $1000). Most clients will attempt to do fine tuning themselves rather than pay this extra money to the outside consultant.

A final benefit is that internal problem solving creates an extremely effective training ground for future executives. An internal troubleshooter's deep involvement in most or all company functions and activities, coupled with broad exposure to many of a company's key executives, can furnish background and experience few managers attain in the normal channels of career growth. As a matter of fact, some internal consulting groups request that their company's management institute rules to keep their best people from being "stolen" by cunning senior executives.

ASSIGNMENTS AND PEOPLE

Before going on to discuss the kinds of jobs internal problem solvers can handle, and the type of people a company needs for each job, I should mention that some types of assignments are simply not appropriate for internal problem solvers. One such category is the "make work" assignment, which can disillusion the problem solvers and undermine the entire internal problem-solving approach. Another kind of assignment that many companies will not give to internal problem solvers involves politically sensitive problems. One internal management consultant told me she tries to avoid what she refers to as "win-lose" situations, such as studies assessing management capability, analyzing one department's problems at the request of a sister department manager, or rubber-stamping somebody's pet project for budget approval.

One trend is apparent, however. As an internal problem-solving system becomes established, the staff involved develop confidence in their problem-solving ability, and become more and more willing to tackle just about anything that an outside management consulting firm will.

Internal troubleshooters, be they full-time consultants, managers on special assignment, or task force members, typically get involved in an extremely wide variety of problem-solving assignments. The listing below represents just a sampling:

- Acquisition analysis
- Long-range planning
- Inventory control
- Purchasing value analysis
- Management reporting and control
- Job enrichment
- Profit improvement
- Executive search
- Consumer analysis
- Management information system
- Work simplification
- Market analysis
- Organization analysis
- Systems analysis
- Computer selection
- Strategic planning
- Sales forecasting

The specific background and experience of the people assigned to be internal problem solvers, either permanently or for just a project or two, should depend on the nature of the problems themselves. Skills of the problem solvers must match the company needs. One company may need a great deal of work simplification skill while another needs data processing expertise or planning knowhow. More important than specific experience and background, however, are the individual's general attributes. You want people with:

- *Broad Mental Abilities:* Well-developed analytical, numerical, creative, and verbal skills are essential.
- *Diverse Interests:* A broad interest base usually entails diversified business and personal skills.
- *Emotional Maturity:* Problem solving is demanding. Ability to accept frustration, as well as self-discipline, are necessary.
- *Leadership:* Problem solvers should be able to motivate people and generate enthusiasm.
- *Independence:* Initiative, resourcefulness, and self-reliance are needed in unstructured problem-solving situations.
- *Drive and Stamina:* The personal motivation for seeing a project through to completion may be more important than any other attribute.
- *Communication Skills:* Both verbal and written communication skills are critical.

THE WAY TO APPROACH
A PROBLEM

Management consulting firms have a rigid set of rules and procedures, almost a protocol, they use in their relations with clients. Much of this protocol is based on the good business sense that is a part of any seller-buyer relationship. For example, if a client requests a change in an engagement while it is in progress, the outside consultant will ask that the request be put in writing, or the consultant will verbally agree to the change and then confirm the change in a letter to the client. Strict protocol is important because consulting services are complex, and consulting procedures are often misunderstood.

Even when consulting services are being provided internally, there is a need for protocol in the relationships between problem solvers and client. In most companies that have established problem-solving systems this protocol begins with a requisition for consulting services written by the client. The requisition is addressed to the head of the internal management consulting group or to the executive that will institute the special assignment group or management task force. (In a small company, the requisition, and the formalization of the appropriate problem-solving system, are combined in a memo from the president or manager of the client division.)

The problem-solving unit should respond to the requisition with a specific proposal, containing most of the same elements that would be included in the proposal of an outside consultant. At a bare minimum, the proposal should include the methodology to be used, the assistance required from the client, the cost (if an internal billing system is used), and a statement of anticipated accomplishments. After the client reviews the proposal and necessary modifications are agreed on, a written go-ahead should be issued.

Communication during the course of a study between the problem solvers, the client, and any other affected departments or individuals is extremely important. Management consulting firms accomplish this with telephone calls to clients, interim meetings, progress letters, and even with informal chats over dinner. Internal problem solvers must do the same things. The last thing a conscientious problem solver wants is a surprised client at the presentation of the final report.

Management consulting firms have a "rule" for report writing that goes something like this: "Tell them what you're going to tell them, tell them, and then tell them what you told them." The reason for "telling them what you're going to tell them" is so that when you do "tell them" formally, they already know what to expect and will not be surprised. This philosophy of report writing extends into study-in-progress communications. Frequent formal or informal progress reports are a must. One internal consulting group I know has instituted a policy requiring weekly progress reports.

If frequent and meaningful communication takes place during the course of a study, the final report's primary purpose is not explanation, but documentation. Documentation is important because it ties the entire study together and puts the recommendations and implementation steps into proper perspective. Final reports should be complete and clearly written, so they can be used for reference whenever problems of a similar nature arise.

The implementation phase of any business problem-solving study is the essence of the study. Many companies with internal problem-solving systems give just and proper emphasis to implementation by separating it from the rest of the study program. This is probably a sound practice if for no other reason than that it is often difficult to estimate accurately the extent or the nature of the implementation phase before the study is started.

As I have said many times, one of the most critical issues associated with implementation is *who* will implement. Should it be done by the problem solvers, by the client, or through a joint effort? Rather than implementation being the total responsibility of either consultants or clients, a happy middle ground should be sought. Some internal management consultants refer to this middle ground as *guided application:* The internal consulting team guides the client in applying the implementation steps.

ESSENTIALS OF PROBLEM-SOLVING SUCCESS

No matter which problem-solving alternative you choose, several ground rules for creating a sound system should be followed. The final section of this chapter presents and discusses each of these ground rules.

Get Total Support of Top Management

On several occasions, I've been involved in management consulting engagements that became mere academic exercises because the client, typically a middle manager, never had, or lost, support for the project by top management. Internal problem solvers are even more vulnerable than outside management consultants to the consequences of a lack of top-level support, primarily because the very presence of outsiders lends a measure of credibility to the process.

It is essential for top management to give support to the internal problem-solving system at two levels. Initially, support must be given at the system level. That is, top management should initiate whatever system is to be used with a policy statement accompanied by a brief description of how the system is to function and what type of problems it will be used for. Following this, support must be given to each specific project until the system is well understood and accepted throughout management ranks. Project support can be shown in many ways, including attending project kickoff and final presentation meetings, assigning well-respected people to task forces, and facilitating prompt and effective implementation.

Earn the Acceptance of Operating Units

An internal problem-solving system can only be effective if its value and merit are recognized by the operating units. Internal problem solvers should project a willingness to work with operating people—to listen to their ideas and suggestions—and should also make sure that they communicate frequently and openly with all interested parties.

A case I'm aware of in a large manufacturing company illustrates the right way to gain the acceptance of operating units. This company, after several years of declining earnings, had finally acknowledged that a good deal of their problems were associated with their aimless, scatter-gun approach to planning. Operating divisions were simply going their own way with little or no regard for overall corporate objectives. Top management assigned its newly created internal management consulting group the difficult task of developing and implementing a cohesive, long-range planning system. The internal group, primarily because of its newness, suggested a collaborative effort between its staff and an outside consulting firm. The suggestion was accepted by top management, and a study team composed of three inside and two outside consultants was formed.

The team knew that it had to avoid being viewed as a threat to the long-standing autonomy of the divisions. Examination and questioning of current division planning practices would have to be done diplomatically. The first step was to develop a preliminary outline of a possible planning system. With this outline in hand, the team carefully worked its way through every division, getting from operating management at all levels their ideas on what might constitute good corporate planning and how it might be instituted.

In the course of the six-month study period, the team met three times with top management. After each session, they met again with the operations people to compare notes, draw out further opinions on the current status of the proposed plan, and reinforce the sense of participation. Gradually the operating managers came to accept the project as their own, rather than as an edict from the top. And in accepting the new planning system, the operating units also accepted the new internal consulting group.

Keep a High Reporting Level

Almost all people who have experience with internal problem-solving systems suggest that inside problem solvers should report at a high level in the organization. Many feel that internal problem solvers should report directly to the president or executive committee. In small companies, reporting at the presidential level is probably always best, but in a large company, it may be appropriate for the problem solvers to report at one level below the president. Advocates of this method say that it prevents the internal problem solvers from being viewed as an elite extension of the president's office. In any case, internal problem solvers must report high enough in the organization for proper acceptance by operating management.

Establish Confidentiality

I have repeatedly emphasized the importance of confidentiality in the relationship between management consulting firms, their client, and their interviewees. Confidentiality must also exist in any internal problem-solving system. All dealings between internal problem solvers and the clients who use their services should be kept confidential if the problem solvers are to do the job properly. In some organizations this means that *only* the client gets the final report, not top management. Personally, I feel that this is unrealistic. Surely if a manager hired an outside firm to do a job, the report would be available to his or her superiors. And, in fact, it might even end up being used as a "wedge" to get budget approval to implement the recommendations!

In any case, an internal problem-solving system cannot exist if top management is not willing and mature enough to accept confidentiality. If confidentiality is not accepted, the problem solvers will be labeled as executive auditors, or worse yet, as spies.

Avoid Company Politics

Specific examples of politically sensitive issues that are not appropriate for internal problem solvers are presented in Chapter 16. It is sufficient to point out here that, whenever possible, a study with potential political implications should not be handled by internal problem-solving systems.

Maintain Objectivity

One of the traditional reasons for hiring outside consultants is to gain objectivity—which, at times, is lacking within the company. Internal problem-solving systems can also be objective if constituted and managed properly. However, it takes a conscientious effort for insiders to maintain objectivity. Insiders must work to develop a reputation of objectivity and fairness, and must constantly be on guard to prevent this reputation from being tarnished.

Start Slowly

The final essential ground rule for business problem-solving success is to start slowly. Initial assignments should be of the type that will help build the group's reputation. These include any problem which can be easily defined and quickly analyzed, and which will produce highly visible results. It is probably better to wait for "ideal" problems to come along than to force more complex problems into a system that is not ready or able to meet the challenge. In the beginning, a problem-solving system's reputation and the confidence of the internal problem solvers are both best served by a cautious and methodical start.

16
When to Seek Outside Help

> *Fools need advice the most, but wise men only are the*
> *better for it.* — BENJAMIN FRANKLIN

> *To accept good advice is but to increase one's own*
> *ability.* — GOETHE

In some situations, it is unwise to attempt to solve a business problem internally. Any one of the following factors is enough to suggest that outside assistance might be appropriate, and, at times, a combination of two or more of them will remove any doubt about the need for an outside management consultant.

1. When specialized expertise is essential
2. For a politically sensitive issue
3. When impartiality is necessary
4. If time is critical
5. If anonymity must be maintained
6. When the prestige of an outside firm would be helpful

SPECIALIZED EXPERTISE

Some business problems do require a measure of expertise to arrive at a sound solution. Most of the expertise needed is accessible to anybody who will take the trouble to do the necessary research. But *application* of expertise can be difficult. In certain situations, it is probably best to call in an outside consultant who has the required expertise and who is experienced in applying it. Some types of studies in which outside consulting services might be required (this varies a great deal, of course, depending on the internal knowledge base of the company) include:

- Data processing
- Plant location
- Production control
- Operations research

When you feel you need outside assistance because of a lack of internal expertise, you should go about acquiring this expertise knowledgeably. If you don't have the proper method and purpose, a management consultant will simply submit a proposal, keep you informed of his or her progress during the course of the study, and then make a final presentation. All you'll have to show for it is a fancy report and (hopefully) a solution to your current problem. But you can gain much much more from such an experience with a little bit of effort on your part.

Instead of allowing a consulting firm to attack the problem alone, I would recommend strongly that you insist on a partnership between your company's people and the consulting firm's people. A collaborative effort will provide your company with the following benefits:

1. *Confidence in the Solution:* This confidence is gained through your in-depth understanding of the problem-solving process. And, if the consulting firm fails to live up to expectations, a personal knowledge of the study's course will prevent you from accepting conclusions and recommendations that a more naive client might unknowingly accept.

2. *Better Implementation:* If implementation is accomplished by extending the collaborative effort, it will go more smoothly because people in the company will understand why the particular implementation steps were chosen over other alternatives.

3. *Gaining of Expertise:* Your firm may gain enough experience so that the next time this problem, or a similar problem arises, you will be able to solve it internally.

Recall the study of the production and warehousing facilities of the small company that manufactured specialty paper products (Chapter 14). This company bought consulting services because they felt they didn't have the necessary internal expertise. But they bought it incorrectly. They didn't get involved in the problem-solving process, and, therefore, they didn't learn from the experience. All they had at the end of the study were:

- A superficial explanation of what the consulting firm did (that even I now have trouble following—and I did the study and wrote the explanation)
- Results and conclusions
- An implementation schedule

If they had insisted on a collaborative effort, they could have learned a great deal that might have been invaluable to them in the future. For example, they could have learned how to make equipment replacement decisions, how to adjust personnel levels in their new warehouse, and how to modify plant layout when necessary.

Don't make the mistake this client did. Get involved when you buy outside consulting services. Then, when the study is completed, your company will possess expertise in areas it previously had no knowledge of.

POLITICALLY SENSITIVE ISSUES

As is true with several of the other reasons for seeking outside assistance, the "politically sensitive issue" reason can be blown out of proportion. That is, *any* important business problem has some implications for the internal politics of a company. There are always people in favor of doing one thing, and others in favor of doing just the opposite. And once a course of action is chosen in any problem situation, there are always apparent winners and apparent losers. This is true in organization studies ("Why did she get that position and not me?"); in executive search ("I could have handled that job. Why did they go outside?"); in studies of marketing strategy ("Our competition is going to have a big laugh when they see this."); and in acquisition analysis ("You'll be sorry we bought that outfit!"). It's almost always true.

Obviously this does not mean that almost all problems should be turned over to outside consulting firms. But it does mean that the impact of a problem on internal company politics should be considered before deciding how to handle the problem. Ultimately, there is only one way to make the choice between using your internal problem-solving system or turning to outsiders in a specific case—by "feel." There is no pat rule for making such decisions, only common sense. There are, however, some useful guidelines:

1. If the issue has made tempers and passions flare and caused closed door meetings, it may be too hot to handle internally.

2. If the problem cannot be separated from personalities, outside consultants may be best.

3. Interdivisional or interdepartmental problems are more likely to have major political overtones.

I remember one study in which all three of these guidelines were relevant. A major division of a large corporation needed a multimillion dollar capital outlay to expand into a product area that was unrelated to its business activities at the time. The president of the division was openly dismayed when the executive committee balked after reviewing his new product plan and capital expenditure request. He felt that they were overconservative and therefore missing out on a great opportunity.

The division president continued to push his proposal and succeeded in winning over the corporation's chief operations officer. But the chief executive officer and the executive vice president, who made up the rest of the executive committee, remained unconvinced. At one point in a knock-down-and-drag-out session the division president threatened to resign if he didn't get his money. He saw the negative verdict on his proposal as a personal vote of no confidence.

The first time we met with these four executives, we would not have believed that they were at each other's throats over the issue. Later, when we interviewed each of them separately, their true opinions and prejudices surfaced. Fortunately for everyone, they all agreed to live by the verdict our consulting firm brought in, which, given the situation, was the only sensible course of action.

This case illustrates a situation in which it was obvious that outside management consultants were appropriate. You will come across others. You must screen your internal problem-solving system's incoming work load for likely candidates.

IMPARTIALITY

There is a close relationship between a politically sensitive issue and problems which require an impartial opinion. In the last example, we saw how a politically sensitive issue was resolved by seeking an outside opinion. But the search for objectivity goes beyond matters involving company politics. In some situations that are totally *without* political implications, it is still impossible to find objectivity within the company environment. Some company problems involve everybody on the payroll, making it difficult to find any objective people.

One study which exemplifies the need for objectivity involved a major rubber company. One of its divisions was involved in the production and marketing of specialized vinyl products. The division was not doing well, and the management of the rubber company asked for our opinion. Specifically, they wanted to know if they should stay in the business of specialized vinyl products or get out. The jobs and security of the people in the division were riding on the answer, and they were in no position to make an objective decision. They wanted to stay in the business and expand it, and they had the "facts" to demonstrate that this was the only intelligent course of action. The corporate people were no bastion of objectivity either. All their executives had been intimately involved in critical decisions involving the vinyl products division over the past several years, and several of them had made their way up through the vinyl division.

The information we gathered in our study strongly suggested that the only wise decision for the rubber company was to get out of the business. We found the market to be saturated, stagnant, and highly price competitive. None of our client's competitors were making any money either. We had no choice but to make a recommendation that was consistent with our findings. Corporate management accepted our conclusion and initiated action to phase out the vinyl products division. This is a case where I doubt if the client could have made the proper decision using internal advice.

Remember that objectivity is not necessarily present just because an independent management consulting firm has been retained to solve a problem. Outside consultants have their prejudices too, and, further, may be hesitant to recommend a course of action they know will be unpopular. If you hire a consulting firm to get objectivity, emphasize that what you really want is objectivity. Most consultants will get the message.

WHEN TIME IS CRITICAL

If you need a study done in a hurry and you don't have the personnel to staff the assignment internally, it's a good idea to turn to an outside consulting firm. Independent consulting firms can usually offer a very quick project completion time. Consulting firms typically complete most assignments in a period of two to four months, and, when real expedience is required, many kinds of assignments can be completed in two to eight weeks.

Management consulting firms can offer quick turnaround times on assignments for several reasons. First, they are trained to "gear up" fast because a slow start can result in a budget overrun and therefore in loss of profit. Second, if you select the firm wisely, they probably have someone on staff who has participated in a project similar to yours and who will know what pitfalls to avoid. Third, consulting firms can usually juggle client assignments and personnel allocations to find enough staff days to complete a rush job.

On one rush assignment I was involved in, we went so far as to ask a consultant to cut her European vacation short by several days so she could work on a high-priority engagement. Then, after she agreed, we had the gall to send her all kinds of background material to read on the plane so when she walked into the office she'd be primed to start.

Even if you do go outside to get a rush project completed on time, don't overlook the possibility of a collaborative effort with its attendant advantages.

Some words of caution. Rush assignments with outside consulting firms should be avoided if at all possible. Even though most consulting firms can work miracles with project completion dates, rush jobs invariably end up costing the client more, and more important, usually result in work of lesser quality. In a rush situation, the consultants assigned to the project just don't have time to communicate properly. Coordination usually suffers, with the result that repetitious work is done in some areas and holes are left uncovered in others. Further, rushed consultants don't have the necessary time to absorb all the pertinent information and analyze it thoroughly. Finally, be wary of insisting on a quick completion time when the consulting business is humming along, which often means that consulting firms are understaffed and overworked. In these circumstances, many consulting firms make the mistake of accepting too many demands for quick completion, and are then forced into doing less-than-outstanding jobs in order to meet agreed-on deadlines.

ANONYMITY

An independent consulting firm can protect your company's identity as the sponsor of a study. This can be important in studies which require marketplace interviews, such as acquisitions analysis, marketing strategy studies, and new venture analysis. Let me explain this with several specific examples.

Suppose that a large company is interested in an acquisition analysis of another company. Often, for competitive reasons, neither company wants the fact that a merger may take place to become public knowledge. But a thorough acquisition analysis requires interviews with customers, distributors, and competitors. One way to solve this dilemma is to hire an independent management consulting firm to do the study and interviewing, using only its own name for all contacts. Anonymity in acquisition studies is also important if one or both of the companies involved is publicly held. In this case public knowledge of an impending acquisition could obviously affect stock prices.

One study I did in which anonymity was crucial involved a company that produced and marketed filters for cleaning the lubrication fluid used in metal-cutting machines (for example, milling machines and lathes). These filters, which made it possible to recycle lubricants, were produced by most companies as separate units that serviced one machine tool. But our client's major competitor, the industry leader, Lube Filter Products, had, over the last five-year period, successfully introduced two new filtration machines that utilized a central systems approach. Groups of ten, twenty, or more machine tools were serviced by a single large filtration unit. Our client was planning to introduce a similar central systems machine, but they felt a need for some specific information before they planned their product line in order to develop a sound marketing strategy. Basically, they wanted to know all we could ethically find out about the market success of Lube Filter's central systems units. Our client wanted to know:

- Annual sales volume by machine type for Lube Filter
- The end-use industries that had purchased the units and why they had been purchased
- Trends in the use of central systems

Obviously, successful completion of this program would require a fruitful interview with Lube Filter Products, and our client's identity would have to be protected for the interview to have any chance of success. The interview was arranged by calling the marketing manager of Lube Filter Products and saying, "Hi! My name is Ken Albert. I'm with a consulting firm in Chicago and we're doing a study of machine-tool filtration systems. I'd like to stop in and chat with you on the subject sometime next week if I can." The whole thing went smoothly. Our anonymity had allowed our client to gather information from a source that they could not have reached themselves.

PRESTIGIOUS RECOMMENDATION

Sometimes a problem situation requires more than a correct solution—it requires a *prestigious* correct solution. Take, for example, the case where a company president knows that he or she will need the recommendation of a well-known firm like McKinsey and Company or Booz, Allen and Hamilton if the board of directors is to be convinced to make a certain acquisition. In such a case, a recommendation to acquire generated by internal analysis, no matter how exhaustive, would be useless. A recommendation to acquire submitted by a lesser-known, yet competent, management consulting firm might be equally useless. So when the source of the recommendation is as important as the substance of the recommendation, there is good reason for using a well-known independent management consulting firm.

In conclusion, there *are* some valid reasons for utilizing the services of qualified independent management consulting firms. They occur in a variety of business problem situations, but they do occur. In this chapter, I've described the primary reasons for seeking outside assistance and tried to suggest some pointers for establishing a meaningful relationship with an independent consulting firm. In the final chapter, I expand these pointers so they can be used as a "purchasing guide" to management consulting services.

17
How to Buy Management
Consulting Services —
When Necessary

> *Every man has a right to his opinion, but no man has*
> *a right to be wrong in his facts.*
> — BERNARD M. BARUCH

In my years in the consulting business I've heard a lot of comments made by fellow consultants concerning the lack of judgment clients demonstrate in purchasing management consulting services. Here are some typical ones:
- "I can't believe we got this study. Two of the other firms that our client considered were much better qualified than we."
- "This client is so useless. If they'd just make up their minds once in a while we could make some real progress on this study."
- "Would you believe they're paying us $35,000 for this. It's only about a $15,000 job."
- (Said with a sense of surprise and relief after a final client presentation): "They bought it! They bought it hook, line, and sinker."

Quite simply, the purpose of this chapter is to prevent your company from eliciting comments such as those.

The selection and proper use of management consultants requires conscientious effort in:
- Identifying qualified firms
- Soliciting proposals
- Evaluating consulting firms
- Making a selection
- Working with and controlling consultants

IDENTIFYING QUALIFIED FIRMS

Remember the Darwin Industries case that was used to illustrate the basic management consulting approach to business problem solving? Well, Darwin did some things correctly in selecting a consulting firm, but they also made some mistakes. The main thing they did correctly was to make a wide search in their attempt to identify qualified firms. This is always a critical first step. The major mistake that Darwin made was that it didn't identify enough qualified firms. In fact, of the six firms that Darwin solicited proposals from, only one (which happened to be my firm) was truly qualified. It turned out that Darwin had overlooked some very basic sources for names of qualified consulting firms. You'd be astonished at how many major publicly held corporations make the same mistake.

If your company does not have an ongoing relationship with a number of highly qualified consulting firms, it should use the following primary sources to compile a thorough list for a particular assignment.

- *Directories:* Most management consulting associations publish membership directories. There are also specialized directories available like the *Consultants and Consulting Organizations Directory* (Gale).

- *Associations:* Telephone your industry's trade association director, and talk to the directors of the management consulting associations.

- *Companies:* There are a lot of companies who have experienced problems similar to yours. Call up your counterpart in those companies and ask for consultants' names.

- *Friends and Acquaintances:* People within and outside your company should be contacted.

- *Nationally Known Firms:* Don't be afraid of, or intentionally avoid, the big companies (such as A. T. Kearney, McKinsey and Company, or Booz, Allen and Hamilton). They may be expensive, but at least you can be pretty sure they're qualified.

SOLICITING PROPOSALS

If you have more than three or four consulting firms on your list of potentially qualified firms, it's probably unwise to ask all of them to submit comprehensive proposals. Boil down your list using the following procedure. Telephone each of the firms and ask if they would be interested in the assignment. Then send each firm that has responded affirmatively a letter asking for:

- The firm's areas of specialization
- Examples of specific past assignments in the problem area under consideration
- The number of people on their staff and their backgrounds, including biographies of consultants most qualified to work in the problem area of interest
- A brief outline of the approach they would propose using on your problem

Specifically tell each firm to limit its response to three pages plus biographies. With these responses in hand, you can cut down your list to three or four names.

Now you can get down to the business of soliciting proposals. I would start this process by preparing in writing a brief request for a proposal. This exercise will help you to focus on the important aspects of the problem, and will guarantee that you will be providing the same basic information to each management consulting firm. Your request for a proposal should include:

- The background of the problem (reason for needing the study)
- Overall objectives
- Scope of the study (for example, products to be included, divisions involved, geographical territory)
- The basic information being sought or questions that need answering
- The expected accomplishments
- Required completion date

I strongly recommend a personal meeting with representatives of each consulting firm as part of the process of soliciting proposals. No matter how good your request for a proposal is, nothing can substitute for face-to-face contact. Conducting preliminary discussions with each firm costs you nothing except the time spent in each discussion, and it gives you a chance to benefit from a series of exercises in problem definition. These meetings will also enable you to evaluate consultants in person before making a selection. Often personality compatibility is an important factor in selecting consultants.

You should expect thorough proposals in response to your requests. Each should include a clear restatement of the objectives to be achieved and the scope of the assignment, and should outline what specific end products will be offered. For example, the statement of the end products of an organizational planning study should make clear whether results will be solely in the form of organizational charts or whether detailed position descriptions and personnel assignments will also be included.

A thorough proposal will also include a specific description of the approach that is being recommended. This description should break the project down into logical steps and indicate the methodology to be followed in each step. Details are important here. They suggest a conscientious planning effort on the part of the consulting firm writing the proposal. Look for specifics like the identification of information to be secured, type and number of interviews to be conducted, and the type of analysis to be performed. A good proposal will also be specific about staffing. After all, consulting firms don't do the work—individual consultants do. You have a right to know who is going to do the work, who is going to manage the project, and who is going to take overall responsibility for the project's successful completion. You should be provided with sufficient information about these people so that you can judge the appropriateness of their education, background, and experience.

And last but not least, a good proposal will conclude with firm estimates of the time it will take to complete the project (from date of authorization) and the cost. It should be clearly stated that the fee will not be exceeded unless your firm authorizes an enlargement in the scope of the program.

EVALUATION

The evaluation process should focus on the proposals themselves, the people to work on your specific project, and the overall position and reputation of the consulting firms involved. Try to address the following questions for each of the firms submitting proposals:

- How well do the proposals convey an understanding of the background, objectives, and scope of the study?
- Are the detailed aims of the study clearly stated and understood?
- Which methodology seems to be most appropriate to my company's specific needs?
- Which firm has the strongest relevant experience base?
- How do the qualifications of the individuals to be assigned from each firm compare?
- Are there any consultants that are so outstanding as to override other considerations? Any so weak so as to preclude consideration?
- Are the cost and time estimates similar? If not, what accounts for the differences?

Remember how much emphasis was placed on reference checking in Chapter 12, Executive Search? Checking references—of both the individuals that will work on your project and of the firm itself—is just as important in evaluating consulting firms. Start by asking each firm to supply a list of four to six companies that are familiar with individual consultants and with the work of the firm. Ask for the name of the firm's prime contact at each company, and emphasize that you're interested in companies that are not too different from your own.

Begin the actual reference checking by telephoning the people that have been supplied to you by each firm. Tell each contact who you are and what company you're with, and say that you're calling because you're thinking about engaging one of several consulting firms under consideration. Then ask each contact about *each* firm you're considering and about the individuals at the firms he or she expresses familiarity with. Ask questions like the following.

- How well do you know the firm? The people?
- What specific experience do you have with them?
- How satisfied were you with their work?
- Would you consider engaging them again?
- Is there anything I should know that I haven't touched on?

Don't forget to ask for the names of other companies the firms in question have worked for. Then call these companies and repeat your question sequence. Often reference checks made with sources not supplied by the consulting firms are very enlightening.

MAKING A SELECTION

You may feel the need for a second meeting with one or more of the firms under consideration before making a final selection. If so, don't hesitate to request it. To minimize the consulting firm's expenditure of additional time and travel expenses, it may be advisable for you to visit their offices for this meeting. Don't be shy about asking difficult questions, either at a meeting or on the telephone. If something you discovered in checking references is bothering you, confront the consulting firm with it. If you feel their qualifications are not exactly appropriate, ask how they expect to complete the assignment successfully with their experience level.

Some companies use a spread sheet to compare the proposals, individual consultants, and consulting firms before making a final selection. This may be especially helpful for large, important projects, or in situations where you want to demonstrate to higher-ups why you're recommending selection of a particular firm.

Cost is one comparison that can be made quite easily. But don't make the mistake of being a price buyer. The overall quality of the people and the firm is much more important than a savings of 10, 20, or even 40 percent. Be especially wary of quotations that are well below the norm. The pricing structure in the consulting business is such that an unusually low quotation means either that you are purchasing substantially fewer staff days of work or you are purchasing the services of less-qualified consultants (who have lower salaries and lower daily billing rates).

Hopefully, you will be making your choice between two or more outstanding firms, each of which submitted excellent proposals. If your overall selection process has been carried out correctly, this will be the situation. If you didn't execute the process correctly, you may be forced to choose between one good firm, one fair firm, and, say, two basically poor ones. Obviously, this is not a good position to be in.

WORKING WITH
AND CONTROLLING
CONSULTANTS

Once you have selected an outside management consulting firm, it is wise to involve yourself and your people in the study to the maximum extent possible. If you fail to do this, don't expect to get full benefit.

Begin by giving the consultants all relevant data you have. These include memos, reports, letters, catalogues, price lists, production records, and so on. Some companies make the error of withholding information from consultants "to see if they can find out the same thing" by themselves. This practice is a mistake and a waste of money. You have done your best to select a competent and capable consulting firm, and now you are obligated to work *with* them to solve your problem in the most efficient way possible. It is always better to tell the consultants too much than to tell them too little.

A long, detailed discussion of the problem and all the circumstances surrounding it is also essential to getting the study off to a good start. Provide your consultants with easy access to any people that they need to see in your company—either to collect and decipher data or for the purpose of interviewing. You can do this by assisting them in making appointments. Another approach is to write a memo to each person in your company that the consultants plan on contacting. Briefly explain the purpose of the visits and ask for cooperation.

To facilitate coordination between your company and the outside consultants, let them know who their prime company contact will be during the course of the study. In most cases this should be the same person who solicited the proposals and spearheaded the selection process. If company people are to work with the outside consultants, make specific and definite assignments, and then follow up to make sure your people are doing what is expected of them. Outside consultants are trying to establish and maintain goodwill, and you cannot expect them to "point the finger" at uncooperative employees.

If one or more consultants are to be working at one of your company's facilities, provide adequate space and equipment. I would suggest a private office equipped with telephones, for each consultant. If sufficient space is not available, let them use offices of employees who are out of town. It may also be necessary to provide such things as adding machines, calculators, or even drafting tables. It is to your benefit to make working at your facility as convenient and comfortable as possible. After all, you're paying a good deal for each day of consulting time. Adequate space and equipment will go a long way toward ensuring that you get the most for it.

It is essential to keep the consulting team informed of changes and new developments that could affect their work. If your marketing group institutes a price change during the course of a marketing strategy study, inform the consultants. Don't let them suddenly find out when they interview one of your distributors or customers. If documents or data that were provided to the consultants at the beginning of a study are updated or changed, give them the revised information so it can be incorporated into the analysis and final report.

Insist on frequent oral or written progress reports from the consultants. Major programs should have scheduled interim meetings at which the consultants make presentations covering the tasks that have been accomplished and the problems that have been encountered, and reiterate that the project schedule is being adhered to. At these meetings, expect to be informed of the major aspects of the consultant's findings and recommendations, even if these have yet to be clearly formulated or finalized. You may also want others in your organization to have the opportunity to be apprised of what is likely to be recommended when the study is actually completed.

Always make sure that you get in the final report what was promised in the proposal. Consulting firms will usually do all they can, within reason, to please a client. Their reputation and the promise of repeat business are in jeopardy if a study is completed unsatisfactorily. I know of several instances where consulting firms have repeated major portions of a study, at no extra cost to the client, in order to make it right.

This brings us to the subject of cost and payments. A study should never cost more than the upper range quoted in the proposal—unless changes which you are aware of and have agreed to result in extra work or expense. Most management consulting firms submit monthly invoices covering professional effort and out-of-pocket expenses. It's common practice for some consulting firms to "prebill" somewhat at the beginning of a study. For example, the first month's invoice for a four-month study may amount to one-third of the total cost, even though less than a third of the work is finished. This is usually done for two reasons: (1) to improve the firm's cash flow, and (2) to give the impression to the client that the firm is working hard on the study. This practice should not be of serious concern to you; it does not mean that you will be overbilled in the end.

If you are embarking on a major study, or if the problem area and efforts required for solution are difficult to define, it is sometimes wise to request that the firms submitting proposals break down the overall effort into two or more separate phases. Each phase should have its own objectives, its own expected results, and, most important, its own cost. This will allow you to delay or terminate the study if it isn't progressing as expected. I would recommend that you always use the separate-phase approach in the implementation efforts, even if the consulting firm can accurately estimate their cost at the beginning of the program.

IN CONCLUSION

You should not hesitate to hire an outside management consulting firm when necessary. But to gain maximum benefit, you must select the firm wisely and carefully. And, once the study is under way, you should monitor progress and work closely with the consultants to help them do a good job for you. With proper planning, you can solve problems using outside consultants just as well as you can those that lend themselves to solution through the efforts of your internal problem-solving system.

Index

Acoustic Research, 86
Acquisition analysis, 80, 82–89
    external, 80, 85–88
    internal, 80, 88–89
Acquisition screening, 81–82
Allen, James, 11
Allis-Chalmers, 3
American Motors, 113
Analysis and conclusions, 4, 49–61
    qualitative analysis, 57–59
    quantitative analysis, 50–56
Association of Consulting Management
    Engineers (ACME), 12
Association of Internal Management
    Consultants (AICM), 176
Association of Management Consultants,
    The, 12

Bacon, Francis, 38
Baruch, Bernard M., 196
Bethlehem Steel, 97
Booz, Allen and Hamilton, 3, 12, 197
Booz, Edwin, 11, 12
Bowles, Chester, 175
Brower, Charles, 90
Business problem solving and executive
    search (see Executive search)

Caltron, 99–100
Chrysler Corporation, 113
Clay, Henry, 49
Client assignments:
    size of, 14
    types of, 14–15
Clinton Corn Processing, 58
Collaboration, 179–181
Collins Corporation, 99–100
Compensation system, executive, 153–160
Consultant licensing, 20–21
Consultants and consulting organizations
    directories, 197

Corporate growth planning, 69–79
    formalizing the growth plan, 74–75
    growth alternatives, 73–74
    internal audit and setting objectives,
        71–72
    market audit, 72–73
    selected opportunities, 74
    (See also Strategic planning)
Cresap, Mark, 11

Darwin Industries, 27–37, 59–61, 63–66
    analysis and conclusion for, 60
    information gathering for, 44–48
    proposal for, 31–37
    recommendations and implementation
        for, 64–66
Demosthenes, 111
Dun and Bradstreet (D&B) reports, 40, 41,
    82, 88

Economics of consulting, 16–18
    (See also Purchasing consulting services)
Equipment analysis, 161
Executive compensation system, 153–160
Executive search, 136–152
    advertising, 141–142
    assessing the problem, 137–138
    basics of, 137
    contacting likely candidates, 143–144
    guidelines for, 150–152
    interviewing, 144
    making an offer, 150
    making a selection, 150
    planning and scheduling the search,
        140–141
    preliminary search, 141
    presenting candidates, 147–150
    reference checking, 144–147
    screening resumes, 143
    sourcing, 142–143
    writing specifications, 139–140

Facilities planning, 161–172
Field, Marshall, 101
Fisher, 86
Ford, Henry, 101
Ford Motor Company, 113
Franklin, Benjamin, 54, 184
Fry, George, 11

Gathering information, 4, 38–48
　sources of information, 38–41
　　client personnel, 39
　　client record and files, 38–39
　　the government, 39–40
　　the marketplace, 41
　　publications, 40
　　trade associations, 40
　ways of, 41–44
　　focus groups, 43
　　mail surveys, 44
　　personal interviews, 41–43
　　telephone interviews, 43
General Motors, 113
Goethe, Johann Wolfgang von, 189
Growth planning (see Corporate growth
　planning)

Hamilton, Carl, 11
Holmes, Oliver Wendell, 11
Home electronics acquisition, 85–88
Hotpoint, 119
*How to Pick the Right Small Business
　Opportunity*, 7

Idaho Specialties, 92, 94
Identifying information needs, 26
Implementation (see Recommendations
　and implementation)
Incentive compensation, 2
Information gathering (see Gathering
　information)
In-house acquisition analysis, 88–89
Institute of Management Consultants,
　The, 12
Internal management consultant, 5,
　175–176
Internal problem-solving systems, 175–188
　collaboration, 179–181
　full-time internal management
　　consultant, 175–176
　special assignment, 176–178
　the task force, 178

Job descriptions, 130–131

Kearney, A. T., 12, 197
Kitchen cabinet acquisition, 83, 115

Limiting the scope of consulting
　assignments, 23
Lincoln, Abraham, 80
Listing questions for the study program,
　25
Little, Arthur D., 12
Longfellow, Henry Wadsworth, 69

McKinsey, James O., 12
McKinsey & Company, 197
Management consulting approach, 3–6
Market Research Green Book, 197
Marketing-related problem, 1
Marketing strategy, 101–110
　basics of, 106–108
Maytag, 119

New product and new venture analysis,
　90–100
　basics of, 90–92

Ore-Ida, 92–94
Organization:
　designing an improved, 125–131
　present (see Present organization)
Organizational alternatives, 127
Organizational interview form, 124
Organizational planning, 120–135
Organizational study, staffing an, 121

Paget, Richard, 11
Patton, J. A., 5n.
Plant layout design, 161
Plant location studies, 161
Polk, R. L., 41
Pollack, 22
Predicast, 41, 82
Preparing a schedule, 27
Preparing a work plan, 26
Present organization:
　analysis of the, 123–125
　defining the, 121–123
Problem, defining the, 4, 22–37
Proposal(s):
　preparing, 27
　sample, 31–37
　soliciting, 197–199
Purchasing consulting services, 196–203
　evaluation process, 199–200

identifying qualified firms, 196–197
making a selection, 200
soliciting proposals, 197–199
working with and controlling
consultants, 201–203
Purposes of this book, 2–3

Qualitative analysis, 57–59
Quantitative analysis, 50–56

Recommendations and implementation,
5–6, 62–66
steps to successful implementation, 66
Reference report, sample, 146
Rogers, Will, 1
Roosevelt, Theodore, 136
Ruskin, John, 161

Sales compensation system, improving,
154–157
Sales forecasting, 111–119
causal models, 112–113
combination approach (modified Delphi
method), 114–119
example of, 113–114
qualitative methods, 112
time-series analysis, 112
Scott, 86
Scrutton, T. L., 120
Securities and Exchange Commission
(SEC), 10K reports, 40

Setting objectives, 24–25
for market-oriented acquisition analysis,
24
Society of Professional Management
Consultants, 12
Sources of information (see Gathering
information)
Sourcing, 142–143
Special assignment, 176–178
Specifications, executive search, sample
of, 139–140
Staley, A. E., Company, 58
Steinmetz, Charles P., 38
Stevensen, Robert Louis, 153
Stowe, 49
Strategic planning, 75–79
good, example of, 77–79
poor, example of, 75–77

Task forces, 178
Tiorio, 120
Todd Shipyards, 97
Trends in management consulting
business, 19–21
Twain, Mark, 153

Wall Street Journal, 81, 142
Warehousing and physical distribution,
161
Work plan:
preparing a, 26
sample, 44